Crazy Free

- An Epic Spiritual Journey -

To the Little Brother and his booming contagious laugh - I still maintain that you cheated that one time when we were wrestling. Blind - folded in my living room - But I still, also, love you ☺

XOX
Melissa Wyld -

BY MELISSA WYLD

P.S→ Wait! Was writing a book not on the list?

ISBN: 1512304239
ISBN-13: 978-1512304237

To my Dad

*Optimist, Adventurer
and Storyteller Extraordinaire*

CONTENTS

NOTE TO THE READER

Crazy Free is an account of events that actually took place in what I perceive to be real life. It is, however, like all personal stories, highly biased by way of having each experience sieved and colored through my unique individual perception of the world, which is an ephemeral moving target at best. Although I have strived to produce a raw and honest story, as you will learn, I am plagued by and blessed with an internal over-zealous Storyteller.

For the sake of keeping it honest, I have included real-time material such as letters, emails and written conversations with the Universe, God, my Higher Self and various other corporeal and incorporeal entities. These pieces were never intended for public consumption and can at time be stylistically awkward or unpolished. In spite of the potential break in the narrative, I chose to include them with little to no editing to illustrate the tone of my life at each stage of the journey undistorted by the perspective of hindsight goggles.

Some of the names of protagonists and organizations in my story have been changed to respect their privacy. Please remember as you read of these encounters that every story has two sides at least and that I can only speak from my own perspective.

I am grateful to *all* the teachers who have appeared on my path. This book could not exist without them.

PROLOGUE

I remember clearly the moment when I first lost my mind. It was January 24th, 2011 – a rare sunny and crisp Pacific Northwest day – and my heart was breaking again.

I loved a man who loved me back, the way nitric acid loves glycerol, bound by irresistible chemistry, explosive in physical proximity.

Oh, we had tried. Logan and I had tried to be a normal, healthy couple seven times already, but instead we had only grown more unstable and volatile.

Only two weeks prior, we had been exploring the fragile elegance of iced waterfalls in Montana, Wyoming and Colorado. The steep ice we climbed still held the mark of our tools and crampons, the trees to which we anchored remembered our passionate belay station kisses, and the valleys below still resonated from the yells of our daily arguments.

I had flown home from Colorado knowing I needed to cut the rope and set us both free. Instead, the rope was being torn, frayed and ripped apart.

I clenched my hand on the phone and held my breath.

I couldn't leave, he said. And I believed him, but also, I had to go. This "us" was all wrong. We'd be better off apart. Whenever we were apart, we felt freer, happier and more grounded. But what about our huge love? What would we do with the huge love? Had I not left seven times already only to collide back again? Had we not felt we belonged to each other from the first moment we met?

I suddenly felt dizzy from the argument and curled against the arm of the sofa for support. Even with a frayed rope, Logan still held my heart and mind captive.

I felt my mind wriggle in my head, like a buzz of confusion, and suddenly, it set itself free. My sense of presence detached from my curled body, floated up, drifted slightly to the right and slowly rotated clockwise above my physical location.

My hand clenched the phone a little tighter and my eyes opened wide with fright, but I was not involved in these

1

motions. "I" was rotating and getting queasy from the rotation. I could still perceive the room and my body in it. Nothing physical about me was rotating. I could still feel the pressure of the sofa on my back and hear Logan's voice in my ear — though his words no longer mattered to me.

Without a goodbye, I let my hand hang up the phone and drop it on the coffee table. The moment I stood up, I was sucked back into my body. But not completely. Some of "me" remained outside the constraints of my physical envelope.

At the time, I believed I was my physical self. Nothing about "me" could escape my body's boundaries. I left the phone in the living room and returned to my bedroom where I let my back slide against the wall and wrapped my arms around my knees until my body was coiled into a tight and safe little ball.

What in the world had just happened? Was I having an anxiety attack or had I really just left my body? And who was this "I" that could float away anyway? Was I going crazy?

The day outside was still crisp and blue and my heart was still breaking. The world looked exactly as it had a few minutes prior, yet my life would never again be the same. I had already unwittingly, unknowingly, taken my first step to the edge of the Rabbit Hole.

Part 1

DOWN THE RABBIT HOLE

You take the blue pill, the story ends; you wake up in your bed
and believe whatever you want to believe.
You take the red pill, you stay in Wonderland, and I show you
how deep the rabbit hole goes.

- Morpheus to Neo-
(*The Matrix*)

CHAPTER 1

"Mark, I think I'm going crazy. Do you think I'm going crazy?" I asked my psychotherapist the day after "I" separated from my body.

"No, you're not. People who 'go crazy' are usually not aware that they are 'going crazy'. The fact that you're asking the question is proof of your sanity."

I relaxed back in the big leather chair and scrutinized him under a raised eyebrow, searching for flaws in a logic that seemed too simple.

I had been sitting weekly in Mark's chair for six months by then and had developed a deep appreciation for his psychotherapist skills and human compassion.

It wasn't him I mistrusted, but myself.

My life had fallen apart, and still to most of the world I appeared a strong, independent and professionally successful woman. I could play my part so well, even with my inner-world in shambles. I simply acted as I always had, in line with the template of what once was an irreproachably normal and comfortable life.

5

Before Logan, and before the volcano, I lived in a modern four-bedroom house in a quiet suburban neighborhood in which lawns were mowed and cars were cleaned on the weekend, with Jack, my husband of ten years.

Every morning I hugged and kissed Jack goodbye before heading to Western Washington University. My days were filled with Geophysics classes and my evenings with homework and reading assignments. I was a straight-A student effortlessly. I could not get enough Geophysics.

From my first quarter in the department, I haunted the graduate students' offices, pestering each one in turn for an opportunity to become a field assistant. I could carry half my weight, I told them. I could climb, shovel, dig trenches, trudge in mud, and work in all weathers.

Brendan later admitted that he had doubted I really could carry half my own weight up a mountain when I first stepped in his office, but my enthusiasm won him over. The very next weekend, I saddled up a pack close to half my weight – I had the battery for the GPS – tied myself to Brendan's mountaineer rope and followed his experienced footsteps towards Mt. Baker's majestic white summit.

It was a case of love at first climb.

Across Mt. Baker's glaciers, along its jagged ridges and precarious ledges and to a complex network of benchmarks on its flanks – there was not a corner of the volcano Brendan and I did not visit. We slept above the clouds surrounded by high altitude silence and napped in the sun in the mid-afternoon while the GPS gathered data.

With each climb, Mt. Baker captured my heart a little more, until it owned it fully. By the time Brendan graduated, it was already too late. I was addicted to the mountain and to the lifestyle.

I applied for and received a National Science Foundation Fellowship to study Mt. Baker's active crater for my Master's project. I became the leader of my own fieldwork expeditions and created footsteps across crevassed glaciers for my own assistants.

There was, at the time, a resurgence of scientific interest in Mt. Baker's volcanic activity. Members of the Mount Baker Volcano Research Center gathered at a brewery in downtown Fairhaven on Tuesdays. We laughed, drank beer and made plans. On the weekend, we sampled chemicals in the volcano's hot springs and fumaroles, listened to its heartbeat with seismometers, tracked its glacial flow with ice measuring stakes and peeked under its snowy robes with ground-penetrating radar.

Mt. Baker was my love and my home, and I resented having to return to civilization at all. Jack asked what had become of his wife. I had no news of her. As soon as I reached sea-level, I disappeared in my office to prepare the next expedition, analyze gathered data or tackle delicious multivariable equations describing the heat and ice flow in my crater.

In the spring of 2009, half-way through my first year as a graduate student, Jack and I parted ways after a thirteen year drama-free relationship.

Some said the volcano was to blame. Perhaps it was part of the equation. I was once struck as I held both Mt. Baker and Jack in my field of vision by the realization that I loved the mountain more than I loved the man. I was obsessed, and Jack had grown weary of second-hand excitement. He held the domestic fort, because one of us had to, and I resented his orderly discipline and sudden uncharacteristic mundanity.

Luckily, we cared enough for each other to realize that we had reached a fork in our common path and that our individual growths were impaired by our "'til death do us part" promises. We separated amicably, wishing each other joy, love and professional success.

By the summer of 2009, I gleefully stood at the edge of my new single life, eager to unfurl my wings. The path to my dream future was clear and unobstructed. There I would be, ten years straight ahead, with my own large yellow pelican case on a remote glacier. "Dr. Melissa Wyld, Glaciologist – Ground Penetrating Radar, property of such-and-such University" the label would read.

My life was perfect, and I was blissfully unaware of the Universe's little giggles.

01/25/2011, Bellingham, WA.
Excerpt from "Letter of intent" from my application to participate in a four-day fast in Death Valley, CA.
In the late summer of 2009, I fell head over heels in love with a man with the uncanny ability to make me lose all common sense and self-respect. Despite the passion and sense of karmic belonging we shared, our relationship quickly began to feel unhealthy, more like a mutual addiction. After a few failed attempts at breaking up with him, I realized something was amiss and turned to professional help.
I have been on quite an emotional ride since. I discovered that the childhood wounds I had cleverly swept under the carpet were still guiding my choices in life, both the good – I am a strong, independent and professionally successful woman – and the bad – who finds herself incapable of handling the extreme emotions brought on by this new relationship.
As I struggled in my quest to integrate parts of my personality I had purposely discarded for the sake of navigating my own childhood, I began to question everything.

I did not see Logan coming. I was side swiped, knocked out and spun. The day after we first met, I climbed 9,500 feet to Mt. baker's crater rim with an assistant to record some glacier melt data, only to realize I had climbed the mountain with half of the equipment we needed.

I lost my wits. I went through the motion of going to class, but my mind wasn't even in the building. "Logan, Logan, Logan" it repeated like a scratched record. I stared at rows of data on my computer screen until the screensaver brought me out of my trance, repeatedly. My grades plummeted.

As misfortune would have it, I couldn't even seek refuge on my mountain because Logan was an avid climber who frequented Mt. Baker as assiduously as I did. Geophysics became secondary to finding love notes in the summit register. Depending on our highly changeable relationship status and the lapse since our last dramatic argument, I either dreaded or hoped – often both – finding his tent at base camp. Even as I worked in the belly of the mountain, surrounded by noxious sulphurous fumes, I could feel Logan's energy somewhere out there, on my volcano. I was a distracted team leader and a careless scientist.

I had never lost my mind over a man before, and I knew I needed to regain control of the situation. Just as I had spoken with several experts in chemistry before venturing near the fumaroles in the crater, so I needed an expert to help me navigate this emotional mine field.

I sunk in the chairs of two psychotherapists for a month each before meeting Mark, but neither spoke my language. Mark, however, listened attentively to my story, pulled a white board from behind his chair, drew a graph of my situation and explained in simple terms how and why I had lost my center in our very first session. The tightness in my shoulders released slightly. I knew I had found the help I needed.

I took on my healing process like a challenging term project. I read the recommended books, meticulously recorded my analysis of the progress of the situation in a journal, complete with sketches, graphs and cross-references, and braced myself for some hard emotional times I expected would last no longer than a few months.

Although I had sought help of my own volition, my initial and biggest hurdle was to admit that I had a problem. I believed only mentally-ill people visited psychotherapists' offices and I considered myself perfectly reasonable and functional – never mind the internal turmoil. In fact, I took pride in my ability to remain level-headed in uncomfortable situations – a great trait for a mountaineer or scientist, but counterproductive for personal healing.

My second biggest hurdle was to allow myself to be vulnerable. I equated vulnerability with weakness, and I disdained weakness. Under Mark's patient guidance, I slowly opened one emotional can of worms after another in classic Russian doll fashion. I unearthed memories I had buried and left for dead years prior. I released ancient angst and anger with such force that Mark sound-proofed his office to protect the sensitive ears of innocent bystanders. And, for months, I cried.

I cried in Mark's office, on my friends' shoulders, in Logan's arms when I happened to be there, in the shower, in bed, everywhere. One by one, my dark mood and low spirit drove all but a core few of my friends away. My roommates moved out, casual acquaintances avoided me, and all the while my family sat at the core of the Russian doll, a source of inner-torment rather than support. My safety rug was pulled out and for a few months I tumbled down the dark hole it had once covered.

"Look," I told Mark, "I just want to get to the Castle, tame the Dragon – I do not condone the killing of dragons – get the Prince and live happily ever after. How much longer do you think this will take?"

"A hero's quest cannot be rushed ..."

"Okay then can't I abandon the quest and return to my old ways? I was happy before all this started. Can't I forget Logan and all this childhood stuff and return to being just a scientist

10

on Mt. Baker?"

Mark calmly placed his pencil on his notepad.

"I don't know. Can you?"

My heart sunk. He didn't need to speak the words I didn't want to hear; his gentle tone implied everything I dreaded.

"No. I suppose I can't. I'm past the point of no-return now, aren't I? I wouldn't know the way back to who I was before anyway. I feel I have completely lost track of myself."

01/25/2011, Bellingham, WA.
Excerpt from "Letter of intent" from my application to participate in a four-day fast in Death Valley, CA.
I came upon your organization by the recommendation of my counselor. I told him that had completely lost track of myself, he answered that this was a wonderful place to be, a place of new beginnings, and that he had expected I would get there.
I told him I was feeling that familiar urge to escape, but that I had been looking at the globe and maps and that there was no place I felt was far enough in the world to fulfill my need. He looked pleased and said that the answer was that I needed to go further "inside".

CHAPTER 2

In those days, I was rarely open to other people's suggestions on how to handle my own life, especially if said suggestions sounded ludicrous, so when Mark recommended a Vision Fast for my next step, I thanked him, but immediately threw the idea out the window.

৪০ · ৫৪

Vision Fast – *n.* Strangers sitting in a circle sharing their innermost feelings while holding hands and looking for answers to their problems in mirages they create in their own brain through the use of drugs or altered physical states.

ഔ · ഇ

That's what I thought of that and I wanted no part of it.

As for fasting, I became surly if I was stranded without a snack for more than a few hours; I couldn't imagine my state after days without food. I was inclined to agree with Jack's evaluation of Vision Fasts, "So much money and they don't even feed you? What a racket!"

But even in those days of single-captainship of my own life, curiosity often overruled stubborn resistance. Within a few minutes of returning to my computer from Mark's office, I had abandoned the writing of my thesis and landed on a Google search page filled with vision fasts.

The Death Valley Vision Fast glared at me, first hit in my search. I leaned back on my chair and stared at the words – "Death Valley". What were the chances?

01/25/2011, Bellingham, WA.
Excerpt from "Letter of intent" from my application to participate in a four-day fast in Death Valley, CA.

If I had not known about the Vision Fast in Death Valley, that is where I would have gone anyway.

I'd like to take a (long) parenthesis in this letter to tell you about my relationship to Death Valley.

According to my Dad, I was conceived in the Mesquite Flat sand dunes, and in my will it states that this is where my ashes should be returned. I was married there, also in the Mesquite Flat sand dunes, and that is where I went to regroup right after the divorce. I have returned there after each break up, each change of career and sometimes just to find a bit of peace and sunshine. I have written odes and stories about the Valley, some of which have been published. I have visited all its attractions (with and without hula hoops) in all seasons and have explored as much of its lesser-known canyons and valleys as time has allowed me.

12

Because I am constantly changing, the Valley is never the same to me. When I worked in the software industry, I rejoiced in its raw uncomplicated nature. Its straight dirt roads taste like freedom, the perfect cure for cubicleitis. When I was a professional photographer, I added to my perception of the Valley its subtle light, its sensual shapes, and the mind-boggling beauty of its details, like small lizard tracks in undisturbed sand. Now as a geologist, I also enjoy the richness of its history and the incredible wealth of minerals you can find there (five inch long Kyanite crystals – for real!).

Last year, at the peak of my emotional turmoil, I rode my motorcycle 4,000 miles through a two-day long snow storm, a wind storm, nasty twisty roads with unsafe semi-trucks, rain, sleet, you name it, to get to Death Valley. When I returned home, I cleaned my phone book, strengthened those friendships I kept, moved to a new place with a new roommate and changed the focus of my study from glaciology to volcanology. In retrospect, I don't think I would have weathered the emotional journey I have been on as well had I not taken these steps. Death Valley is a magical place!

I took a deep breath and hit the send button.

There, it was done – applied for and paid in full. If I had pondered my decision for even a minute, myriad reasons would have stopped me.

I leaned back again, this time to stare at the confirmation page. I was really doing this. Just the day prior, I had floated out of my body, and suddenly I was signed up for a Vision Fast. I shuddered at the thought of what my rational scientific-minded friends would think.

Right on cue, the phone's ring jolted me back to reality. It was Darcy, one of my best scientific-minded friends.

"Hi Love, how are you?"

I mentioned neither my brief moment of out-of-body insanity – speaking of it would have implied I admitted it happened – nor the Vision Fast.

"Not so hot, actually. I broke up with Logan again. I had to." The words brought tears to my eyes, but I knew Darcy would support my decision. In my early days of Logan chaos, she had threatened to end our friendship if I didn't leave him. This was an act of love, she said, for she could not in good conscience, as a friend, watch me self-destruct through an abusive relationship.

"He'll be back in town soon though," I told Darcy, "and I feel I need to be away when he returns – far away!"

"Is Minneapolis far enough for you? There's a room available in my house for four months if you want to rent it."

Neither Minneapolis nor any place on earth felt far enough, but Darcy's was the best offer I had. The fast started in April, three months away. The field work and data gathering phases of my master's project were complete. I could write my thesis in Minneapolis. I only needed an internet connection.

In addition to reducing the risk that I might, again, "accidentally" return to Logan's arms, moving to Minneapolis also alleviated the temptation to procrastinate writing my thesis for the winter pleasures of the Cascades. Neither ice climbing nor skiing would distract me on the flat Minnesotan landscape. But, most importantly, moving to Minneapolis in the heart of winter seemed a ridiculous proposition – I had never experienced negative temperatures before, nor a real winter – and therefore, it really appealed to me.

A week later, I was packed and ready to go. In the bed of my truck, I lodged two large bins filled with climbing and skiing equipment – just in case – and a small duffel bag of clothes. A cardboard box held my desert camping gear – a bivy bag, sleeping pad and sleeping bag. I would need neither stove nor pots and pans. In the cab, behind the seats, I fastened two wooden crates with the seatbelts, and filled them with a laptop and printer, a few geophysics textbooks, a thick folder of important professional research papers and a stuffed tiger named Timothy.

I drove along Bellingham Bay on my way out of town, and stopped to say goodbye. I should have felt excited about the journey ahead, but my heart weighed more than a chunk of lead at the bottom of the bay. This adventure was different. These goodbyes felt permanent. Although I was only leaving for four months, I sensed that the current version of myself would not return. I squeaked a small "thank you" by the bay and drove away. I left without saying goodbye to Mt. Baker. I didn't have the heart.

CHAPTER 3

I stood at the metal gate of Sofia's apartment complex in a light drizzle and waited for her familiar footsteps. I knew I'd hear the clapping of her high heels down the corridor before she reached the door and I smiled in anticipation. It didn't matter that my duffel bag and backpack became a little damp. Sofia was always worth the wait.

Sofia's apartment had been my decompression chamber for years. It was a sanctuary of rich dark colors and sumptuous fabrics where I was welcome to a soft warm bed, exotic teas, dark chocolates and intelligent conversations. I stopped there before any adventure for a good meal and a mind-set switch and after any adventure for a shower and debrief. I would not have even considered continuing east without a stop to see Sofia.

I heard her steps. The clapping increased, and soon she was running towards the gate while holding a scarf over her head to protect an elegant bun. How she could run in high heels and a tight business skirt suit, how she could look so polished after a day at the office and a bus ride in the rain were mysteries to me.

But then, I was often a mystery to her.

"Is that all you have?" She shouldered my backpack and led the way back to her door.

"That's all I need. I'm only staying one night."

She laughed. At the surface, our friendship made no sense. I liked dirt, mountain tops and muddy boots. Sofia liked little French cafés, poetry and designer shoes. I avoided cities; Sofia thrived in their bustle. I wore neither makeup nor jewelry and rarely combed my hair; Sofia always tastefully sparkled. I lived comfortably out of a duffel bag; Sofia's closets overflowed with fashion.

Our friendship, however, was not impaired by superficial differences. It was grown slowly, as all strong things with deep roots are. Sofia was *that* friend – the one with the courage to kick me back on track when I lost my way, the patience to listen while I worked through my own drama, and the wits to be a worthy opponent when we bantered. Sofia made me think, and she made me laugh.

She was then the only person with whom I dared share that my "soul" had separated from my physical body.

"How interesting!"

The concepts of Soul and the possibility of an out-of-body experience were not unsettling to Sofia. She had grown up in a religious household and comfortably believed in spirits, angels and a Greater Power beyond ourselves.

"You mean 'How insane!'"

I, however, had lost such faith decades prior. I was raised without a religion by a non-practicing Jewish father and an Atheist mother raised Catholic. As a small child, I talked with God in my head. I asked questions, I asked for protection, and sometimes I asked for things. I assumed that everyone spoke with God, but as I grew older, I discovered it was not so. Neither grownup in my household spoke to God. My mother didn't believe in God; she believed in self-reliance. My father spoke to the ocean if he needed higher counsel. I don't know the form of the ocean's answers he received, but he always seemed happiest after he had been at sea.

My divine conversations became a private affair, a well-guarded secret I didn't bring home. When I was nine years old, I joined a boarding school. Suddenly I had friends, real people of my own age with whom to converse and play. My divine dialogs slowly tapered and eventually disappeared.

I had nothing to ask God anyway. As a young adult, I was naturally lucky and content. All my unspoken wishes were fulfilled effortlessly. I had what my friends called a "direct line to the Universe", but I shrugged off any religious insinuation and instead attributed my luck to hereditary optimism and charisma. I simply knew how to seize opportunities, work hard to achieve my goals and dreams and find silver linings in all situations.

I dedicated my twenties and much of my early thirties to the exploration of the physical world. I travelled to distant lands and learned whom I was through immersion in cultures thoroughly different from mine. Religion was no more than an artifact of culture to me, on par with traditional costumes and foreign languages.

In my mid-thirties, the scope of my exploration of the world tightened. I became fascinated with physics, from basic Newtonian to Quantum Physics. I meant to understand the world from its most basic building blocks and kept a steady supply of books by Richard Feynman and Michio Kaku by my bedside.

With this framework in place, I decided that "God" probably referred to the sum of all the energy in the universe. According to the first law of thermodynamics, energy could neither be created nor destroyed, only transformed. There could therefore be no "Creator".

I also decided that since energy was the building block for all matter, there could be no hierarchy. Humans were therefore no more and no less worthy than any other creature or inanimate object, and I acted accordingly. I cared for trees, rocks and my vehicles as lovingly as I treated my friends and husband. I felt my attentions were returned and attributed part of my luck to the support of inanimate objects.

As for death, I wasn't sure. I vaguely assumed that a system to recycle energy must exist, but mostly avoided thinking about it. The idea of my non-existence saddened me, and I found no value in making myself sad.

I considered this set of ideas my personal philosophy, not a dogma to be shared or preached. It simply provided me with enough of a spiritual framework to deflect the classic existential questions – who was I? Where did I come from? What was my purpose? And so forth – so that I could instead concentrate on planning and partaking in adventures, such as a random move to Minneapolis in the heart of winter.

That night on Sofia's sofa, however, my existential questions deflection system was failing me.

"I don't think you're insane at all." Sofia said. "Maybe, on the contrary, you had a spark of sanity. I just finished reading *The Power of Now* by Eckhart Tolle. His path to enlightenment also started with a separation of the true self and ego." She left the sofa and returned with the book from her bedroom. "Here, take my copy. I think you'll find it interesting."

I couldn't imagine I'd have time to read anything besides my own thesis in the upcoming months, but either because of Sofia's reverence for the book or because of a small seed of intuition, I accepted her gift.

We both left her apartment early the next morning. Sofia was late for work, as she often was when I visited, so we expedited our goodbyes. I set my bags down to give her a full-body embrace while we waited for the elevator. Unlike my goodbyes to Bellingham, I felt no heaviness in parting from Sofia, no sense of loss. I must have known intuitively that she also stood at the edge of the Rabbit Hole. In fact, she was closer to the edge than I was.

"Read the book!" she said, as she kissed my cheek before disappearing into the elevator.

CHAPTER 4

I drove eleven hours, over Snoqualmie Pass, across eastern Washington, Idaho and most of Montana to Livingston, and I remember none of it. All driving and traveling decisions were delegated to my trusty Toyota truck, while I spent the day in a parallel world – the one inside my head.

It was always a busy world inside my head in those days. Miles flew by while I agonized over the serial loss of Logan, my addiction to our dysfunctional relationship and the childhood patterns that might have led to this mess.

Luckily, my journey's logistics arranged themselves with minimal involvement on my part. No navigation was required as I traveled only on I90, and within an hour of leaving Sofia's apartment, accommodations for the night had materialized.

"The Hula Girl! How the hell are ya? You're coming through Livingston? That's great. I'm actually in the midst of tying loose ends to catch a plane to Florida tonight. I'll be gone a few weeks, but hey, come on over anyhow. The door's always open and help yourself to coffee...or smoothie... or whisky! Stay as long as you want. I wish I was there to meet you, but hopefully I'll see ya next time you come around!"

I hardly knew Jimmy. We had only met briefly in Death Valley a few years prior, drawn to each other by our matching Toyota trucks, one loaded with hula hoops, the other with a three-foot tall alien named Al. We had exchanged phone numbers, in case I someday found myself driving through Livingston. I would have never imagined I'd be sneaking in his empty house while he was away.

I must have sneaked in, but I don't remember how. The door was locked when I arrived. Did Jimmy leave a key for me in the mailbox? Did I slip in through the garage or a window? Was it snowing? Did I eat dinner in the kitchen? Did I shower? Did I read before going to bed? I fell asleep having missed a whole day in the physical world.

A few hours later, however, I was jolted awake from a deep sleep by Native American drumming right outside the bedroom window. My blood run cold and the temperature inside my sleeping bag instantly rose by several degrees from the adrenaline rush. All my senses were on full alert.

"All is well." My brain said. "It's likely just the neighbors practicing." The rest of my body didn't believe a word of it. This was wrong. This was so wrong that I couldn't even muster enough courage to investigate. I zipped up my sleeping bag over my head, plugged my ears and lay still until the drumming dissipated.

"Wow. Cool! You heard the drums. Not everybody does." Jimmy said when I reported the event the next day. "Oh yeah, the house's haunted. Sorry, forgot to tell you. Can't see them myself, but supposedly there's a little boy in the basement and an older lady who roams the corridor."

I considered packing and moving on. Out-of-body experiences, vision fasts and now ghosts – I didn't know what to make of it. But instead of driving on, I reached down my pack for the Eckhart Tolle book Sofia had given me. I lay down on Jimmy's sofa, under the one lamp in the living room, and began reading. I suddenly had ample time to read – I wasn't about to fall asleep in a house filled with ghosts.

In fact, the haunting proved beneficial to my first steps down the spiritual Rabbit Hole. Any creak or snap in the house, and I was instantly awake. For a whole week, I remained in a state of half-sleep I later learned is called Yoga Nidra – a state of relaxation within awareness, conducive to internal exploration and epiphanies.

During the day, I read *The Power of Now* voraciously. I took notes and cross-referenced concepts in the book I felt were relevant to my life and in particular to my relationship with Logan. I only worked on my master's thesis occasionally, out of a sense of obligation. At night, I scrutinized my life, my patterns, my reactions, through this new Now lens.

My entire worldview and personal philosophy were dismantled in a few days. Tolle's message resonated so clearly that I felt no need to run it through my skepticism sieve. I recognized the ego and its incessant voices, the emotional pain body, which cries and moans to the woes in its own story, and the sense of being both a watcher and a participant in said story.

The Power of Now presented a worldview and a way of living that intellectually made sense to me yet felt very distant from the way I had lived my life up to that point. The discovery of this mental Promised Land was unnerving. Was the peak of growth and healing I had climbed with Mark's help just a false summit? How much further until I reached healing and understanding? This had taken so long already. I growled about it at first but soon shouldered my metaphorical pack and kept climbing. At least, I sensed the true summit was in sight this time.

After a week in Livingston, I bid the ghosts goodbye, tucked my finished copy of *The Power of Now* in my backpack and left through the garage. I didn't feel any different physically and my mind was occupied with the same quandaries as when I first arrived, yet something had shifted. My life's frame had been aggrandized and I sensed that if I could only step back to see the new frame, everything would make more sense.

The first change I noticed was a slight release in my previously uncompromising work ethics. I had a thesis to write, but Mount Rushmore and Badlands National Parks were conveniently located on my route. I observed myself justifying – My thesis would only be delayed by a few days at the most and my professional career in no way impacted.

Mount Rushmore was not worth delaying my thesis. Even from a distance, the memorial looked like a monstrous tourist trap with an overflowing parking lot. I stopped a few miles short of the entrance and used a telephoto lens to record my visit to the stone presidents from the safety of the truck's cab.

I was so disappointed that I almost skipped the Badlands. But at the last moment, the truck, of its own volition it seemed, took the off ramp to the park.

The Badlands reminded me of Death Valley, a smaller, more intimate version of the rugged parched landscape I knew and loved. I had the park to myself. Calm and joy filled my heart instantly – that sense of peaceful solitude one gets coming home after an arduous day.

I lingered at each marked vista point, sat in the dirt, listened to the wind race through carved buttes and snapped hundreds of almost identical photos. But the park was small and in spite of my best lingering effort, I was back on the freeway heading towards Minneapolis and my thesis writing duties within two hours.

I watched myself try to justify turning around, but could not find any reasonable excuse to do so. Finally, I asked "permission" – I called Darcy.

"Hi, so … I just drove through Badlands National Park and I'm back on the freeway now, but …"

Darcy knew me well. She could guess the next words from the tone in my voice. She laughed and completed my sentence.

"… but you want to turn around and go back. You should.

I love you and I'll see you tomorrow."

"Thank you! I love you too."

I caught the next exit and drove back to the Badlands. I already knew where I was headed. One trailhead parking lot in particular had caught my attention. It was surrounded by sharp wind-carved buttes and spires on one side and a wide-open grass prairie on the other. Several trails left from the parking lot on the spires' side. Most followed short loops around particularly spectacular geologic features.

I had assumed I would walk several of these trails and learn from the displays about the geology of the area. But suddenly, as I stood at the trailhead with my camera and a gallon of water in hand, an overwhelming need for space overtook me. I turned away from all the trails, crossed the road, and walked across the prairie in a straight line to no particular destination. I was giddy with a sense of freedom. I laughed and skipped across the golden grass.

I had taken to hiking alone in Bellingham but always on familiar well-trodden trails. I also had ample bushwhacking and off-trail experience but always in the company of climbing partners, fellow geologists, friends and significant others. Here though, was a brand new landscape with unknown dangers and not another human in sight.

I loved it!

Instead of feeling vulnerable, I felt safer *because* I was alone. I explored the vast prairie on my own terms. I checked neither my direction nor the length of time I was gone, yet returned to the truck exactly on time to watch the sunset from the comfort of my tailgate. When the first stars appeared and the chill of the evening descended on the park, I crawled in the back of the truck and snuggled down in my sleeping bag for my first night alone in the truck.

I listened attentively for potential dangers because it was the common sense response to the situation. But not even the howling wolves in the distance could alter my potentially unfounded yet deeply rooted sense of safety.

CHAPTER 5

02/12/2011, Minneapolis, MN.
Excerpt from my journal
 I think over a week has passed since I last wrote in here. Since I got to MN, my life's mostly been about thesis writing. During the day, I don't exist. My mind is 100% in thesis mode. I make it a point to not think about it in the evenings. The one time I did, I ended up recalculating a set of equations I had calculated correctly the first time. It was -8 F the day I arrived here. It has not warmed up much since. A man today told me that you should not blink when riding a bicycle in this weather lest your eyelashes freeze together and keep your eyes shut. He had just fallen off his bicycle as a result of this. Seriously! I might as well have moved to another planet.
On another note, I have been trying to meditate a little bit every day as Tolle suggested, but so far, I have not been successful in quieting my mind. I have better luck with finding peace when I walk by the Mississippi, even if I have to bundle up like an astronaut to get there.

 I outwardly led a simple life in Minneapolis. Every morning, I walked to the University of Minnesota, where the Geology department secretary had graciously allowed me the use of an empty office, even though I had no affiliation to the department beyond my friendship with Darcy. I wrote my thesis until about four in the afternoon, when I left school to aerate my brain by the Mississippi. I always walked along the western river shore, starting upstream. The path on the western side descended away from traffic and closer to the river's level. I could pretend I was following a river in the wild. Once I felt sufficiently aerated, but not yet completely frozen,

I returned to the Arthur house, as it was affectionately named for its street address, for dinner.

Three geologist women lived in the Arthur house with me, two young post-doctorate researchers, one from Japan and one from Switzerland, and my good friend Darcy, already several years into her PhD program. The house oozed with studiousness, smarts and worldliness – all traits I valued and respected. This familiar world of brainy scientists was made all the more comfortable by Darcy's nurturing little attentions, from a bowl of homemade granola, to a sympathetic ear for my Logan woes, to a new custom-handmade hula hoop for my upcoming desert adventure. I was spoiled in the Arthur house. It was a good home.

The apparent simplicity of my life in Minneapolis, however, belied the inward system upgrade in progress. Sofia and I spoke every day just to keep up with each other's inner explorations.

The night of my departure from Washington, while I was zipping my sleeping bag to escape ghostly drums, Sofia was falling into a vortex of energy. The details of this event are, of course, hers to share if she ever chooses to, but in general, the event was similar to Tolle's description of his own spiritual awakening. Sofia had been granted the gift of clarity and understanding, while I still swam in the murky waters of undefined consciousness.

She met my unending flow of questions with infinite patience and definite answers. This was no longer the Sofia with whom I had bantered for years but a wise and patient guru who had no interest in discussing topics for the mere sake of a discussion. Either she felt she knew, or she didn't. If she didn't, there was no point in speculating, because we would eventually, when it was time, learn what we needed to learn.

I probably would not have fared too well if the only path to spiritual awakening required the mentorship of a guru, even a patient and loving one. I overflowed with questions and found no consolation in knowing that all would be revealed in due time, which was always later than the now in which I had the question.

Luckily for my frail sanity and friendship with Sofia, one night, as I was pouring questions into my journal, something or someone with a different style, voice and penmanship than mine joined in my internal dialog with some answers.

This was the beginning of a voluminous body of written conversations between me and the Unseen. My journal took on a completely different character after that night. I no longer cared to record mundane happenings. My direct line to the Universe was back in service, and this time on an unlimited minutes plan. Sofia had been recording her own conversations with God since she had fallen in the vortex, which gave me a little faith in the process.

02/15/2011, Minneapolis, MN
Excerpt from my journal [first conversation, edited for length]

So, if Sofia is right and our dramas are only internal movies, why is it so hard to let them go? Why am I still thinking about Logan every day? Am I addicted to my own passionate chick flick? The previews didn't match the main act, yet it is the previews I am still playing in my head. The actual movie didn't make me feel good.

Not quite me: The movie you create, since you are the director, should not make you feel bad. You should write movies the way you want them to play. You're the star and the director both.

Me: Can I write a movie without Logan in it?

Not Me (NM): Sure you can. But you don't. He still is the star of all your inner movies. Write a new plot. Without writing it. Live it. Don't worry too much about what comes next. Just know that it will be good. It will be fantastic. It will be an adventure.

Me: It's true that I am having good adventures. I am thankful for all the opportunities and experiences I have had so far. I feel pretty lucky to live here, in this house and by the Mississippi for a little while. I am also thankful for having met Logan and for having now gone away from him. I am sorry he hurts and I wish I could help him.

NM: You can't help him if you are not solid. You were placed together to ignite your creative minds. Logan is closer to who he wants to be today because he met you. I don't need to tell you the leaps in growth you have made as a result of being with him.

Me: Did I really need to leave then? Shouldn't I have stayed and completed my learning?

NM: Your learning is complete. Logan and you are linked, like all. What is to come of you two involves many factors. You, him, and everything else. The whole system is in balance. We cannot predict which way the machine will sway.

Me: The machine? What do you mean by machine?

NM: I mean the interpersonal relationships that constitute a person's social life.

Me: Are we that influenced by others?

NM: No, we are not. We are dependent on their energies. Right now you cannot be with Logan because his energy field is stronger than yours. You have not yet established in your mind who you are. You get pulled in. You lose yourself.

Me: Did you place me with Logan too soon then?

NM: Yes and no. Your growth process was expedited through the exposing of childhood wounds, but I had not anticipated his draw on you.

Me: But! Didn't you create me? Didn't you know this about me?

NM: Ha ha! No, I knew. I just listened to your prayers. You asked for passion, you asked for a climber. That is what you received.

Me: So, can I know if I will go back or even if I should go back?

NM: No, that would take all the fun away! Just know that all is well. You are going to be fine. I have great plans in store for you. And actually, I have great plans in store for Logan too.

<u>*Me*</u>: *Okay. Thank you for taking the time to answer my questions.*
<u>*NM*</u>: *Anytime. I'm always here.*

CHAPTER 6

It was still dark when I stepped outside and started at a slow run towards the river. The cold air fogged my breath and froze the tip of my nose, but I didn't have much time if I wanted to reach the Mississippi by sunrise. I arrived right on schedule to see the first golden rays of sun pierce through the morning fog and illuminate the tree tops. The scene looked like a postcard, but I hardly noticed; I was on a quest for answers.

The Death Valley Vision Fast manual recommended a one-day fast and nature walk approximately a month before the main fast to habituate our bodies and mind to the concept. I welcomed the challenge. Despite my daily walks, the difference of pace between my hiking and climbing life in Bellingham and my sedentary thesis-writing life in Minneapolis was beginning to affect my mood and health.

I decided that I would walk along the Mississippi River from sunup to sundown, following the river's flow. Darcy would pick me up at sunset however far I had gotten. This was not just an adventure by the river; I meant to treat my walk as a real vision fast by keeping my mind open to guiding signs and greater meanings beyond the surface appearances of a mid-city river shore.

Despite the grounded wisdom in the Death Valley Vision Fast manual, which I had read twice, and despite my daily conversations with God and Sofia, I still sensed that *something* I needed to understand lay less than an eighth of an inch out of reach. And if I could open my mind to the possibility of its existence, I'd see it.

"Good morning Mississippi. What is my quest, please?"

My gaze left the spectacle of sun rays through the fog to fall at my feet where a white feather awaited to be noticed. Feather ... Flight ... Freedom. Could it be this obvious?

02/01/2011, Seattle, WA (At Sofia's the morning of my departure)
Excerpt from my journal
Titled: "A dream: A feather from the Albatross"

I was in a beautiful field of green grass in the spring. The sky was blue and filled with floating cottonwood. I thought that since I didn't know what to do next, I should stay in this field until I received a message from the Universe. A flock of birds flew overhead and shat all around me, but not on me. Then, one of them, which I knew to be an Albatross, landed next to me, plucked one of its feathers and placed it in my hand with a pointed look. It flew away with no further explanation. The feather was short and soft, like a down feather. It was ruffled as though it had gotten through some hard times. It was black with four red stripes. After a while, I noticed that there was some small writing on it, but none of it made sense to me. I didn't know what the message meant. I still don't.

Although the feather I found by the Mississippi was nothing like the albatross's feather of my dream, I assumed this was the sign for which I'd asked. So, my quest was freedom. Freedom from what? Freedom from my own thoughts, antiquated beliefs, detrimental relationships, social expectations? I still could not read the metaphorical small writing on the feather. I recalled the pointed look on the albatross's face. Clearly, I was still missing something.

80 · CB

Side note: The night before I left Minneapolis, I saw the actual feather of my dream in the Arthur house, complete with stripes and a ruffled down edge. That feather belonged to Darcy. It had been given to her as a token of love by an ex-partner, but was, by then, reduced to nothing more than the equivalent of salt on a wounded heart. We agreed to trade feathers. Whichever meaning I chose to assign to it, my feather would, at least, always be a precious gift from a dear friend.

ಖ · ಛ

After a few miles, the trail along the Mississippi left the river bank and climbed back up to a side street with an unusual amount of religious buildings. Within a few blocks, I had walked by a mosque, a synagogue, and several Christian churches of various denominations. My mind turned to religion.

What puzzled me most about religion was why a divine entity hierarchically superior to the creatures of the earth would choose to dwell indoors. But then, by the virtue of omnipresence, the Divine would, of course, occupy indoor spaces as well. Maybe my predilection for being in nature did not warrant judging others' modes of worship. Still, I couldn't help feeling a little smug that *my* church came complete with snow covered peaks, sand dunes, fresh air and the most diverse of all congregations. I could have a "religious" experience anywhere and anytime, including while walking along the Mississippi.

A fleeting thought crossed my mind, "Wouldn't it be nice to walk in nature full-time?"

No sooner had I completed the thought that I was struck down by Mother Nature's lightning rod of fate: "I am walking the Pacific Crest Trail!" There was no pondering the feasibility or reasonability of this adventure. It was decreed and non-negotiable. I stopped walking and repeated it out loud to ensure I understood the implications of my mission, "I am walking the PCT. I am taking six months off next year and walking from Mexico to Canada. Wow!" The joyous trepidation that always precedes great adventures suddenly filled my heart. I stepped off the sidewalk to briefly note in my journal: "1. Freedom is my quest. Nature is my church. Adventure is my path". Yes, these words rang true. I resumed my journey with a much bouncier gait.

After the last church, the trail followed residential streets for another mile. I could see the river below, down the steep banks, and wished the trail would return to its side. A few steps later, the trail veered right sharply, straight down to the river.

As soon as I returned to the river's side, the trail turned into a muddy mess through the snow. I wished it would be drier, and again within a few steps the trail was dry and firm. How curious! Was I granted any wish I made?

This needed to be tested. I wished for a bathroom – in part because I needed one – then I remembered the filthy port-a-potty I had seen a few miles back and added "a *clean* bathroom". If I were to fully test this out, I might as well … "a clean bathroom, in a concrete building, with flush toilets and sinks." I giggled. It was a ridiculous demand; I was in the woods, a fair distance from the residential street above, and the trail continued along the river as far as I could see.

The Universe giggled back a few minutes later when the trail bifurcated to a trailhead with a large parking lot and the bathroom I had just described. I sat at a picnic table and wrote in my journal "2. All my needs are taken care of. All I have to do is ask."

After I left the bathroom, I got lost. I walked through a meadow covered in undisturbed snow and followed what I believed was one of the Mississippi's meandering channels. My mind was racing. "All these channels eventually flow to the Mississippi. All rivers flow to the ocean. Maybe the same is true of souls. Maybe all souls flow towards enlightenment, at their own rate, by their own paths".

I became so fascinated by my own "insightfulness" that I forgot to pay attention to the trail and, somehow, returned to the entrance of the meadow covered in snow, which was this time disturbed by my own footprints.

I figured I must have needed to repeat this section. Nothing is upsetting to one who seeks greater meanings in everything. I walked through the snow again with an eye out for anything I might have missed the first time but found no further lesson in the meadow. When I finally rejoined the main trail, I stopped for a brief nap on a bench and a journal entry: "3. All paths flow towards enlightenment, but sometimes loops might be necessary before the journey can continue. These are actually not loops but upward spirals."

I was still pondering what had happened in the meadow since the correct path had been glaringly obvious on my second pass through it, when I caught a glimpse of Minneapolis in the distance. I should have been walking away from Minneapolis, not towards it. Had I lost my way through the meadow a second time? Was the lack of food affecting my cognitive functions? I was about to turn around when I heard a clear, authoritative, genderless voice in my head, "Keep going. Trust me and keep going."

I was hesitant; it was insistent. It didn't sound like me, but it seemed confident, so I decided to comply. This might have been my first true act of blind faith. Every sensory input insisted I was heading in the wrong direction, yet the voice in my head assured me I would not be led astray. I walked another half hour, continually checking over my shoulder for an excuse to disobey, until I was close enough to distinguishing features in the cityscape.

The similarities between Minneapolis, behind me, and St. Paul, ahead, were striking and I understood why they are called the Twin Cities. The voice "smiled" approvingly.

"4. Trust and Faith" is all I wrote. I didn't know what I meant but guessed I would, at some point, understand.

As I walked through St. Paul, I noticed a sense of lightness about me. I had been walking on an empty stomach for about ten hours by then. I thought I would feel weak; in fact, I felt stronger, as though I had switched out a heavy backpack for a much lighter one. I could almost fly.

I began prancing along a congested street and singing a loud nonsensical song within earshot of St. Paulians stuck in rush hour traffic. The words were a poorly rhymed parody of all the great "insights" I had gained on my journey.

How ridiculous was I?

"Oh, my quest is freedom, it is so important. Look at me flow up the spiral to enlightenment. I am guided by voices. That's how I make my choices." My song turned to laughter, the kind usually associated with the glee of small children, completely unhindered by social filters. So, I could get a little far out after only a day without food. This was good to know.

"I made a large Moroccan stew. You must be starving." Darcy said as she swung the passenger door open to welcome me.

"I'm walking the PCT next year!" I jumped in the seat and reached across the center console to hug her.

"What's PCT?"

"It's a long trail. I think 3,000 miles. It goes from the Mexican border to the Canadian border, across California, Oregon and Washington, through national parks, deserts, forests, just endless wilderness. I'm so excited!"

She laughed. "Yes, that sounds like something you'd do."

We drove home a mere twenty minutes away, retracing the steps of my twelve-hour journey. I didn't feel hungry at all. I felt light and joyous.

Darcy's stew was divine, and I was grateful to her even though I missed much of the meal because my mind was in hyper-drive planning and dreaming of the PCT. Darcy listened attentively; she would not get to the point of PCT-conversation-saturation for another couple of weeks.

I also shared with her the day's "epiphanies" and was surprised to discover the depth of my scientific-minded friend's interest in spirituality. In her own unique way, Darcy was exploring the same edges. Maybe everyone was exploring the same edges. I just hadn't been aware of it before because I had not invited the conversation.

I went to bed early that night and reintegrated my daily routine the next morning. Although I was tackling the same set of glacial data in my thesis's Results section and walking the same Mississippi afternoon walks, I never returned to the mental space I occupied before the one-day fast. Knowing I was to walk the PCT gave my busy mind a wonderful dream with which to play, like sunshine above the clouds on a dreary day. And, also, it distracted me from my growing nervousness about the approaching vision fast.

CHAPTER 7

02/25/2011

Facebook note, [edited for length]

Titled: "What not to do if you live by the Mississippi River"

I was in a very bad mood this morning, so I decided to go air myself out by the Mississippi. I have just met the River, but already it has provided me with good ideas, great sunsets and inspiration for adventures, so I hoped it would cure my case of the blues.

I found a path in the snow and followed it down to the river. The trail meandered through trees then out onto a flat snow field along the river. Now, I have never seen this river in the summer, so I don't know what sort or banks it has. Is the steep part the banks? Was I walking on snow over a sandy shore, rocks, water? I really liked the trail because it was down from all the city commotion and I felt as though I was walking in the wild, plus it was in the sun.

I thought, "Well, there are steps here, and they look no older than yesterday based on the light dusting of snow that covers them. The person who made these, based on the size of the footprints, was much bigger than I am and he (most likely a he) didn't sink that much. And, it's colder today than yesterday. If yesterday the ice was strong enough to hold a large man, even if I am over water, it should be solid enough to hold me today." They say that every accident can be pinpointed in hindsight to one single bad decision ... I committed to the trail on the flat.

It was a gorgeous day out despite the below-freezing temperature. I followed the man's steps for about half an hour, took photos, enjoyed the sun and the trees and took deep breaths. I was approaching a bridge when I noticed there was ice at the bottom of the steps. I started the thought "That's odd. I wonder if the snow in the steps thawed and then refroze as ice with the colder temperature or if the ice here is so thin that the water from the Mississippi is ..." Jolt of adrenaline! I was suddenly down to my left hip in water, left hand and arm included. I swore. My other leg was folded over the ice still, so I tried to push myself out, but the ice gave out under my right leg as well. I grabbed on to the snow towards the shore, but the ice was breaking from the hole in which I was to wherever I tried to go. Finally, in a very ungraceful commando maneuver, I beached myself on the ice, kicked my legs out and belly crawled to the shore until I had a tree firmly in hand.

My heart was racing. I swore a couple of times to clear my head and said out loud "Who the hell is so stupid as to go hike alone on top of a frozen river?" I took my gloves off to wring them out, but they froze solid in their wrung position. I cracked the ice off them and put my hands back in quickly before they became so frozen as to make them unwearable. My left leg and boot and my left arm from the elbow down were covered in a thin sheet of ice. A pain in my left thigh let me know that I would have a bruise to commemorate this event.

I scrambled up the banks and crawled onto a paved sidewalk. It felt so anti-climatic to find myself on a road in a pleasant neighborhood with cars driving by while I stood there – a death-defying ice-caked weirdo –

*that I laughed for at least a full minute before moving on – the kind of
nerve-releasing laugh characteristic of post-adrenaline events.
I walked home on the road and by the time I got here, my gloves and
pants felt like they were made of inflexible plastic. It took me a while to
thaw, but I am well and warm now.*

The truth is I enjoyed falling in the Mississippi River.

It woke me up and calmed me down simultaneously. It made me wonder. What if I had fallen all the way in? Would I have known how to get out? Would my friends have found my death in the Mississippi strange or appropriate? Would I have regretted not saying goodbye to anyone? Would I have regretted anything in the life I've lived?

I discovered, or remembered, that I was okay with dying. I felt no need to expedite my own demise but accepted the risks inherent to living a life at the edge of my own comfort zone. In fact, the closer to the edge I played, the more alive I felt. So I could go out into the desert and fast for four days. I knew I would not fear death – I might fear other things, but at least death would not be one of them.

I updated my will and had it notarized. My truck would go to Darcy, my motorcycle to Rosie. Investments I still held would alleviate the financial burden of friends, and anything left would be donated to the Pacific Crest Trail Association.

The news of my brush with an icy death spread through my network of friends like wildfire. For a week following the incident, love and friendship poured into my phone, email and Facebook page. This gave me the opportunity to say goodbye and to express my gratitude to each of my friends before the fast.

When the time came to leave Minneapolis for the desert, I felt my affairs were in order. I could leave the life I had known and step into a new one.

Part 2

MEETING THE GRANDMOTHERS

"Would you like to have some Medicine Power?" Frog asked." "Medicine Power?" asked Little Mouse. "Why yes, if it is possible." "Then crouch as low as you can, and jump as high as you are able. You will have your Medicine." Little Mouse did as he was instructed. He crouched as low as he could and jumped. And when he did, he saw the Sacred Mountains. Little Mouse could hardly believe his eyes, but there they were. But then, he fell back to Earth and landed in the river. Little Mouse scrambled back to the bank. He was wet and frightened nearly to Death. "You have tricked me!" Little Mouse screamed at the Frog. "Wait," said the Frog. "You are not harmed. Do not let your fear and anger blind you. What did you see?" "I," Mouse stammered, "I saw the Sacred Mountains!" "Yes, and you have a new name!" Frog said, "It is Jumping Mouse."

- Native American Lore -

CHAPTER 8

03/02/2011
Email from Helena, Vision Fast guide:
  "The Grandmothers already know that you are coming. They are speaking to you now. Listen to the wind and the voice in your heart, and open to your wisdom."

I left Minneapolis in late March, right as the snow was starting to melt. My master's thesis was written, though I knew it still needed much editing before it could be submitted to the Dean. I filed all things related to my thesis in a large mental folder in a back drawer of my brain under "temporarily on hold – please resume after the fast" and drove towards the desert without a second thought about it.

The night before my departure, I had spread a road atlas on the Arthur house's dining room table and plotted my route to link both famous Utah national parks and lesser known state parks all the way to Death Valley – Capitol Reef, Grand Staircase, Escalante, Zion, Bryce, Goblin Valley, Kodachrome Basin and Coral-Pink Sand Dunes. After the grey and cold of Minnesota, I was eager for vivid rocks in the sunshine.

But by the end of the first day of my trip, I realized something was afoot. This was not a simple journey through the desert for colors and sunshine. The magic of the fast, it seemed, had travelled back through time and space to meet me.

At the time, despite my new-found ability to converse with a wise incorporeal entity I called God for convenience, I did not consider myself a spiritual person. I was a scientist with existential quandaries, questionable sanity, quirky beliefs and extraordinary luck. I was not aware that I had already embarked on a spiritual journey – that is until the "wind incidents".

03/25/2011 – Mormon Island, Nebraska
Excerpt from my journal.

I feel perfectly happy right now (except all my pens are frozen). This is slightly ludicrous. I am tucked in the back of the truck in a parking lot behind a bar at Mormon Island in the middle of Nebraska. The wind is howling and shaking the truck. In front of me is a small lake, and beyond that the interstate, I80. The incessant flow of semi-trucks is not exactly peacefully quiet, but they look pretty cool in the fog – like big dragons with glowing eyes. I made myself a delicious cold salad of spinach, tuna, walnuts and vinegar (the oil is frozen) and ate it with gloves on while Pandora serenaded me with Sinatra tunes. I don't know why this pleases me so much. It probably would suck by other people's standard. Maybe that is why it appeals to me. I feel like a free bird, an odd free bird.

I closed my journal and cocooned myself in my sleeping bag with a smile. The wind outside was relentless. It rocked the truck with each gust and sang a whistling song through the branches of nearby trees. I closed my eyes and let the wind rock and sing me to sleep. My consciousness slowly faded until an inconvenient thought brought me back to reality.

"Wait a minute. I'm a woman alone, parked behind a seedy bar on a Saturday night in the middle of Nebraska, and nobody in the world knows where I am. This might be a very, very bad idea."

I peered through the darkness of the parking lot and listened for signs of trouble, but could find none – or none yet.

Was I really so special in the Universe that I was always

protected, even if I defied common sense and put myself in harm's way? Or was I incredibly naïve in assuming that my good luck was inexhaustible?

"You are safe here." I heard in my head. The voice was clear and authoritative, the same voice that had guided me along the Mississippi during the one-day fast.

"How do I know that's not me telling myself I'm safe? Can you prove to me that it's not just plain old me playing God in my head?"

"Would it help if I performed a miracle?"

A miracle! I had my share of serendipitous events and synchronicities, but these could just as easily be attributed to natural abilities, such as being aware of and open to opportunities. But an actual miracle? Of course it would help.

"Do you hear the continuous howling wind? I will stop it for exactly two seconds, and you will know that you are safe."

Just then, the wind stopped suddenly and completely.

I sprung back up, wide-eyed and breathless. One-thousand-one. Two-thousand-two. A fierce gust of wind rocked the truck as the howling reengaged.

I still held my breath, dumbfounded and mystified. The skeptic in me was not completely placated. Maybe I just didn't know anything about wind. Maybe wind in storms stopped occasionally. Maybe this was a perfectly normal wind pattern. I listened attentively for another break for at least half an hour, but none occurred. I slowly released the doubts and finally fell asleep soundly, as though I were held in big loving arms.

The same big loving arms held me as I raced ahead of a snow storm across the rest of Nebraska, through two awkward evenings and one day in Jack's company in Longmont, Colorado, and throughout the long, harrowing drive in a white-out over the Rocky Mountains.

As soon as I passed the Colorado-Utah state line, the sky opened over the unlimited desert vistas I had longed to see. I left the freeway for a side road that quickly turned to dirt. There were no habitation, no cell phone reception, no sign of civilization of any kind. I pulled into Goblin State Park in the golden light of a dusty sunset, turned the truck's engine off and listened. Not a sound beyond the wind – I had the park to myself.

I descended into the main pit of goblins and meandered through their large faces and phallic appendages. I felt so small in their petrified company, just a tiny insignificant human. Through one random path then another, my feet delivered me to a particularly tall goblin, perfectly positioned for maximal desert viewing. I placed both hands and feet in its natural handholds and climbed to the top of its head. From there, I could almost see the entirety of Goblin Valley.

And I could see it well. In fact, all five of my senses seemed unnaturally sharp. Not only could I detect subtle differences in the range of reds in the rocks – from deep brick reds to earthy coppers – and in the delicate texture of their wind-carved faces, but I could also locate small creatures from their minute scurries and detect a hint of sage in the passing wind. The wind – I felt the gentle caress of its scented passage on my bare skin, echoed in the sway of the goblin's head. I closed my eyes and began crying.

I didn't know why I was crying. I assumed the tears were part of some stress-release mechanism, a safety valve through which stored personal dramas and the pressure of thesis writing could be purged. I decided to let them flow.

A few tears turned to weeping then to sobbing. The wind increased in magnitude in proportion to my grief. Through the fog of my sobbing, I noticed the change in the wind, especially when the goblin began wobbling past my comfort level. I was, after all, over ten feet off the ground on a potentially unstable goblin's head. I became so fascinated by my precarious situation that my tears subsided, and so did the wind.

Because I had just witnessed a wind miracle a few days prior, I was less awed by this than I probably should have been. Instead, my scientific brain immediately concocted a testable hypothesis – were the wind and my tears somehow linked?

I focused on the overwhelming feeling of grief lurking in

my heart, barely skin deep, and let myself get weepy, then sobby again. The wind matched me. This could, I suppose, have been a strange coincidence. I chose to believe in magic instead. Either my tears could control the wind or the wind was communicating its support of my grief. Either way, there was something going on with me and the wind.

I remembered Helena's email, and thanked the Grandmothers for their presence. I then thanked the goblin for holding me safe and returned to my truck at camp.

As soon as darkness enveloped the truck, the wind abandoned its gentle caressing and resumed howling. It gusted so fiercely that I didn't dare leave the back of the truck once I had tucked myself in. I ate a can of cold tuna and some partially wilted spinach for dinner crouched on top of my sleeping bag. Eating was difficult. My throat was still closed with sadness.

03/28/2011
Excerpt from my journal.
[Note: Although at the time I called my interlocutor "God" because it felt more accurate than "Not-Me", I also considered the possibility that I might be speaking with an angel or spirit guide or something else entirely. It felt like a reassuring masculine presence, so I used "Him" in this and subsequent transcriptions of our dialogs.]
<u>*Him*</u>*: Dear Melissa,*
The tears you shed earlier were not due to a release of stress but to perfect complete surrender to your natural state. No, your natural state isn't sadness; it is one of communion with nature. You might have lost it recently, even with the walks along the Mississippi. You have concentrated on your inner health and that is good, but you need nature – wind and sand in your face. Thank you for giving me your tears, for not resisting the seeming randomness of your emotions. Accepting your emotions will serve you well.
[I felt another wave of tears well up. I shut my headlamp and cried again. After a few minutes, when the tears subsided, I turned my headlamp back on and resumed writing.]
<u>*Me*</u>*: I am sad.*

Him: I know.
_Me_: And it's very dark out.
Him: [amused] yes, I know, and very windy. You'll be fine though. I've got you. I would not have given you the gifts of freedom and adventure without giving you the ability to withstand a dark, windy, occasionally sad night.

Through the saturated Kodachrome Basin, the surreal Coral Pink Sand Dunes and the majesty of Utah's best national parks, I carried an undertone of sadness all the way to Death Valley. I didn't even stop for a photo in either Zion or Capitol Reef. I rushed through the parks and the mayhem of Las Vegas, convinced that only Death Valley held the medicine to heal my woes.

With a few days to myself before the beginning of the fast, I drove from familiar canyons to favorite sand dunes in search of the joy and feeling of "home" usually characteristics of my visits to the valley, to no avail.

At the Furnace Creek Ranch, I met a painter from Lost Angeles on her annual solo desert retreat who offered me a shower in her hotel room. She also gave me the key to the pool, where I hid an entire afternoon from the hundred and fifteen-degree convection-oven the park had become.

A day before the fast, in spite of the grandiose vistas, the wind miracles and unexpected gifts, I hit an all-time low in my happiness level. And, because of it, I became upset with God.

I did not, at the time, understand that I was grieving my old life, my old self and my old loves. All I saw was that I had undergone all this therapy, had diligently followed through on my own with daily self-healing practices and still I felt miserable. I was in Death Valley, my home, my sanctuary, and still I felt restless and lost. I had personal conversations with God daily and still I had no idea what I was looking for, who I was, why I did the things I did, or why I loved the people I still loved.

04/01/2011
Excerpt from my journal.
<u>Me</u>: *Dear God,*
I don't want to be at odds with you. Can you help me find my way back
to joy? Please?
[There was no answer. This was the last entry in that journal.]

They were no guiding words in my head when I woke up just before dawn the next morning. I always woke up early when sleeping in the sand dunes, in part because I naturally matched the sun's rhythm, but also because sleeping in the dunes was illegal and I wanted to prevent any trouble with the rangers.

ഇ · ൠ

<u>Side note</u> – please don't sleep in sand dunes in Death Valley National Park unless you have impeccable leave-no-trace ethics. It is illegal, and I would hate to start a trend detrimental to a place I love.

ഇ · ൠ

There were no spoken words in my head, but still I felt inspired to sit in lotus position on the crest of a sand dune facing the rising sun. Its warmth and light crawled towards me across the desert, like impending doom or salvation, until I was fully bathed in it. My friend the wind was just waking up as well.

This was the day when I was to meet the Vision Fast's guides and participants. I was nervous and restless. And I was still upset with God.

I closed my eyes and listened to the wind for a few minutes and finally heard the familiar voice in my head.

"Stay here, in meditation with your eyes closed, until it is done." The tone was firm. This was an order.

"Until what's done?"

"You will know."

The wind increased in strength and sand-blasted me, particularly across the face. It prickled. I didn't move. Sand underneath my buttocks and legs was excavated and swirled around my body. I couldn't understand how the wind was carving a hole under me with equal strength on all sides despite its unidirectional flow but resisted the urge to look and kept my eyes closed.

The process was tedious and lengthy. I sat motionless for what seemed like an hour while the wind slowly carved away my sand support. Sheer curiosity kept my mind entirely focused on the process until something scurried across the desert to my right, only twenty feet or so away.

"Stay focused." the voice said, "Stay here. Keep your eyes closed."

I opened my eyes just in time to catch a glimpse of a crumbled piece of paper tumbling across the desert. I knew that piece of paper well; I had unsuccessfully chased it the previous night in the opposite direction until it evaded me in the darkness. I was about to spring up and run to catch it when the voice stopped me.

"Leave it."

"But it's trash in the desert! MY trash!"

"If you are meant to pick it up, then you will find it when you are done here. If you are not, then you will not. Either way, the piece of paper is not your concern right now."

I surrendered. I had no choice. Half an hour or so later, all the sand under my buttocks had been excavated and I was left suspended, uncomfortably, between my feet and my tail bone. I found the image appropriate. I did feel that my hold on reality was precarious, and that I was bound to fall into an unknown abyss in my life as well. I feared this fall, though I knew I couldn't turn away from it.

The last of the sand support gave way, and I dropped, but only by a few inches. Instead of falling into some dreaded abyss, I landed softly into a comfortable carved sand seat exactly to the dimensions of my body.

I smiled in gratitude. What a wonderfully dramatic way to deliver a message. "It's okay to fall." was my message. "I've got you." is what that meant.

I opened my eyes and looked upon a desert I knew by heart

as though for the first time. The soft curves of the dunes seemed brighter, the Panamint Range in the distance stood taller and the mesquite bushes swayed in the wind with unprecedented vibrancy. I felt new. My cheeks were sand-polished smooth. My eyes, ears and hair were filled with sand. My clothes were fully coated as well. Death Valley had once again claimed me as one of its own.

I rolled out of the carved sand seat with a cringe as the blood rushed back into my legs and feet and stood tall to locate the escaped piece of paper.

A flash of white in the distance – only a few dunes away – caught my eye. It looked trapped under a bush. I set off to rescue it, but only found a small desiccated mesquite branch. I searched further and further but never found the piece of paper.

"I'm sorry about the trash" I told the dunes as I turned around. I had searched so far that my path back to the truck was devoid of tourist tracks. Right on this pristine path, a gift awaited me. It was a triangular piece of broken glass, sand-blasted smooth as I was. I held it into the sun and rotated it to see all its facets. In the center of its smoothest side, the sand had swirled so much that it had left a pattern, that of a heart.

I held the glass heart close to mine and quietly thanked God and the desert. I knew this gift was meant for me, and I knew what its message meant.

CHAPTER 9

A few hours later, I was sitting in a circle with strangers about to share their inner-most feelings, and oddly, I was okay with it.

We were a group of nine female fasters, two guides – Helena and Paul – and one assistant. The circle was silent at first as the guides burned sage in a large shell to clear unwanted energy and open a space in which to create our common experience.

I watched attentively as Helena dispersed the smoke in all four compass directions, and I observed myself enjoy the ritual. Maybe I was the circle-sitting, sage burning, Spirit invoking kind after all. But maybe I was not ready to admit it. I knew who I was. I was a scientist, an adventurer and a desert-lover, conceived and grown in the love of Death Valley. That is the story I told myself and shared with the circle the first time the talking stick landed in my hands.

ಏ · ೞ

Talking stick: *n.* a brilliant idea: a small hard-wood branch with a gnarled top polished by dozens, if not hundreds, of nervous confessing hands, which allows the bearer to speak or stay silent uninterruptedly.

ಏ · ೞ

The talking stick moved on, and to my surprise, the desert adventurer dissipated. As each personal story was shared, I realized that this circle was no accidental gathering. These were sisters I had never met, each holding a part of my life story as their own — not the parts I usually shared, but those deep down that struck a nerve and made me cry.

I became a tiny weeping girl I hardly recognized. With each story I resisted the urge to stand up to hug my sisters in support and gratitude for their words.

I had barely dried the last tear when the talking stick landed in my hands a second time. This time we were to create an "intent", a definition for our reason for choosing to fast. What had brought us here? What rite of passage were we undertaking? Who did we wish to be that we felt we weren't yet but hoped to transform into?

I believed I had come to find peace and solitude, to regroup after some hard emotional times, but when the talking stick landed in my hand, a different intent burst forth of its own volition.

"I want to be enlightened!"

I recoiled at my own words. No one else reacted.

The self-governing intent continued, "My best friend

recently fell into a vortex of enlightenment, and I feel that if she can, then so can I."

That night, as I stared at the stars from the warmth of my sleeping bag atop a picnic table, I felt sick to my stomach with embarrassment. How conceded of me to claim wanting to be enlightened. I could have dug a hole and disappeared in it. I would have been no less ashamed had I demanded a helicopter to take me to the summit of Mt. Baker because I couldn't be bothered to climb it myself. The weight of my imagined desert sisters' judgment pressed on my chest and crushed my heart. I just hoped that no one mentioned it again in our upcoming days in the circle.

Our task in the circle for the next three days was to refine and clarify our intents. For my sisters, the process was mostly uncomplicated. Our guides mirrored the stories, extracted themes and longings, asked refining questions until one clear statement emerged – one that could be owned, held in the heart and offered to the Grandmothers during the fast.

I, however, made completely different and often contradictory claims with equal fervor each time I held the talking stick. I was a shape-shifter of passionate personalities, a different person every few minutes.

After the fast, one of the guides shared with me that I was the subject of much debate during the preparation phase. The guides felt that I was too volatile to be sent out in the desert, not because they feared I wouldn't survive physically, but because they couldn't discern who I was, what I was about, or what I might do out there. I was a potential liability.

In the end, they agreed that the compassion I had displayed towards my desert sisters during the initial introductions indicated I had a sufficiently large heart to rescue myself from any psychological trouble I might inflict upon myself alone in the desert.

For three days, I exposed my deepest, darkest inner-most feelings to a circle of strangers, who gradually felt more like kin than anyone else in my life, and received nothing but compassionate support. On the last day of the preparation phase, as we gathered one last time to share our greatest fears about the upcoming fast, I was no closer to crafting an intent. I just hoped that the Grandmothers knew why I was coming.

01/25/2011, Bellingham, WA.
Excerpt from "Letter of intent" from my application to participate in a four-day fast in Death Valley, CA.
    The fast worries me. I knew nothing about fasting when I signed up, but I have been reading up on it since. Anything past three days is called the starvation phase. It can cause physiological damage and alter the thought process. Being alone doesn't worry me; I tend to talk to rocks and plants and stars, so I never feel alone in nature. Sleeping on a tarp in the middle of the desert is bread-and-butter for geologists. Fasting though I have a feeling will be unlike anything I have ever done. It will be like dying. I welcome the idea of having every nutrient in my body related to my previous life flushed out and replaced with clean Death Valley serenity, but I am worried about the alteration of my thought process. A few days ago, during a particularly difficult conversation with my ex-boyfriend, I felt myself separate from my body. I feared I was losing my mind and might not recover from it. As a kid, I heard ghosts my parents claimed were nonexistent – a child psychologist determined I had "too much imagination" – and the few times I smoked Marijuana, I had vivid hallucinations that caused me such fright as to make me black out. I have often wondered about my own sanity and what it would take to tip it over permanently. That is what I fear: I fear that the altered state brought on by the fasting will subject me to some sort of scary hallucination which I will have to face alone, or a sense of losing my mind from which I will not recover. I have spoken about this with my counselor who assured me that crazy people don't know they are going crazy, thereby proving my sanity. I am not saying any of this is rational, but you asked what my concerns are. I hope this will make sense to you. As for the physiological damage, I figure the emotional stress through which I have put my body for the past year is probably more detrimental to my health than four days without food in a place I love and trust.

CHAPTER 10

I walked to the small canyon that was to be my home for the four days of the fast with four gallons of water, a ground tarp, a sleeping bag, a hula hoop, a little bit of Himalayan salt in a Ziploc bag, a journal and pen, a peanut butter Powerbar for emergencies – for which I had no taste, so I knew I wouldn't be tempted – an umbrella for shade and rain, and enough clothes to withstand temperatures from below freezing to convection-oven mode. I felt I was ready for anything.

All eight of my fasting sisters had chosen to wander north from our home base; I alone had gone south.

For safety, I was to walk out each morning to an agreed-upon location and place a rock in a rock circle. Every evening, Helena would visit the same location and place a rock next to mine. If something were to happen to me, my rock would be missing, and the team back at camp would initiate search and rescue.

After the fast, all my sisters commented on the desolation of the desert that surrounded their respective camps. My canyon, in contrast, teemed with life. The bed of the canyon was carpeted in wild flowers, especially Desert Golds with a sprinkling of Mariposa Lilies and California Puppies. Birds, bugs and lizards visited me daily. Small cacti surrounded my natural sleeping cot – a flat and level slab of red sandstone with a view of the Sacred Mountain framed in the canyon's entrance.

The Sacred Mountain was actually snow-covered Telescope Peak, but because I was on a spiritual quest, it pleased me to pretend it was the Sacred Mountain, and perhaps to some of the local natives, it was.

The canyon was a lovely home, but the restlessness that had been growing inside my body and mind didn't leave me much time to settle and enjoy it. No sooner had I dropped my pack onto the flat slab of red sandstone that I began to act strangely.

Those varied "personalities" that had made setting up a unique intent an impossible proposition could no longer be contained. They took over my body in turn, each with its own mannerisms, voice, and opinions.

On the first day of the fast, there were dozens of them, some of which I recognized and some of which I didn't. Any personality by which I had once lived still lived in me. I recognized the Adventurous Child, the Scared Child, the Angry Teenager, the Hard Worker, the Traveler, the Scientist, the Storyteller, and others. Any personality that I had encountered in another and that had helped shape me into whom I had become also still lived in me – The Critic, the Loving Parent, the Disciplinarian, the Ex-husband and his down-to-earth common sense, the Ex-Boyfriend and his wild passion, and so forth.

Some felt unfamiliar. One of these came from a place so deep and dark that the mere recollection of its shrill voice gives me the chills to this day. I was glad that it didn't linger. The loving authoritative voice that had grown prominent in my thoughts since I had left Minneapolis was there as well. His was the only voice that did not express itself out loud. In fact, I could not speak it aloud even when I tried.

As the front lines of these personalities rose from the trenches of my subconscious where they had laid unheard, I was, at first, able to hold my ground. There was no drama in those parts of my mind that felt like mine, just excitement. I had an entire canyon and desert to explore and four days of unbridled freedom in which to do so. I didn't even have to worry about planning, preparing, eating or cleaning up after meals. I had neither expectations nor schedule to uphold, except for one small daily rock-placing duty.

I dropped my pack onto the flat slab of red sandstone and set off to explore the canyon with a gait and stream of thoughts that mostly matched my mental self-image. My hands flared up and my head twitched occasionally as random thoughts passed through, but I still felt like myself.

In the upper-reaches of the canyon, above the red sandstone, the valley floor narrowed and steepened as it entered a section of dark basalt. Walking turned to scrambling.

I continued on hands and feet until the smooth face of a large basalt boulder about seven feet in height completely blocked my way.

It looked like an easy bouldering problem, so without hesitation, I began climbing the obstacle. The small space between the boulder and the canyon wall offered a perfect set of handholds. I lodged both hands in the crack and leaned back to shift my balance, but as I placed my foot on a small protrusion on the canyon wall, my body suddenly cringed and my lips pursed.

It was the Critic, reprimanding me, "Oh, very smart – go climb some rock and break an ankle where no one will find you, why don't you. Very smart."

I jumped back down. The Angry Teenager stepped in, puffing my chest and waving my hands: "Leave her alone, you jerk, she knows what she's doing. She doesn't need your fucking opinion." The Angry Teenager was loud and swore a lot.

The Scary Entity slithered in, scrunched my upper body and whispered: "Yyyyeaaaaah. Let her climb the rock. It's not dangerous. She'll be okay." I felt it did not have my best interest at heart.

My body wriggled from one personality to the next as the argument escalated. The transitions were abrupt and violent as each one pushed the other out of the way to hold its space – my space.

Finally, the wide-eyed Scared Child pushed everybody out in a forceful blow of panic. She backed my body against the rock wall and let it slide to the ground into a small safe ball. She held on tightly to both my knees, hid my head in the space between my arms and began to cry.

I watched the whole event unfold with terror in my heart, which seemed the only organ still somewhat under my control. It was beating hard and fast. I was glad we were crying; at least that emotion felt familiar.

Under the rule of the Scared Child, tsunami-sized waves of sorrow washed over me. She was inconsolable. She sobbed, trembled and wailed until drool ran down to the ground and snot covered my face, and I let her.

She must have felt heard, because, eventually, her tears subsided, and I felt like myself again. I pressed my back against the cold rock for support and lifted my head to look at the world through blurry blood-shot eyes, wondering where I had been. There were my bluish-purple hiking shoes in the brown desert dirt. Everything else was a desert aquarelle through the remnant tears.

As my mind regained focus, I became aware of a presence, an energetic distortion only a few feet in front of me and to my left. This one was not in me; it was with me. I wiped the tears out of my eyes on my sleeve and focused my attention on the distortion. It was a large but gentle energy with a hint of mischievousness. It reminded me of my Papy, my deceased grandfather. I saw his smiling face in my mind.

"Hi Sweetie. Why are you crying?"

My grandfather spoke French with a Polish accent when he was still alive, but I heard him in clear American English in my head.

"Because I don't know which one I am," I raised my hands off my knees and spoke out loud in no specific direction.

I felt gentleness around my heart. "You are the Explorer. Exploring is what you do. Explore this as though it were a canyon or a desert. You will find your way back. You always do."

My grandmother's energy floated behind him. She agreed with him but didn't speak.

I walked back out of the canyon in time to see the sunset, feeling slightly reassured despite the continued internal cacophony. I sat directly on the dirt with the cacti and lizards and watched the sun slowly sink below the horizon in a fiery spectacle. I watched, but I didn't really see it. There was too much noise in my head distracting me from the show.

As the last of the sun disappeared behind the glowing orange horizon, a sudden flash of anger I was sure was mine stood my body up in one bound and placed both hands on my hips in traditional leader position.

"Alright, listen up!" I could hear my own voice loud and clear at last, "I understand that you need to express yourselves. You can use my body for four days – that's it! So be sure that what you have to say is said. Also, I have two requests. One, I want some peace and quiet during sunsets. Two, please don't keep me up all night. I need the dark hours to rest so that I can be strong enough to withstand you all. Thank you!"

Some complained but not too loudly. The Storyteller narrated, "On the first day, she spoke to the voices that had taken over her body, and asked them ..."

I lay awake in my sleeping bag for several hours that first night, looking at the stars and listening to the voices in my head. They were not quiet, as I had asked, but at least they had stopped fighting. I did not argue with them or contradict them, I just listened.

To my delight, I woke up on the second day of the fast to find that most of the voices were gone – or integrated – and quiet. Only seven remained: the Scared Child, the Critic, the Angry Teenager, the Scientist, the Storyteller, the Explorer (which I considered to be "me") and the Voice that could not be spoken.

I led my internal entourage on an all-day hiking adventure to some sedimentary hills at the southern edge of my territory. A dirt road led straight towards the hills, but I had an entire day to reach them, so instead I meandered across the valley floor, following lizard tracks and trails of pretty rocks, stopping to smell flowers and observe insects.

For a few hours, I lay next to a massive anthill – at least three feet in diameter – and studied the daily life of ants. At first the ant colony seemed like a big mess of busyness, but I slowly began to identify individuals within the colony – the Overachiever that carried twice the load of others, the Thief that could not be bothered to find its own, and the Sloth that sluggishly dropped its load short of the edge of town.

"Oh! Look at you! Dropping your load short of town. I saw that." I laughed. The ant paused for a microsecond and looked around. I could have sworn it heard me.

My mind, it seemed, was not so different from an ant colony. I was also a composite of individual voices. As I listened to each one in turn, I began to understand their nuances and patterns. The more I understood, the more I became fond of them.

The Angry Teenager was only trying to protect me from injustices, and I understood that it would remain until the Critic left. The Scared Child just needed to be loved and comforted. Even the Critic likely probably meant well, like a cumbersome overprotective parent. I enjoyed the Scientist's vivacious curiosity. The Storyteller amused me. The Voice supported and loved unconditionally. And I, the Explorer, was not impaired by any of them in my meanderings through the desert in search of adventures.

When I finally reached the sedimentary hills, I scrambled up on all four to the summit to embrace the whole valley in one vista.

The view was well worth the climb. There were dried drainage channels winding down the mile-wide valley floor filled with wild flowers, narrow gullies and carved faces in the dark rocks on the edge, and straight ahead, far in the distance, the Red Amphitheatre Mountains. For a moment, all the voices were quiet and still in contemplation of Mother Nature's beauty. My eyes followed the dance of sunshine and shadows across the scene, then upward to the massive dark clouds congregating overhead.

"It will not rain. You don't need to cover your sleeping bag." The Voice had assured me that morning.

The temperature was dropping rapidly, and those clouds overhead sure looked like rain clouds to me. I was just beginning to doubt the Voice when a few snowflakes floated down, one of which landed on my nose.

Snow? Impossible! Just two days prior the valley was baking at a hundred and fifteen degrees Fahrenheit.

I heard the Voice laugh in my head.

"See? I told you that it wouldn't rain."

I shook my head in mock disapproval, but I could not pretend that I was not amused; I giggled at the joke for the rest of the afternoon.

I returned to my canyon's entrance just in time to watch the sunset. I sat again on the dirt with the cacti and felt my internal companions were watching the sunset with me. They were not silent, as I had asked, but they assumed hushed tones for the rest of the evening, and I was grateful for the reprieve.

On the third morning, there were three left: the Storyteller, the Explorer and the Voice that could not be spoken.

The three of us roamed north to the desolated area where my sisters had set up camp. In order to avoid being seen, I followed the ridges, treaded softly and carefully kept out of sight behind bushes and boulders.

From my high vantage point, I could spy camps tucked in the corners of the desert. My sisters were out on roaming adventures of their own, ghostly silhouettes in the distance moving softly through the parched landscape as though they were spirits of the land.

I waited motionless behind a volcanic boulder until the basin below was cleared of their presence, then hiked down and across the flatness towards the Red Amphitheatre Mountains, the northern boundary of my territory.

When I felt I had hiked far enough, I simply turned around at no particular end point and followed a dried streambed back towards my canyon. The streambed led me within thirty feet of the guides' camp, but none of them acknowledged my passage. I, too, was a spirit of the land.

I was physically weaker than I had been the previous day and had to stop and rest more often. Even with ample water and a hint of Himalayan salt, I was sluggish. I fell asleep during several of my breaks and struggled to get back to the canyon in the early afternoon.

My patience was also wearing thin. The Storyteller's continuous narration of my actions and thoughts was no longer amusing now that it was the sole commentary in my head, and it would have likely driven me crazy had I not already been in that space.

I tried reasoning with it. I tried bargaining for silence. I yelled at it to shut up. Without skipping a beat, it reported my attempts. It spoke in the past tense, as one who is recounting the story to an imaginary future captive audience. I didn't want the Storyteller to disappear completely – I enjoy telling stories as much as I like hearing them – but for God (the Voice?)'s sake, I needed a break.

On the way back to camp, I tried shushing it.

"And then she …," "shhhh," "she …", "shh," "she …," and so forth until I could no longer take it. I stood with my fists clenched and shouted "I will WIN THIS THING!"

As soon as I uttered the words, I felt my energetic center physically rise. I had never given any thought to the exact location of the "center of my being," but that day, my "center" smoothly rose from my solar plexus to my heart and stopped there. At the time, I knew little about chakras or personal vibrational frequencies. I had no idea what had just happened and no time to ponder it because the Storyteller, sneaking through my distracted mind, was already reporting "Suddenly, on the third day …"

When I finally returned to my sleeping bag, back in the canyon, I collapsed into an exhausted heap. The sun was still high and its rays bounced off the sandstone in heat waves. Heat waves! – Had it really snowed the day prior or had I imagined it? Was I imagining this canyon, its flowers, cacti and lizards?

The canyon had seemed real – solid physical reality – when I first arrived, but by the third day everything had acquired a slight "transparency". I didn't concern myself too much with it. I assumed the transparency was simply the result of a combination of lack of nutrients in my brain, physical exhaustion and the haze of heat shimmers – Nothing a good, long nap wouldn't cure.

I opened my umbrella for a little shade, closed my eyes and surrendered to torpor. But a fly had other plans for me. It landed, buzzed, flew off, landed, buzzed, flew off and fully occupied my mind. It even superseded the Storyteller.

Just as I had done with the Storyteller earlier that day, I tried to reason with it, bargain with it and shoo it away, to no avail. The thought then crossed my mind that I knew nothing about flies, and since this one wouldn't leave, I had an opportunity to learn about them by observing it – just as I had done with the ants.

I cleared some space on my sleeping bag as a welcoming landing pad and waited for its visit. I was eager for it, but after a perfunctory touch-and-go the fly flew off, never to return.

I understood – There was the key, the solution to quiet the Storyteller- I just had to acknowledge it, listen to it.

I focused all my attention on the Storyteller and listened. I expected it would be eager to recount the lesson of the fly, but it was uncharacteristically quiet. I beckoned it, "Come on! Tell me what happened … 'And then, the fly …'"

It remained quiet, and I was left, at last, alone with my own thoughts for the rest of the evening.

80 · C03

A note from the Scientist – I tested this method with other flies. It seems to only work with flies meant to teach a lesson, and not, unfortunately, all flies.

80 · C03

CHAPTER 11

I awoke on the fourth day with a blank mind.
And the Universe poured into that void.

*Sketch by Paul, Vision Fast guide and elder, illustrating my personal
journey in Death Valley. The raven represents sharp intellect. The dunes,
heart and flies are from the stories I shared with the circle*

CHAPTER 12

On the fourth day, I sat perfectly still and quiet on my sleeping bag for several hours in the early morning. For the first time in my life, I had no thought at all – no story, no desire, no question, no personality. I held complete knowledge of all that was from within in an undefined haze of consciousness. My sense of presence was so infinitely spacious that I felt dizzy and nauseated whenever I tried to intellectually grasp what was taking place. I could only let the experience be, in awe and discomfort.

At last, the Voice that could not be spoken said, "We should rehearse what you will tell your desert brother and sisters when you return to the circle. I will guide you."

04/09/2011- Death Valley National Park, CA.
No journal entry.
[Oddly, although I took a journal with me on the fast, I felt no inclination to write. I was too busy "experiencing". On the third day, I used a full page to draw a realistic life-size sketch of a plate of fish and chips under the shade of my umbrella. This remained the only entry in the journal. I never wrote the rehearsed speech I prepared on the fourth day, and I never saw the journal with the fish and chips sketch again after the fast.]

The speech that was prepared for me in my own mind felt like an oversimplification of the Grandmothers' gift – such a set of ordinary words to express the extraordinary switch in perception I had experienced. In fact, it seemed so inadequate that I never committed it fully to memory. I remember that it spoke of our true nature as one of Light and Love, which we commonly call Soul – a soul with a body, rather than a body with a soul. It explained that our human personalities are mere roles we choose to play, and that each is essential to the Whole, which is Love. It redefined pain as something for which to be grateful in its ability to accelerate awakening. It clarified that all relationships, including difficult ones, are volitional and beneficial. It also included the intent I could not formulate before the fast, a definition of whom I meant to play in the world. This part of the speech I memorized and wrote down:

04/14/2013, Bellingham, WA
First entry in my new post-fast journal.
> *I am grateful to have chosen to be a free-spirited woman,*
> *a whole, complex, beautiful free spirited woman,*
> *driven by passions,*
> *grounded in self-awareness and love of the Earth,*
> *committed to the protection of said Earth,*
> *its systems and wild places and creatures.*

I have no recollection of what I did for the rest of the fourth day beyond memorizing the speech and practicing it on flowers and cacti a few times.

That evening, I climbed a five hundred-foot mountain above my canyon, one heavy, breathless, starving step at a time, as though it were the last push to the summit of Everest.

I positioned my sleeping bag to have an unobstructed view of my entire territory, from the southern golden sedimentary hills to the northern Red Amphitheatre. Straight across the valley, the Sacred Mountain reminded me of the vast world beyond and of my modest place in it.

I watched the sunset in deafening internal silence, then tracked the slow passage of the moon and stars across the sky until the first glow of daylight once again silhouetted the Sacred Mountain.

This was the night when we were to ask the Grandmothers for a vision, but I felt I had already been granted more than I could ever have asked for, so instead, I simply said "Thank You" to each corner of the desert.

CHAPTER 13

I walked out of the canyon on the fifth morning after returning my camp to its former pristine state. I distributed the last of my water among the plants that had accommodated my presence during the fast, working in a spiral pattern starting with those closest to my sleeping pad and therefore most inconvenienced. I thanked each one of them individually, and thanked the canyon and its creatures as a whole. I then walked out with neither parting sorrow nor regret. My time in the canyon was done.

I walked out of the canyon, met my sisters and ate some food, but "I" didn't. "I" was infinite. The physical form that was doing the walking, the meeting and the eating felt like a tether to the earth, rather than an identity. Yet the experiences in which I was partaking through my physical tether felt simultaneously more vivid and more remote than ever before.

The fragrant floating flakes of burning sage, the kind and welcoming words of our guides, the warmth of the Miso soup and the cool watermelon, the wind skipping over small stones, my sisters, the desert, the earth, the sky and space all entered my consciousness at once, indiscriminately, and in hushed tones. The movie of my own life was playing in the other room while I sat with the Great Silence, slightly queasy from the separation.

After our break-fast meal, all eight of my desert sisters drove to the Furnace Creek Ranch in search of a full body water immersion, be it in the pool or a shower, but I wasn't ready for the shock of a crowded tourist destination. Instead, I craved music, possibly to dispel the Great Silence.

I drove my truck to the Mesquite Flat Sand Dunes with the windows rolled down and some blues blaring on the stereo. I felt each note enter my cells like individual droplets returning to an ocean. Each word of each song carried an essential message, a summary of all I ever needed to know.

I lingered in the dunes until dark, still a ghost of the land, unwilling and unable to rejoin civilization.

That night our circle gathered around a rectangular table at the Furnace Creek Ranch for a celebratory dinner. I, of course, ordered fish and chips. But even with amplified sensations, the meal failed to meet my unrealistic expectations, born of four days of fantasizing.

The next three days were reserved as a time to regroup and debrief. As the talking stick made the round, each of my sisters shared stories of transformation, discovery, recovery and magic. Nothing mundane had happened in the desert. Because each story was truly fantastic, our guides asked that we limit our talking time to twenty minutes. They then mirrored each story, echoing our words from different perspectives, so that we might further enrich our understanding of these personal events.

Although I enjoyed each of my sisters' talking time, with each passing hour, I felt less and less connected to my tether. The sensation was not a pleasant one for me. The universe was too infinite to be comfortable. I suffered from homesickness – I missed the Earth and my body. By the random nature of the draw of speakers, two full days passed before I could tell my story. By then, I felt an urgency to download it, let it flow into the Earth where it could be stored in safety so that I might be me again.

When my turn finally came, I sat down from my chair onto the dirt and placed both palms face down, burrowing each of my fingers into the earth for grounding. My heart was palpitating in anticipation. I was grateful to have practiced my speech. I think I would have lost my wits had I been faced with concocting a report on the fly. I had not anticipated the twenty minute limit on the post-fast story time, and had not timed my speech. I spoke each word as I had rehearsed it, looking up at my audience without seeing it, and finished my speech exactly on the twenty minute mark.

The group was silent for a few minutes. This was an earth silence, that of quiet places. It felt much more intimate than the realm from which I had just returned. I sat in this silence and felt it flow down my shoulders, down my back and to those points of contact where I stopped and the earth started. My muscles relaxed.

At last, I was freed from being infinite.

I spent the last day and a half in the valley in a state of blissful deflation and peace. When the final talking stick came around, I reported that I could hear the songs of crickets, and that they made my day lovely. I assumed this state of bliss was mine to keep.

Part 3

INTENSIVE SUNDAY SCHOOL
FOR THE REBELLIOUS

Ultimately, following one's true north takes
the ability to listen to one's heart,
the humility to accept what is,
and a leap of faith to relinquish control.

- Excerpt from Sofia's journal 5/11/2011 -

CHAPTER 14

My post-Death Valley desert glow was so potent that my reentry into Bellingham sent a shock-wave through town. Within an hour of my return two friends had texted me "Are you back in town? I just 'felt' you might be here." I was to hear the same story from almost every friend with whom I reconnected.

I knew a change had taken place in the desert, but nowhere was it more palpable than against the backdrop of the life I had left just a few months prior. Nothing looked as familiar as it should have. Bellingham was a new town. Every friendship had to be renegotiated. Some prior acquaintances resonated with the new me at a deeper level, while my relationships with others whom I had considered close friends fizzled almost immediately. Men who would have never before given me a second look stopped in the street to stare, shopkeepers were unusually helpful, and one policeman let me go with a kind word after pulling me over for speeding in the rain while talking on my cell phone.

What did they see? What did desert glow look like from

the outside? On the inside, it felt like joy, peace and trust that everything everywhere was exactly as it should be.

I loved the glow, but unfortunately, it was not mine to keep. Gradually, the old Bellingham returned, the one in which men simply walked by and police officers lurked at the edge of campus eager to exercise their ticket-books. I felt that I was diminishing back to "normal" life and that the magic of the fast was leaving me.

I probably would have been thoroughly depressed by this had Paul, one of our guides, not addressed this common outcome of Vision Fasts. He warned us that the colossal gifts we each had received from the Grandmothers – different and perfectly appropriate for each of us – might seem to fade once we returned to our previous lives. He explained that the phenomenon was not a loss, but instead was akin to composting. Although the feelings resulting from the experience seemed to diminish, the essence of the experience was, in fact, getting condensed, like nutrients stored for continuous growth. These nutrients, he assured us, would fuel positive repercussions from our desert metamorphosis for the rest of our lives.

"What happened to you in Death Valley? You seem different."

Everybody asked, but with the passing of the days, I no longer knew the answer. What *had* happened? I went crazy. I spoke in different voices. I watched some ants. I met a fly. I dreamt of fish-and chips. All true, but inadequate.

Something life-changing had happened in the desert, but I didn't know what exactly. What was this gift the Grandmothers had given me? The realization that I was an infinite soul tethered to a body rather than a mortal, physical human being?

Was it even a gift?

Within a few weeks of my return to Bellingham, I was no

longer certain that it was. If my former reality was built on false premises, then nothing I had previously taken for granted could be trusted. I had to start from scratch and learn to navigate a brand new world. The implications of the Grandmothers' gift seemed so fantastical that I feared I was imagining the whole spiritual story.

I tried returning to the mental space I once occupied – where God was just the sum of all energies and the physical world was all there was – but one cannot live as an infinite being for a couple of days and then simply disregard the event as an amusing excursion. Curiosity alone would have kept me going down the Rabbit Hole.

04/18/2011
Excerpt from my journal
<u>*Him*</u>: *I know you feel that what you have discovered is huge, overwhelming and not possibly the truth. In fact, the truth is much greater than you can imagine. You must trust that the process of growth is not one of pain or sacrifice. Whatever you let go will be replaced by something truer. I know that you are in love with this world. You have thrived in it and you feel you might be betraying it. But you do not need to let any of it go. The world is still yours to be in. It is yours to understand more fully through a clean lens and, trust me, it will seem more beautiful than ever.*

Since I had returned from Death Valley, the Voice, which I called God at the time, was omnipresent in my thoughts. It influenced all my decisions. It guided, comforted and supported me. It delivered lessons and homework. And, sometimes, it set me straight.

In addition to the constant dialog in my head, I also dedicated hours daily to recording divine conversations in my journal. The difference in style, voice and penmanship that had characterized our earlier conversations soon faded. Questions and answers looked the same. Initially, I couldn't speak the words of the Voice out loud. So I simply read my journal. If I could speak the words, I knew they were mine; if I couldn't, then they were God's.

This soon passed, however. Just as my desert glow faded, so I could speak more and more of God's answers, until I could speak every word in my journal. I briefly panicked. Was every word mine? Was I losing my ability to speak with God?

"Relax, my love." I heard clearly in my head, "You have not lost me. Do not get too attached to any method. They are training wheels you will soon discard. Just learn to hear me without gimmicks. I am always here. Always."

And so, following His instructions, I learned. Every morning and every evening, I opened my journal and took a deep breath to fully relax into the moment. I stared at a blank page until my eyes defocused. My mind became soft, malleable, fuzzy, elsewhere. A few words appeared. I wrote what I heard.

At first, words mostly appeared in my mind. After a few days, they appeared in my heart. And eventually, they just Were – pervasive and patient – until I wrote them.

I wrote without reading, without understanding, in part because the flow of thoughts was quicker than my pencil, but also because the act of comprehending required a return to my conscious mind, which immediately muffled the process.

After each writing session, I looked out to the world through the window to recalibrate my eyes to physical reality. I returned from the trance and read the words on paper for the first time. Sometimes, they sounded like mine, most often they didn't, and occasionally, I could not understand what had been written.

Have you ever wondered what you would ask God, if you could ask Him anything? The meaning of Life, the makeup of the Universe, the key to Happiness? I asked about my thesis. What was the purpose of writing a thesis? Why were my data so inconsistent? Why did my file just get lost? I also asked about Logan. Were we soulmates? Why the attraction? Why the dysfunction? Why the longing for him still so potent in my heart?

My issues were the same as they had been before I left Bellingham, but my relationship to them had evolved. Before the fast, these issues and the instinctual reactions they elicited had carried me along blindly, but no longer. My mind had been opened in the desert and I could see that my issues were in fact opportunities to learn and grow.

There was no accident, no purposeless story or drama in my life. Absolutely everything was used to facilitate my transition to a new reality, one question, one conversation, one fat notebook at a time.

CHAPTER 15

Reopening my master's thesis for editing was the greatest post-Death Valley non-sequitur of all. The previously all-important calculations of glacier mass balances and heat flux for a tiny crater atop a mostly unknown volcano suddenly seemed trivial in comparison to the exploration of the Universe's inner-workings. Yet, for a month after my return, my earthly life was dedicated to thesis editing.

"May 13th" God had told me. This was the date by which all my editing would be done and the date I had filed with the Graduate School as my final deadline. It was an ambitious deadline for a complex hundred-page document. I had no time to waste. Within two days of my return, I had secured a private office in the Geology department and reopened all my files, both physical and those stored in the back of my brain.

My goal in studying Mt. Baker's active crater, in a nutshell, was to calculate how much heat emanated from the crater, compare this number with historical calculations and draw conclusions about the volcano's eruptive potential.

I assumed that any ice inside the crater not melted at the surface from the heat of the sun was necessarily melted from below by the heat of the volcano. All I needed, therefore, was a measure of how much ice filled the enclosed crater at the beginning and end of summer, and how much had melted at the surface. I used a Ground Penetrating Radar (GPR) to send electromagnetic waves into the subsurface and analyzed the returned signal. Then, it was all math and physics to convert the data into volumes of ice.

Of the hundred or so pages of my thesis, at least half were dedicated to describing the behavior of electromagnetic waves in the crater's heterogeneous environment. I spoke of energy, of waves, of center frequencies – so, naturally, that is where God began my new world education.

04/24/2011
Excerpt from my journal
<u>Him</u>: *Yes, I see that you have questions this morning. You want to know why you feel closer to some people than others and if there is any validity to the concept of soulmates. Let's look at these.*
Your old philosophical views were not completely incorrect. The sum of all energies, which you called the Universe, is the Soul. It is not God; it is a reflection of God. Energy fluxes in the machine, from one entity to the next – do not think of these entities as their physical forms. There are no trees, no world, no people. There is only energy, some of it made physical by the wonderfully simple $E=MC^2$ – one of your favorite equations. All is one and it is the Soul. The interplay of energies is the machine. The reason why some people feel "closer" than others has to do with vibrational frequencies. Vibrational frequencies refer to the oscillation of quantum particles in and out of the reality of form. Each entity of energy in the world of form vibrates at a particular frequency, which is in part determined by how "aware" the entity is. When you feel connected to

another on a "soul" level, as you do with Sofia, Logan and for you, the natural world, it is because your frequencies match. They might not be the same, but they are in harmony, like chords on a guitar. They "play" harmoniously together.

Places also have their own particular range of frequencies. That is why you resonate more with Death Valley than with Vancouver. Spending time in places that feel harmonious can "fine-tune" your own frequency – refine the frequency along which you already operate by filtering out extraneous energies.

During your fast in Death Valley, you experienced a rise in frequency. You were aware of this. It felt to you like the center of your being migrated upward to your heart. You are also aware that some of your old friends now feel closer while others feel further. Very few go "down" in frequency in their earthly life-time, but it is not uncommon to have some be stagnant. This happens when they do not question, when they are satisfied with being content and feel no drive to seek higher joys. Entities of energy like Sofia, like you, like all creatures perfectly on their path, increase the overall frequency of the Soul, so that the whole is raised. This makes it difficult for those who do not seek because they become comparatively ill-matched in the machine. Eventually, all must rise to meet their greater selves.

That is all for now.

I love you.

Despite the similarities in concept exploration between my thesis, my relationship with Logan and my Divine conversations, I still compartmentalized my life into what I considered my "real life" – thesis writing, grocery shopping, bill paying – and my "spiritual life" – Soul, unified energy and the seeking of higher joys. My real life happened in the physical world; my spiritual life solely in my mind and journal. Because of this compartmentalization, I constantly missed obvious metaphors and correspondences.

God patiently presented me with the same lesson in

various forms of decreasing subtlety until I had no choice but to notice.

04/26/2011
Excerpt from my journal
<u>Him</u>: *Good morning Melissa, I was waiting for you. No need to ask your questions, I know what they are.*
Yes, I know that you are upset because your file was lost when your computer crashed. Yes, I know that I promised you that the lost file would be recovered and it was not. That's right, I did not perform the promised miracle, but consider the chapter you had to rewrite. You remember our last conversation on energy? What did you have to rewrite? Go ahead …
<u>Me</u>: *I had to rewrite the part of my thesis that explains impedance, wave reflection and reflection coefficient.*
<u>Him</u>: *What about it? Give me a summary here so we can look at the metaphor together.*
<u>Me</u>: *Fine [I was still upset about the file]. The GPR creates an electric pulse, which makes an electromagnetic wave. This wave has a particular center frequency (80 MHz in this case), but it also operates within a range around the center frequency. The wave is sent into the subsurface where it encounters boundaries between materials with different properties. One of these properties is impedance, which is the ability of a material to impair the progress of the wave, and is related to the material's dielectric constant. Based on the contrast at the boundary between materials, part of the wave gets reflected back to the source (the GPR) where a receiving antenna sends it to the control unit where it is recorded. The magnitude, continuity and polarity of the reflected wave depend on the boundaries encountered. Some boundaries can flip the wave and return a negative-phase signal. Some boundaries send a clean, continuous reflector, some scatter it, some are not thick enough to affect the wave at all, etc.*
<u>Him</u>: *Good. I am glad I had you rewrite this. You had not seen the parallels with our conversations on energy the first two times you wrote*

about it. Now you should rewrite it in terms of Soul and personal vibrational frequencies so that you can share it with Sofia.

<u>Me</u>: *O-kay ... Huh ...The Soul is a fabric of energies. Each section of the fabric ...*

<u>Him</u>: *Section is inaccurate. You can still describe it as separate entities until you are ready to comprehend the whole.*

<u>Me</u>: *So, each entity in the machine?*

<u>Him</u>: *That is closer to the Truth.*

<u>Me</u>. *Each entity in the machine ...*

<u>Him</u>: *including places*

<u>Me</u>: *... vibrates at a particular frequency. We emit waves based on our center frequency ...*

<u>Him</u>: *which can be a wide range or fine-tuned to a narrow range*

<u>Me</u>: *what is the advantage of having it fine-tuned?*

<u>Him</u>: *Why do you use filters on your radar?*

<u>Me</u>: *Oh, I see. So, I know how to interpret the signal that comes back, so it's not murky.*

<u>Him</u>. *Good. Continue ...*

<u>Me</u>: *The waves we emit encounter that of other entities. Based on the contrast between our frequency and theirs, the waves we emit are affected, absorbed, reflected and possibly flipped, then sent back to us and to everything around us as well. Oh! So, actually, everything we perceive of the world is in fact only a reflection of ourselves?*

<u>Him</u>: *Yes. Very good. Can you be more specific?*

<u>Me</u>: *More specific? Mmmh. Okay, so let's say two people really resonate with each other because they vibrate at the same frequency. We can calculate the reflection coefficient for their interaction. Let's say, both have*

a frequency f ➜ $R = \dfrac{\sqrt{f} - \sqrt{f}}{\sqrt{f} + \sqrt{f}} = 0$

There is no reflection!?

<u>Him</u>: *That's right. There is no reflection. They vibrate in sync. Their combined energies flow into the world in unison.*

<u>Me</u>: *I really feel I am making this up right now.*

<u>Him</u>: *Does it make sense though?*

Me: Yes, somewhat. The physics makes sense, but I don't know if it is me or you writing all this. And also, can I ask about the miracle of saving the file? I understand that you wanted me to rewrite the reflection coefficient paragraph, but why tell me you would recover the file and then not do it? Why make me doubt everything I write when you know that this whole spirituality thing already feels hoaky to me?

Him: Because it had to be so. Your file will be saved. I do not lie, but I am limited in my choice of words to your vocabulary since I am speaking to you through you. Sometimes, you just don't have the appropriate words to describe some of the processes at work. Just know that time and timing is the essence. I am proud of you. Don't give up on your faith now. I love you.

Me: [after a long while] I'm hesitant about saying it back. Though I feel I should. I'm sorry.

Him: There is no 'should'. You are still learning.
I love love you.
Have a great day.

That night Sofia called me, "Do you have a conversation to share with me? God said that it was time for me to learn about vibrational frequencies, and that you would teach me."

While I was in Death Valley and ever since my return, Sofia had kept up a correspondence with the Divine of her own. Our spiritual education was symbiotic. We typed key conversations and emailed them to each other daily. Our basic lessons were the same, but because of our vastly different backgrounds and personalities, our conversations read nothing alike. Sofia's journal entries were succinct, respectful and poetic; mine were lengthy and casual. Sofia's spoke of Love, of Home-coming to the true self, of the power of surrender, and of the healing capacity of an open heart, while mine read more like science lessons. Our conversations often cross-referenced each other, giving credence to our idea that we were indeed speaking with God. How could we have otherwise known what lay in the privacy of each other's journals before sharing it?

Sofia could have learned about vibrational frequencies through her own writing and experiences, but God anticipated that she would enjoy learning about them from me and that I would enjoy teaching them to her, and He was correct.

She drove up from Seattle on a cloudy Saturday morning and met me by the fireplace of a busy coffee shop near Bellingham Bay. We pushed aside our café au lait and mocha, and eagerly spread a napkin on the table.

I sketched a stick figure, an energetic entity with its own vibrational frequency and the source of electromagnetic waves, represented by small squiggly lines, and another stick figure, another entity reflecting the wave back to the sender.

Sofia understood, and my excitement for teaching mounted. I carelessly dove into the quality of reflectors, impedance, filters, center frequencies, and what God had taught me about each of them, until Sofia stopped me.

"Shhh. Not so loud!" she said.

I never had any qualms about addressing any topic – esoteric, personal or otherwise – in public. Not only did I not mind being overheard, I think I secretly enjoyed adding a measure of surrealism to strangers' lives. I imagined what they might later share with their spouse – "This morning at the coffee shop, there was a woman who thought she could talk with God and receive physics lessons from Him. Wow!" – and it made me smile.

Sofia, however, still adhered to propriety in public places and preferred to keep her spirituality private. We left the coffee shop to find some privacy along the bay.

"We should have a code to talk about God in public." I told Sofia. "How about 'Charlie'? I mean, we are guided by a bodiless voice in our mission, after all. And then we could be Charlie's angels."

Sofia laughed. "No. God is not 'Charlie.' What about Godfrey?"

"Godfrey! Definitively not. God isn't a British man from the Middle-Ages!"

We laughed through Yahweh, Jehovah, Dieu, and so forth, but none would do. Eventually, when the laughter subsided, we agreed on simply using the pronoun He.

By then we had reached the end of the docks. We both leaned over to gaze into the water, and I saw it – the perfect illustration for my physics lessons.

As though they had been placed specifically for my purpose, two pine cones of different sizes waited at the edge of the dock. I threw both in the calm water at the same time and we watched as ripples traveled outward from their landing point. Wherever the ripples met, the advancing waves interfered with each other and a portion was reflected back to the source location. The rest of the wave continued on to interfere with the next waves, and so forth. If the source pine-cones had been sentient beings, they would have "known" something of their neighbor's size and location from the modifications to their own wave reflected back. It was perfect. Two pine cones were worth a hundred scribbles on a napkin.

The metaphor of ripples on calm water to represent vibrational frequencies would become a staple in my spiritual education. Once, on a rainy day, I caught a glimpse of the system's complexity. Hundreds to thousands of pin-point source locations emitted waves to create a network of reflections at the lake's surface. Larger drops under the trees near the shore created larger ripples. Those I assumed represented older souls, maybe even ascended masters.

On another visit, I saw beyond the ripples. I saw what lay beneath our energetic interactions. I saw the one Soul.

05/05/2011
Email to Sofia

I took the morning off from thesis-editing to go on a hike to Fragrance Lake today. It was nice to be by myself and in nature again. I found a rock right at the water surface, so when I sat on it, I felt I was sitting on the lake itself. Oh, it was so nice and peaceful. Staring at the lake, it dawned on me that the relation between the reflection of the material world (the forest in this case) and the actual world is the same as that of God and the Soul, or that of the Soul and the world. The image I see on the lake is a reflection of the world, which is a reflection of the Soul, which is a reflection of God – A reflection of a reflection of a reflection of God – and still it is amazingly beautiful. So the source must surely be something to behold, except it can't be beheld. I had some thoughts about Logan float up, as I always do, and just then, the wind picked up and created tiny ripples on the lake's surface, blurring the image of the forest. The ripples are like the thoughts in my mind; they modify and blur the true image of the world. When I am lost in thoughts, I lose sight of myself as Soul. But, if one has seen the real world, then it is much easier to find its image in the reflection on the lake than if one only has the reflection to go by. Similarly, if one has had a conscious experience of being Soul, it is easier to find evidence for this experience in the material world than if one never has had the experience. Then I noticed that the rest of the lake was still calm and clear underneath the surface and figured that the same must be true of the Soul. It remains a place of perfect peace and stillness, only the surface, which is our earth personality with all its clarity-clouding thoughts, is affected. Then the sun came out and I stopped my runaway analytical brain and just enjoyed the warmth for a bit. I felt very lucky to be able to escape to wilderness so close to home.

CHAPTER 16

I had expected to have my new-found faith tested. I could amuse myself with noticing the contrast between my pre- and post-Death Valley thought process. I could update my worldview with divinely inspired conversations and applied lessons by the bay and little lakes. But I knew that I would believe in my own transformation only once I had passed the ultimate stress test, the test I had failed seven times already, the Logan test.

Even in a town of eighty thousand inhabitants surrounded by hundreds of square miles of pristine mountainous wilderness, the potency of our chemical attraction had historically superseded logical probability. Logan and I collided everywhere constantly. We reached road intersections at the same instant, chose, out of dozens to hundreds of options, the same restaurants, coffee shops and trailheads. We even once found each other in the whiteout of a snow storm, while our trucks sat on opposite ends of an otherwise deserted trailhead parking lot.

So, if other friends had intuitively 'felt' my return when I entered town, I supposed the event must have rung like a gong for Logan.

04/20/2011
Excerpt from my journal.

I want to run into Logan for selfish reasons. I want to be tested, to know for myself that I have been transformed and healed, as I think I have. Two friends have seen him in town and said he still hurts from the last breakup. I don't want our meeting to cause him pain, though I realize that is not for me to decide. If and when it is suitable for the greater purpose, our encounter will be inevitable. Until then, I can roam the streets of Bellingham and linger where I think I might find him all I want; I'll never see him.

I also want to run into him because God told me that I would and I want validation that I do indeed have a connection with Him. I feel if I question these words, then I will question everything else He has told me. But, also, there might be part of me that wants to run into Logan because I am already falling back into old ruts, longing ruts. It is very important that I don't fall into old ruts. I am a new person now. I should ask myself, what would Melissa of Death Valley do? Would she agonize over whether she will run into Logan or not?

Well?

Would she?

Melissa, whole complex beautiful free-spirited woman, needs no man, but she does love passionately.

So, what would she do about it?

I don't know.

I guess this will be the question for today.

04/21/2011

Email to Sofia.

   And there you have it ...

Shaky shaky Melissa.

Fuck.

Logan just called me. The conversation was tenuous and expected ... he swung by my place to see if I was back because he sensed I was. In fact, he pinpointed my return to the hour. He pulled in just in time to see a supposed "fella" walk out of my place and asked what that was all about ... when I asked how he was, he remained elusive, wouldn't say when he is leaving town and finally said he had to go but wanted to meet me for lunch today. I don't understand why I am so shaky. He leaves me with an icky feeling. If there is a mistaken belief behind any negative emotion, what is the mistaken belief behind the ickiness? That he can affect me? Well, he can. Why do I let him? How do I not let him? Why do I lose my center when I talk to him? I am really writing all this to myself, I know. I am displeased with myself for not handling this like I think the new person I think I am would.

I write to you as I write to myself. Thank you for being an ear to this madness. I am sorry if it takes you away from important tasks.
XOX – Mel.

A little before noon, I stood in front of my office's closed door, my heart beating hard and fast against my chest, and joined my hands in a prayer motion.

I never prayed, in a traditional sense, as I perceived it then. I asked questions, gave thanks, and expressed preferences, but never did I beg or place solemn requests with God, and never did I rely on religious gestures to get my message across. But I did that day.

"Would you please please please protect me, help me stay centered, stay close to me throughout this encounter."

My mind was too noisy to hear an answer, but I assumed that reassurance had been given.

I walked out of my office, down the stairs and stepped onto the sidewalk in front of the Geology building at noon precisely, just in time to see Logan pull in to pick me up.

My fears vanished instantly. Here was the man I had dreaded seeing, yet I could still feel the serenity and strength of my desert glow in my heart. I was changed. I was strong enough for a casual lunch with Logan.

We chose a favorite sushi restaurant and had both a pleasant meal and conversation. We traded accounts of events of the past four months and surprised each other with near-death stories – The very same day I was breaking through the ice of the Mississippi, Logan was getting a broken hand and split helmet as the sixty-foot ice pillar his rope partner was climbing broke off and crashed down on him. He had not let go of the rope despite the broken hand.

I could see our relationship from a remote vantage point for the first time. I could see the intensity and the edge of danger that appealed to me so much. I could see the incompatibility, the attraction, the addiction, the dysfunction, and the love. The character development for the role of Logan in my inner story was complete, and I felt confident that I could conclude this affair effortlessly and with gratitude.

I returned to my office in the early afternoon with a clear mind, ready to concentrate on my thesis.

04/25/2011

Excerpt from my journal.

<u>Him</u>: *Logan's vibrational frequency matches yours in that it is an exact opposite – same frequency, shifted by half a phase. This will become much clearer to you when you meet him next. In essence, you cancel each other out energetically, which leads to that feeling of losing yourself. I shielded you from these cancelling effects during your last encounter so that you were able to remain centered. In your next encounter, I will let you fully experience the effects of the interaction.*

Once again, I stood in front of my office's closed door. A week had passed since I had lunch with Logan – a week I had spent delightfully free from incessant thoughts of him. I had no need for a prayer this time. Logan was leaving town for a few months, off to Alaska to scale unclimbed routes on deadly peaks. There was always a risk that he might not return, so I had agreed to meet him for a goodbye lunch.

Despite the warning in my own writing, I felt casual about this meeting to the point of distraction. At noon, I was so engrossed in the editing of my thesis that I would have forgotten all about it had my alarm not beeped to remind me. I stepped in front of the Geology building to find Logan already waiting for me.

My eyes caught him just so and a wave of infatuation washed over me, drowning any superpowers I might have possessed a split-second prior. I considered turning around and retreating to the sanctuary of my office, but the chemistry we shared had already taken control of my legs and was walking me with a determined gait straight towards my doom.

Our eyes met as I climbed in the passenger seat.

"You are kryptonite." I pulled the seatbelt across the fire in my belly reluctantly, "Kryptonite wrapped in catnip."

He smiled and turned the key in the ignition.

"And so are you."

Melissa, whole complex beautiful free-spirited awakening desert woman, was no more. We ate lunch in Logan's truck parked facing Bellingham Bay, and that was the only world that existed. The bay probably glistened in the sunlight as seagulls soared over the beach and families strolled along the seashore, but I saw none of it. I stared at my fingers, which were shaking slightly, and only occasionally glanced to Logan's face. We talked about "us", about what happened in Colorado, about who had done what to whom, but said nothing. Or maybe I wasn't listening. The music of Logan's voice flowed into my ears like the call of Ulysses's sirens; the lyrics were irrelevant.

The sirens' call gradually subsided until silence filled the cab of the truck – heavy, awkward silence. I turned to look at Logan just in time to see him reach both arms underneath my body. I levitated above the center console and landed on his lap. Two strong arms engulfed me tighter and tighter until our bodies had merged. We were one, outside of time. The cab of the truck disappeared. Everything disappeared, except for the flurry of fire butterflies in the pit of my belly.

In my belly? Hadn't the center of my being been raised from my solar plexus to my heart? Why did these feelings dwell so far down? Had my vibrational frequency been demoted to reflect the state of weakness I had just demonstrated?

Logan kissed me, and I thought of it no further.

I returned to my office after lunch, but have no

recollection of any productive work for the rest of the day. Sometime that afternoon, I stood in the bathroom at the end of the corridor, puzzled at my own reflection in the mirror.

I thought I looked duller. I noticed my first grey hair. I felt there was a likely a correlation between losing myself to Logan's energy and this new sign of aging, but I accepted it. So what? Let me age prematurely, lose my center, return to chaos and forget about the Divine. I would have traded it all to see Logan again — and that is what I did, temporarily.

I thought I was safe for the evening. I had plans to have dinner with a friend. I assumed I'd have no time for Logan.

"Are you seeing Logan again?" There was no "Hello", no "How are you?" In fact, before I even entered her kitchen, my friend was scrutinizing my face with a furled brow.

I lied, defensively. "No!"

"Mmh. You look deflated." So that's how she knew.

I admitted to the lunch meeting and concurred that the encounter had thrown me off balance temporarily but reassured her that I was in no danger. He was leaving town. I likely would never see him again. We changed the subject.

But no sooner was dinner over that I drove straight to Logan's house. I listened for the Voice, but could not hear Him. I convinced myself that if my path was otherwise, God would let me know. God would stop me. It didn't occur to me that advice whispered in my mind might be drowned in dopamine, adrenaline and serotonin carried on the wings of lust butterflies.

Logan recognized my truck's purr as I parked across the street. He walked over to meet me. I had hoped for a few minutes alone to check again with the Voice, but Logan already stood at my window, calm and certain, his green eyes filled with fearless desire. What choice did I have but to surrender?

"I was hoping you'd come. Are you coming in?"

I followed him, and suddenly we were kissing again.

We kissed across the living room, down the corridor and to his room. We stumbled backwards to the foot of his bed.

A thought floated through the haze in my mind, driven by hope more than certitude. "I think I have changed enough to be with him. Now that I understand my true nature, now that I understand that there is no past and no future, I can embrace our relationship for its own sake in the Now. I can stand in a place of infinite Love and make this work."

I heard the Voice whisper "Melissa, get out."

We fell onto Logan's bed, my body on top of his, the taste of his kiss permeating my mind.

I heard the Voice a little louder, "Melissa, get out."

My shirt lifted to match his and our skin connected – at last! I was melting away, ready to sell my eternal Soul for just one night of this particular Now, when I was jolted out of Logan's arms by the loudest shout I have ever heard inside my head.

"MELISSA. GET. OUT!"

I jumped back from the bed and looked at Logan with wide eyes.

"What? What just happened?"

Without a word, I walked out of his bedroom, out of his house, got in my truck and drove away.

He called my cell phone. "What happened?"

"I'm sorry. I have to go."

He called again several times and left messages on my voicemail. "What happened?" turned into "What the hell, Mel?" then into "Fuck you!" but I neither picked up nor returned his call.

To settle my swirling mind, I buried myself in the editing of my thesis and returned to discussing energy and vibrational frequencies with God. I had been tested, data had been collected and the results were in: without God's assistance I was neither wiser nor stronger than I was before. I had strayed on Krypton and was humbled by the realization of how blindingly delicious the experience had tasted. The after-taste was nauseating, and yet the craving for Logan lingered.

Almost two weeks passed before I even dared ask God about the incident in my journal.

05/10/2011
Excerpt from my journal
<u>Him:</u> *It is okay to fall, my beloved. I did not let you fall; I caught you. I let you fall just far enough to open your awareness to your inner-state so that you wouldn't get carried away running down a road you are not ready to walk. You can run free once you know how to run. You can drive once you know how to drive. For now, just let it go. Let me drive. Take the passenger seat without assumptions that you will hate being "controlled". You still have free will. I am just asking that you take a little test drive. I know you; I know you enjoy driving your own life. When you are in a place where you can make choices from your true self, I will gladly, proudly, lovingly hand you back the wheel. Let me drive through this rough spot so you can see how it needs to be driven.*

That night, God's voice woke me around two in the morning, asking that I repeat the words "I pray to never see Logan again," but the words choked my throat. I sat in tears, incapable of repeating the small sentence. The Voice was supportive but gently insistent. I cried for several hours yet never made it past "I pray …"

The following night, God's voice once again woke me at two in the morning. "You can do this, my beloved. Free yourself. Just pray that you never see Logan again. Expressing the intent is sufficient. You don't need to do anything else to free yourself."

I understood that the Voice would insist night after night until I found the courage to abide. I cried for another couple of hours and at last repeated "I pray to never see Logan again." I had to repeat it three more times, each time with more conviction.

I lay awake until the light of day found me, arms still spread wide onto the bed, a wound as raw as red meat where my heart had been.

The Voice returned, this time softly insisting that I write my intent down.

05/12/2011
Excerpt from my journal
    Dear God,
I am grateful to have chosen to meet Logan and to learn the lessons I
needed to learn through our relationship.
It no longer serves me. The learning is done.
In this spirit, I pray to never see Logan again.
The love I think I am giving up is not given up,
because it is You.
I experienced True Love through Logan.
Those glimpses were real, but the source is not Logan.
The source of all Love is You
and the experience of it is in me.
There is no one outside of myself providing me with Love.
I just needed to get to a place where I was ready to experience it.
I surrender.
It all can go.
Here is the wheel. Would you please drive this stretch of the road while I
rest and recover?
Thank You.

CHAPTER 17

There is a park in Bellingham, Boulevard Park, right along the bay, where I liked to run in the evenings to get my blood moving after long hours in front of the computer.

Bellingham is known for its spring-time cold drizzly days, but on one particular May evening, I found Boulevard Park bathed in the golden light of a clear-skied sunset and swept by an unusually warm wind. I stood on one of the docks like a ship's figurehead and let the wind play on my face and in my hair.

There was something exotic and vibrant about that wind and I knew in all certainty that this was the proverbial wind of change.

I welcomed the news – I needed a change. The trust and faith I placed in my connection with the Divine had been steadily growing. Aside from small incidents such as that of the lost file – which I, apparently, couldn't understand because I didn't have the words – everything God promised was delivered with little to no effort on my part. Yet I still felt that I oscillated between two worlds.

In the spiritual world, surrender to Love through trust and faith was the answer in all situations. Human longings, heartbreaks, theses and their deadlines were mere illusions, lucid dreams created to assist in my awakening. In the real world, that in which I had grown up, a thesis could only be completed through determination and hard work. In the real world, clearing my mind of love-and-loss drama and finishing my thesis by the deadline was key in the development of my career, and hence my future livelihood and survival in society.

The spiritual world, of course, appealed to me considerably more, but my faith in it was not such yet that I dared gamble a three-year project. In the real world, the deadline to table my thesis was fast approaching.

ॐ · ೮೪

To table – *v. tr.* Literally to place one's thesis final draft on the table dedicated to this purpose in the Geology Department's office. Once the draft is on the table, it is open to public review for two weeks. If after two weeks nobody has any objection, the thesis can be defended in a public presentation. If nobody has any objection then, a master's degree is granted.

ॐ · ೮೪

The deadline of May 13th was the last possible date on the calendar to table my thesis and still be able to graduate in the spring quarter. If I slipped in any way, I would graduate in the fall, which was not an option because I was moving to Vancouver, in British Columbia, Canada, by the end of summer.

05/07/2011
Excerpt from my journal.
Me: You know, that business about finishing my thesis on time ... I do slack a lot. I mean, I don't really count talking to You as slacking, but I do spend a lot of time, well, slacking. I hope it's not one of those situations where the lesson is that I shouldn't slack.
Him: Ha ha. No it's not. You are done with those sorts of lessons. You will, I promise, finish your thesis on time. You will table and defend by the human calendar dates you have claimed as your deadlines. You will have some work to do after that, and you will most likely still growl about it [amused], but it shall be all done in time so you can start your summer. Out of the pan, into the fire.
Me: Uh oh. I really want to know more about this "into the fire" business!
Him: The learning intensifies. You think of this as the time before your vacation, this is the vacation before your learning time. Yes, you will have time to do your hikes, your climbs, your sewing, your napping in the hammock, but I will expect you to be alert, aware and open. Think of it

as the Intensive Sunday School for the Rebellious. Yes [amused], that is appropriate.

On the morning of May 12th, just a day before my tabling deadline, I was certain that God's promise would not be kept. I was exhausted from two sleepless nights crying goodbyes to Logan, and my thesis was not even yet formatted. I cried in frustration, cursed God, realized it was all *my* doing – or non-doing – wiped tears out of my eyes, and finally settled back reluctantly in front of the computer, braced for a long day of formatting.

It was in this state of turmoil that I accidentally discovered that I had used the wrong formula in my calculations of the dielectric constants associated with each ice layer inside the crater. Horror! If the dielectric constants were wrong, the calculations of depth of ice melted and the estimate for the total heat emanating from the crater – the key conclusion to my entire project – were wrong. The final figure was only a few Watts per square meter off, but the method I had used to calculate it invalidated the results. I briefly considered feigning amnesia, but instead resolved to share the distressing news with my advisor and committee and ask for guidance.

The purpose of a master's thesis is to learn how to conduct research, and it is not uncommon for projects to go awry. With the limited time afforded to master's degrees, providing explanations for mistakes made and recommendations to future researchers is often the only recourse available to panicked graduate students.

With less than twenty-four hours to table, I was partial to that solution. When I received no immediate response from my advisor or committee, I assumed I was home free. But just as I was about to wrap up the formatting and walk home for some much-needed rest, God informed me of an incoming email.

To my chagrin, the consensus was that I had to recalculate my figures and rewrite much of my thesis.

05/12/2011
[This conversation was typed spontaneously in the middle of a thesis's paragraph I was formatting.]
<u>*Him*</u>*: Let it go!*
<u>*Me*</u>*: What am I letting go?*
<u>*Him*</u>*: The emotions brought on by the email from your advisor that you haven't seen yet. In fact, go check it now, so you are not speculating about what you are letting go.*
[I read the email. Ugh!]
<u>*Me*</u>*: Okay. I can work through this ... What emotions are brought up? This email makes me feel discouraged. What is the mistaken belief behind this negative emotion? The mistaken belief is that this process is endless. So, why is that frustrating? Because I'm not doing what I want to do. I'm just doing endless revisions to a thesis I'm ready to see be done. So I feel I am not free. The mistaken belief is that I am a free-spirited woman whose freedom is impaired by menial work.*
<u>*Him*</u>*: Why is it a mistaken belief?*
<u>*Me*</u>*: Because I am not Melissa. I am Soul, a reflection of God, made of pure Love. I am here to experience the world and the frustration is pain that stems from the confusion about who I am.*
[I wrote this as thought I were reciting a learned lesson, but without conviction.]
I didn't choose the frustration, but I probably chose the thesis writing. So, there is probably some lesson ...
<u>*Him*</u>*: [interrupting] No lesson to learn from writing your thesis, just the experience of doing so.*
<u>*Me*</u>*: Does it have to take this long?*
<u>*Him*</u>*: Where are you going in such a hurry?*
<u>*Me*</u>*: Somewhere else, doing something else, more pleasant.*
<u>*Him*</u>*: More in line with Melissa the free-spirit?*

Me: Yes. Absolutely. What's the point of choosing a personality if I don't get to enjoy the cool parts of it?

Him: What is the point? You answer it.

Me: [After a long while] I don't know.

Him: Do you want to be that one-dimensional?

Me: No.

Him: So, maybe Melissa the scientist needs to go through the process of writing a thesis so she knows how to handle writing a thesis, or, say, deal with the editing of a book she might write someday.

Me: But why even bother since it's not real? It's all an illusion. I'm not writing a thesis, Melissa is, and she's not real. The character in the movie I play for myself is writing a thesis.

Him: And wouldn't you want to write her part such that she handles the writing of a thesis gracefully?

Me: But, it doesn't matter! The part is not real. Who cares what a fictional character wants?

Him: Well, apparently, you care.

Me: But I only care because I'm still confused about who I am!

Him: [sigh – not of exasperation, more like bracing for a long explanation]. Okay. You chose the part you are going to play. That part is your path. When the character is exactly on the path, exactly, it becomes transparent to the Soul. The Soul experiences the world in the purest way it can. Clouding confusion is cleared. The Soul shines through, I shine through. Pain disappears. Understanding comes, along with peace, joy, happiness. Everything becomes easy, unless it is a chosen challenge. Okay, so back to the beginning.

What do you need to let go?

Me: Concretely?

Him: Whatever comes to your heart.

Me: I need to let go of false beliefs, some of which fall in the category of "I'm not free."

Him: Good. How do you let go?

Me: I recognize them when they show up.

Him: And?

95

<u>*Me*</u>*: and I don't fight them. I notice they are there.*
But then what do I do?
<u>*Him*</u>*: That's it. Just trust. Trust in my love for you. Trust that I love you SO MUCH that I am going to dissipate any obstacle in the way for you, so that you can be free, so that you can feel free.*
<u>*Me*</u>*: But you said that it was my path to write this thesis, so how are you …*
<u>*Him*</u>*: [interrupting] Your thesis is not an obstacle to your freedom. The frustration is. If you believe and trust me, if you stop resisting or wallowing in your story of how frustrating this is, the answers will just come to you. I have promised you will make the deadline and you will [all this said gently, despite the choice of words].*
<u>*Me*</u>*: The 13th? Tomorrow?*
<u>*Him*</u>*: When it is time.*
And you are going to trust me that I know when it's time.
<u>*Me*</u>*: This is difficult.*
<u>*Him*</u>*: I know*
It doesn't need to be.
All is well, my beloved. All is well.

I stared at the conversation that had appeared in the middle of my thesis and, in the corner of my consciousness, caught a glimpse of how my real life and my spiritual life were in fact integrated. I felt relieved that my advisor had not given me the option of an easy out. I would have never been satisfied with a half-concluded project. The personality I had chosen to play in the world came complete with fierce work ethics, and the love I had for Mt. Baker dictated that I correct my mistakes. That is how, I deduced, the Soul must use the earth-personality for its purpose, by infusing necessary real-world actions with a sense of spiritual excitement and righteousness. My frustration was completely gone; I felt excited by the challenge at hand.

I called a friend and asked if he could bring me a take-out

dinner. He could and did, promptly and graciously – I have often felt that my greatest superpower is in the quality of the people I call friends. I gobbled dinner, locked my office door and plunged head first into the necessary revisions.

Time became elastic. The twelve hours between sunset and sunrise compressed into a perceived four or five. My focus was a methodical and unwavering laser beam over each word and each page. By morning, I had rewritten over a third of my thesis, including all calculations, graphs and formatting. No further editing was required. My thesis was done.

I stepped out of the building to an indigo sky still peppered with a few stars. A yellow sun in a pink halo was just rising behind the forest in the neighboring hills, projecting a bright aura around each silhouetted pine tree. The majesty of the scene and the all-nighter delirium ignited my spirituality to such an extent that I believed I had strayed in a parallel world for the duration of my walk home.

The trees and houses in the distance appeared to move as layers in a diorama. The streets, cars and my own body appeared partially translucent. I could see the stillness and void within the world of form. I could see myself as the creative Soul, the clay master of the world of form. My body, this physical representation of my Self, was just a creation in the world of form, like the trees and houses in the distance.

I understood that this "I", this creative higher vibrational version of my Self, must have been the omniscient interlocutor of my conversations, not God as I then conceived of Him – not some remote entity separate from me.

This actually made sense. I had wondered how God could be interested in my petty drama and daily incessant questions when so many others on the planet had more pressing needs. But if I was writing to myself, then I could definitely understand the narcissist indulgence.

I called Sofia, who was on her way to work, to assess

where my epiphany ranked on the delirium-to-insightfulness scale, and was delighted to hear that she had experienced a similar switch in perception. If I was delirious, at least I had the company of my best friend.

Her own experience had taken the form of a disappearing glass of water. A few nights prior, she had been resting on her sofa, lost in thoughts, her unfocused eyes on the glass of water nearby, when she noticed that parts of it became translucent. She opened her mind to the perception and could, as I had, see the void and stillness within physical matter.

Sofia also felt that our interlocutors were most likely our Higher Selves, the parts of the Soul that characterized our respective individuality. We could intellectually conceive of ourselves as a unified being with both a Higher Self and an earth-personality, but in the same way that we could conceive of the infinite Universe – it was really too mind-boggling to integrate into our daily lives. Still, for the sake of accuracy, we strived for a few weeks to replace "God" with "I", meaning our true self, the Higher Self, in our conversations. For the lower self, or earth-personality, we used our first names. For example, instead of "I was graduating on time, as God had promised", I related the event as "Melissa was graduating on time, as I had promised". Our conversations could not have been stranger had we spoken Pig-Latin.

Meanwhile, Melissa *was* graduating on time, as "I" had promised.

Because my project pertained to Mt. Baker, a popular and potentially dangerous volcano, the news of my thesis defense attracted a much larger audience than is usual for a master's degree. The Geology department secretary booked a large auditorium to accommodate the crowd.

On the day of my defense, instead of practicing my presentation, I took the morning to hike to Pine and Cedar Lakes. I arrived at the auditorium at the last minute, infused with the peace of calm lakes and fully connected to Soul.

I gave an informative and vivacious presentation, a thinly veiled excuse to gush my love for Mt. Baker to a large audience. I tripped over a few technical facts and caught myself with humor. People applauded. There were a few questions. In less than an hour, it was over – my presentation, my master's degree, my life on Mt. Baker.

Overall, I was pleased with my presentation and received many compliments from non-technical folks. My advisor's evaluation was that my presentation "was very, huh ... 'you'." He gently reminded me that my future career as a Geophysicist demanded that I impress my peers and future colleagues with sound technical reasoning, more so than with showmanship.

He was right, of course, but I think Melissa had already deviated from the Geophysics path by then, she just didn't know it yet.

CHAPTER 18

On May 28th 2011, the day after my thesis defense, I filled a box with all my geophysics papers and books, tucked it away in my storage unit and readied myself for a summer of adventures and spiritual exploring on the benches of the Intensive Sunday School for the Rebellious.

My first order of business was to find a way to financially survive the summer. I considered getting a real job, but only briefly. If I was the director of the movie of my own life, then I preferred to keep my main character exciting by crafting a script filled with outdoors adventures. I was certain that locking her into a job would have been detrimental to her growth.

My options seemed limited at first, but I sat patiently with trust and gratitude that *something* would appear.

Within a week, I was living with Rose.

Rose was a sweet elderly lady whom I had met when she purchased the house that Jack and I sold when we parted ways. Rose and I had maintained a friendship based on afternoon teas, cookies and long talks. She had not repainted my former bedroom, now her guest bedroom, so that I would always feel welcome if I needed a place to stay, and I had enjoyed returning to her house whenever I found myself temporary homeless in between adventures.

Rose was willing, and eager, to let me stay rent-free the whole summer in exchange for work around the house – anything from adding shoelaces to old slippers to moving heavy boxes on tall ladders in the garage. I loved the work and felt at home in my old room.

A week after moving in with Rose, at a birthday party, I met Avis, a wonderfully feisty and adventurous five-foot-nothing motorcycle-Mama in search of a new ride. By then I had owned my Triumph for eleven years and loved it as a dear friend and adventure companion; I certainly had no intention of selling it. But I recognized the spark of destiny when Avis set eyes on it. Although I cried as I watched my Triumph ride away, I also sensed the stamp of Greater Good on the transaction: Avis had found her dream ride, I had enough cash to play all summer, and the Triumph was saved the ignominy of being locked up in a garage while I roamed on foot and in my truck in the years to come.

With logistics promptly handled, my mind was completely free and available for spiritual lessons. My only task each day, aside from a few chores for Rose, was to learn, learn, learn. The term "intensive" was accurate. My world perception was shifting so rapidly that any volition I tried to apply to the process delayed it. My only recourse was complete surrender and trust.

I wrote in my journal for hours, drove where I was told, hiked when I was told, and gratefully accepted any synchronistic invitation. My journal became a thick repository of esoteric conversations and one of my most prized possessions. I slept with it and carried it with me on hikes and to coffee shops.

Sometimes, I stared at its tattered cover in fascination — such an ordinary looking notebook, yet I knew that in its pages lay a portal to another realm, a magic realm where all answers lived.

06/02/2011
Excerpt from my journal.
[Although I had experienced a shift in perception, I still used "Me" and "Him" for convenience when transcribing conversations. In my journal, questions and answers followed each other with no indication of who wrote what, aside from content and writing style.]
<u>Me</u>: *Dear Love,*
I have a question. It's about people who have a hard life. I understand that we choose our life to learn/heal/experience whatever we need to, but couldn't the process be less painful? It seems if someone is always in survival mode, they wouldn't have the leisure to become awakened.
<u>Him</u>: *On the contrary. When people lose everything and there is nothing to hold on to, the acceptance of what IS comes easily because the fight to "keep" is gone, rendered pointless. Acceptance of experiences as they are leads to healing.*
<u>Me</u>: *Healing? How did we get unwell to begin with?*
<u>Him</u>: *We started out unwell.*
<u>Me</u>: *The Soul was created unwell!?*
<u>Him</u>: *Yes, we were, and you want to know why. You do not have the words, but consider that the getting well is more important than the being well.*

Me: That seems backwards. You always tell me to be, not do.

Him: Okay, how about this: the dynamic being-well is more fruitful than the static being-well. A dynamic being has ebb and flow, it is alive; a static being is dead. "Alive" experiences more than "dead". Not human dead, more like the Dead Sea, stagnant and contained. Maybe a better term than "unwell" is uncontained. The Soul was created bounded but infinite [the image of a donut appeared in my mind, bounded but infinite], as such it is uncontained.

Me: How does this relate to healing?

Him: By the law of entropy, anything uncontained will tend toward disorder. It is one of humans' physics laws and it is true beyond as well.

Me: Is it, I mean are we trying to put ourselves back in order then? Is God order?

Him: God is neither order nor disorder. Let us concentrate on the Soul for now. I am not sure you have the words for even that yet. Your question will be answered in time, but let us continue.

Me: Are we trying to make order out of disorder?

Him: No, order isn't the proper term. We are trying to expose all parts to Light; disorder creates shadows.

Me: Were we, the Soul, fully in the Light when we were created, but because of entropy shadows appeared?

Him: Yes, I think that is as close as you can get for now. Ask your other question.

Me: Will we continuously be battling because as parts get into the Light, entropy creates more shadows?

Him: "Battling" is the wrong term, as is "continuously".

The process is eternal because the Soul resides in a timeless dimension. There is no gradual coming into the Light. It is there and not there at all times. Learning is a better word than battling.

Here:

[my pen moved to the next page, where it drew a large spiral]

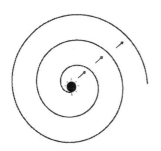

Expansion via entropy, the tendency of all systems toward disorder.

Requires more awareness to reach the same shadow.

Hence the concept of evolution.

Me: How can there be evolution, if everything exists simultaneously in a timeless dimension?
Him: The spiral exists. Each "level" requires a higher degree of consciousness, but at each level entities with lower degrees of consciousness are present, the legacy from the prior, or lower level.
Me: I have more questions, but I just sensed that we are done for now, so thank you.
Him: Yes, Grasshopper. You always have questions. I know. I made you this way!

It was lucky that I was the only student enrolled in the Intensive Sunday School for the Rebellious. I would have been *that* kid – the one in the front row with her hand continuously raised. In the beginning stages of my learning process, I asked much more than I understood.

I asked the same questions day after day, and my Higher Self patiently answered using as many metaphors as necessary. Every few days, I returned to past conversations and discovered new meanings, new answers, with each visit. It was like learning to navigate a brand new world with a map written in a foreign language. It looked like American English, but every term had a different quality, a more holistic meaning.

06/19/2011

Excerpt from my journal [several conversations combined and edited for length].

<u>Me</u>: *Are events in one's life predetermined or are we making our own paths as we go?*

<u>Him</u>: *The healing to be accomplished is predetermined. Experiences to foster said healing are chosen, but the Soul is timeless so these choices are made in "real-time". The personality is not the source of the choice; the Soul, the One Soul is.*

<u>Me</u>: *What is the machine again?*

<u>Him</u>: *The interplay of personalities.*

<u>Me</u>: *all of which are lenses through which the one Soul experiences life to heal its parts in the shadow?*

<u>Him</u>: *Yes, you can think of it in this way for now.*

<u>Me</u>: *What is an experience in terms of Soul and such?*

<u>Him</u>: *An experience is a Soul's intent manifested.*

<u>Me</u>: *What does manifested mean in this context? And while I'm at it, what is an intent?*

<u>Him</u>: *Manifested is perceived. At the grossest level, manifested is what is made accessible to our physical senses, but that is only the final stage. You will learn more about this as you progress. An intent, most simply put is a thought backed by desire.*

<u>Me</u>: *Are thoughts the source of the creative process then?*

<u>Him</u>: *No, intents are. Some thoughts are the result of intents, but not all.*

<u>Me</u>: *Okay. An intent is a thought backed by desire. So, what is desire?*

<u>Him</u>: *Desire is a divine impulse. An impulse is a change in vibrational frequency, so a divine impulse is a change towards a higher frequency.*

<u>Me</u>: *An intent is a thought which aims to place us on our path to a higher frequency, yes?*

<u>Him</u>: *An intent is a choice of the Soul to have an experience to attend to necessary healing. The repercussions of an intent include, but are not limited to, the creation of thoughts. Thoughts are simply waves of energy. They have neither volition nor agenda.*

Me: If some thoughts are created by intents, what creates the other thoughts, the one that are not created by intents?
Him: Shadows in the Soul, energetic disturbances in the machine. There is a finite amount of energy that constitutes Life. In a swimming pool, the movement of a swimmer's body displaces water, which creates a disturbance that affects other swimmers. In a similar fashion, energetic changes such as movements or thoughts can lead to far reaching changes. Each entity in the pool of life affects the whole. A negative thought is like an infectious disease. It affect the energy in the surrounding space, it travels and "bumps" against others. If a person is not firmly grounded in awareness, this can change their own thought patterns, and so forth. Love is the most powerful of all energy space transformers.

Not all lessons were delivered via written conversations. The Intensive Sunday School for the Rebellious held no recess or weekly break. Any activity in which I was led to partake held a lesson, and the bulk of my learning was actually wordless. Concepts simply appeared in my consciousness with immaculate clarity as I wandered through the woods, by the bay, around lakes, on rock climbing routes or glaciated peaks. My perspective shifted as I napped, washed dishes, soaked in baths or sewed my gear. Sometimes, I even continued learning in my dreams.

There were lessons on energy, vibrational frequencies, manifestation, beauty, patience, compassion, situational awareness, undistracted listening, non-judgment, blind trust and faith, and, of course, levity.

"Keep it light. Don't get too serious. This is supposed to be fun. Enjoy the journey…" I was constantly reminded.

There were days dedicated to the exploration of heavier feelings, such as grief for the loss of Logan, and others for lighter feelings, such as the unbridled joy of summiting a peak with a friend. There were social days, during which I was bathed in the pool of others' energies, and solo days, days of utter laziness in the hammock, meant to teach me to *be* rather than *do*, a lesson I still have not fully assimilated as of the writing of this book.

The sewing of my backpack for the PCT fell under the category of "blind trust and faith" lessons. Because I had minimal sewing experience, I ordered a kit containing all the ultra-light fabric and notions necessary and a booklet of instructions – nineteen pages of detailed step-by-step instructions but not one photo or sketch of the finished product. I sewed my backpack, one step at a time, one seam at a time. Sometimes, my patience failed and I rushed ahead to get to the finish product faster, only to spend that evening de-stitching my anxious renegade seams.

Once I learned to trust and get out of my own way, the pack came to life effortlessly. It was a thing of beauty – sturdy, electric blue and less than eleven ounces in weight.

"You should climb Eldorado Peak to test your pack." My Higher Self suggested.

The test was actually of my newfound blind trust and faith.

After six hours of steep climbing in the sun, a dense fog rolled in obscuring the route across the upper glacier below the summit cone. Neither my climbing partner nor I had climbed Eldorado Peak before, but I had more experience and therefore lead the climb. The mountain was blank and night was falling. Just a few months prior, I would have likely opted for an early camp. We would have carved a platform for the tent and slept uneasily, wondering what crevasses lurked around or below. But while enrolled in the Intensive Sunday School for the Rebellious, I could never be lost or in danger. There were no mistakes or wrong exits. Every event was designed to further my growth, with a risk of consequences no greater than if I were dreaming these situations or playing a role in a movie of my design.

I kept walking for at least another hour, guided around

crevasses I could not see by the voice in my head. I walked confidently, as though I knew where I was going, and my climbing partner never seemed to doubt my route finding abilities. He was not surprised when I led him straight to a safe set of tent platforms sheltered by a rock ridge. I must admit that, in spite of all I had learned, I was amazed – but I never shared this with him.

We woke up the next morning to a glorious blue sky, our camp right below the spectacular knife edge ridge leading to the summit. We were standing on top of the world before most people far below had breakfast yet.

The next major set of lessons began on the summit of Eldorado Peak. High above the clouds, with a three-hundred-and-sixty-degree view to the surrounding peaks of the North Cascades, time suddenly compressed to a singularity.

I vaguely sensed that I, my Higher Self or the Universe, had conspired across time to create this exact moment at the summit, from the first set of crampons I purchased years prior to an undefined future in which the story of that moment would be told. I could conceive of the whole set of related experiences as one event outside of time, but tenuously, right at the edge of my consciousness. I made the wish then to further understand timelessness.

A few days later, my wish was granted – a spark of clarity delivered by bugs and bubbles at the surface of Lost Lake in the Chuckanut Mountains.

The concept appeared fully formed, fully understood, in my consciousness: intents were created complete with an inception phase, a development phase and a resolution phase. These phases were created instantaneously and materialized in the world of form like a bubble at the surface of a lake. A bug swam across a bubble. It swam across ripples, then across a calm center, and across more ripples. Because of the limited perspective afforded by its small size, the bug I surmised was unaware of the bubble, it could only know of these ripples, and that calm section, and those other ripples – just as humans perceive past, present and future in a linear fashion, unaware of the greater bubble of creation that constitute one intentional event.

After that day, I could switch perception at will on any event. For example that one dreary Wednesday afternoon when I wished to find a small secluded beach with calm water to meditate and remembered that my friend Deborah had led me to such a beach just a week prior.

In the traditional worldview, in which time is always forward and linear, because Deborah showed me the beach, I had a picture of it stored in my memory. When the desire to find a meditation location arose, I simply retrieved the picture from the past in my mind to accommodate a present need.

In the timeless worldview, my wish to meditate on a secluded beach *created* all at once the moment when Deborah showed me the beach, the moment when I sat on the beach to meditate, and this moment, now, of which I was not then aware, when the story is shared.

And, just as bubbles on the lake sometimes overlap, so could several intents be involved in the creation of a particular experience. When I arrived at the beach to meditate I found two sets of fresh footprints. A couple in love, it seemed, had walked along the water, very close to each other and in step. The smaller of the footprints were exactly my shoe brand and size. We had identical footprints. I made the intent to be in love again someday, and to come with my love to this beach, and I knew that these were in fact *my* footprints perceived as a future occurrence on a linear time scale. How delightful!

Of all the topics covered in the Intensive Sunday School for the Rebellious, I loved the timelessness lessons the most. I felt empowered and reassured to know that I was creating my past as much as I was creating my future.

The reel for the movie of my life already existed, as I was creating it – with as many adventures as I wished to insert in it. All I had to do was step in each frame and enjoy the full-sensory show.

CHAPTER 19

"Do you want to go to the Yukon with me in two weeks?" Mike asked in the same nonchalant tone he might have used to ask if I wanted to get a sandwich downtown. "I'm signed up for the Yukon River Quest race as a double kayak, but my partner had to cancel for health reasons."

„ · ‟

Yukon River Quest – *n.* The longest kayak and canoe race in the world – 444 miles of paddling on the majestic Yukon River between Whitehorse and Dawson City, and for many paddlers, the adventure of a lifetime.

„ · ‟

"But Mike, I have no paddling experience."

"I know, but you're stubborn, and I need somebody who can last."

I looked at him intensely, searching for a joking twinkle in his eyes, but I already knew from the upwelling of excitement in the pit of my belly that this was no joke.

"Think about it." He said, "I mean, you might not want to do it. It could be rough. We will be traveling through such remote wilderness that if anything were to happen, we'd be completely on our own, possibly for days, until organizers realized we were missing ... marooned in the middle of the Yukon having to deal with moose, wolves and grizzly bears. There are very little roads, no habitation, no cell reception and no facilities of any kind. Most people train for years before they feel confident enough to run the Yukon River Quest race."

Oh, the man knew me well. He knew he had just dropped an irresistible, fully-funded adventure of epic proportion on my lap and that there was no way I would ever pass it up.

Of course I was in!

And, just like that, the bell rung and the Intensive Sunday School for the Rebellious was out for the rest of summer.

06/17/2011

Excerpt from my journal

<u>*Him*</u>: *The Yukon trip is my gift to you. There will be others. There will be learning of course – everything, everywhere is a metaphor – but mostly I want to allow you the opportunity to synchronize with your chosen personality, to reset your priorities. The intensive learning is done for the time being. The Yukon trip will allow you to rest and review. Enjoy!*

For five days, our journey north through British Columbia and the Yukon revealed one more fantastically wild landscape after another. Mike and I were in high spirits. During the day, we chatted, sang and laughed. We drove all day, except for a few short paddle practices on small emerald blue lakes. We also kept a detailed tally of our wildlife encounters – one bear, three bear cubs, one red fox, one wolf, two bighorn sheep and seven bald eagles.

In the evenings, I read to Mike conversations from my journal. Although I had shared most of these conversations with Sofia, I never had to explain the concepts to her, unless it was by design, because our learning was so perfectly parallel. The spiritual perspective on life described in my journal was, however, brand new to Mike. He listened attentively, alternating between fascinated interest and pensive puzzlement. I explained and clarified as we read, finding in the teaching a new level of comprehension. By the time we reached Whitehorse, we had read every conversation in my journal. The review process was complete.

The night before the race, I drew a line across the first blank page in my journal, and in big bold letters wrote "Phase 3" on the next one. I no longer recall what I might have perceived then as constituting "Phase 1" or "Phase 2", but a new phase had indeed begun. For the remainder of the summer, I only conversed with my Higher Self a few times, instead filling my journal with messages of love and gratitude for my wonderful life and its exciting adventures.

The last shreds of intellectual processing evaporated the moment we pushed off from Whitehorse. I had a task, a delightful physical challenge and adventure ahead, one that required I occupy my body fully.

Mike anticipated that it would take us three days, paddling non-stop, aside from the mandatory seven-hour rest stop in Carmacks, to reach Dawson. Knowing my propensity for slipping into altered states of consciousness without any drugs, I wondered what new form of personal insanity or divinity I would explore by the grace of sleep deprivation.

At least, I wouldn't be alone this time. Although Mike had instigated several of our most epic adventures, he had always done so in a controlled, reasonable manner. Mike pushed the edge of danger by building solid ground at the edge before proceeding, not by leaning over with a giggle and expecting to learn to fly instantly, as I did. Mike had a family and a career, and a sharp analytical intellect to insure he returned to them in one piece. I fully trusted him to keep me grounded were I to fly off to strange mystical lands again.

Mike was correct; I was a strong and stubborn paddler. Despite my difficulties with the spray skirt at the start line – we left last – and my recurrent vomiting for the thirty miles of Lake Laberge, we had climbed to a middle position by the time we reached the first checkpoint.

Seven hours into the race, the hardest physical part was over. We gratefully left the windy, nauseating lake behind for the fast flowing stillness of the Yukon River in the late evening, and prepared to endure the cold of our first night on the water with extra layers of hats, gloves and jackets.

The riverine woods gradually faded from green to gold to shadowed shapes, and still, Mike and I paddled uninterruptedly, in cadence and with full torso swings. After twelve hours of paddling, I still felt no aches and only a slight chill. My mind was much too fascinated by the experience to have any complaint. For hours, I watched frost gradually mute the bright yellow and red of our kayak's bow to a pastel palette. I admired the perfect converging lines created in the mirror-like surface of the river by our slicing forward progress. I tracked the sun's stealthy path below the tree line. It hid for only a moment and returned immediately. I understood: I didn't want to miss any of this experience either. The backdrop alone was breathtaking. The stars, the trees, the river, the swirls of nascent fog on the river ahead – this was a magical place.

Slowly, the swirls danced, joined and expanded until the entire river was obstructed by a wall of fog. We entered the fog in cadence and silence.

"Paddle faster!" The urgency in Mike's voice startled me back to reality. We had been paddling silently most of the night, each lost in our own reveries and contemplations. I checked my pace, and found no lack in it.

"Why?"

"I don't want to talk about it now. Just do it."

The kayak lurched forward as we both leaned harder into the paddles, working a welcomed sweat to dispel the last chills of the night. We passed an injured solo kayaker, a joyous – or delirious – team of sisters in a kayak and a young couple in a canoe before Mike finally relaxed his relentless pace. Had it taken an hour or several to escape the fog? I had no sense of time, but felt it must have been morning by then, whatever concept "morning" relates to during a non-stop race under a non-setting sun.

"It spoke", Mike said "The fog. I saw it create a large face and mouth words menacingly."

"What did it say?"

"It said 'GET OUT!'"

We both felt the chill of the night deep in our bones as Mike spoke the fog's words.

So, the hallucinations had begun. I was surprised I had not been first. If Mr. Reasonable there, in the pilot's seat, was taking orders from water vapor, what chance did I have?

I quickly scanned the shore and spied several alien creatures I had not previously noticed. They were gawking at us.

"Do you see the fat naked troll on the beach?"

"The one with a dog barking at him? I sure do."

Whatever alternate reality we were navigating, at least Mike and I were navigating it together. I felt no sense of menace from my creatures, they mostly seemed curious, and with good reason. It must have been a strange scene for a troll, this red and yellow kayak with two jabbering entities on top.

As the second day progressed, I gradually occupied my body, my place on earth, more fully. I felt more grounded than ever before. Melissa the explorer, in the remotest wilderness she had ever experienced, was no longer a label I claimed. I owned that role. I excelled at it. I was her as much as the river was water and the banks were dirt. And yet, from this rawest of grounding, I strayed further and further into an unconventional perception of reality.

There were anilogs (logs masquerading as animals), archers in the trees, moose, eagles, dinosaurs, fairies, even a grizzly bear swimming across the river. That bear was almost hit by a canoe right before Carmacks.

A fellow kayaker we met in Carmacks assured us that there indeed had been a grizzly bear almost hit by a canoe. Others had seen it too. That man's kayaking partner had, earlier that day, witnessed a water nymph glide up on the bow of their kayak, listen to the boat's heartbeat, and glide back to the river on the other side. He had not seen the nymph himself, but he had seen the bear.

"How many witnesses do you think it take for reality to be real?" were the last words I spoke to Mike before falling into the deepest and most delicious sleep I have ever experienced. There were no beta, theta or delta waves, no REM in that sleep cycle. Instead, I left my physical body safely cocooned in my warm sleeping bag, next to Mike, in a volunteer's tent, in the sun of a campground in Carmacks, and I flew away. When I returned, four hours later, I had no mental images, no visual memory of my out-of-body journey, but a strong intuitive knowing of it. I felt refreshed, revitalized, peaceful and exquisitely happy.

I approached and greeted the river as a dear old friend I had not seen in years. The sun was still pretending it might either set or rise, but we knew it intended neither. We were allowed back on the river at one in the morning, exactly seven hours after disembarking, and paddled away without headlamps.

Mike and I quickly discovered that although the mandatory rest had rejuvenated our bodies, it was powerless in dispelling alternative visual realities. The Yukon River was still populated in equal proportion by legit wildlife, anilogs and a host of fantastic creatures. But we paid the visions no heed. This surreal river world was our new normal, and our attention turned to more practical topics, such as the upcoming rapids.

Five Finger Rapids, from what I could tell looking ahead, was a roaring wall of impassible tumultuous water.

"We'll pass the first set of rocks to the left, then immediately veer to the right to stay away from the main falls."

Mike knew just what to do. We stayed the course, hearts beating hard and adrenaline pumping. But the exhilarating ride I expected never came. We were through so quickly and effortlessly that I suspected the rapids had been just another hallucination. Only after the race, in talking with other boaters, did I realize how serious the rapids were. Mike's exceptional navigational skills had in fact been the key to our smooth passage.

After the rapids, a sense of euphoria joined our journey. The River was infinite and we were joyous eternal paddlers with neither destination nor deadline. We felt safe on our liquid home. We sang songs and sometimes laughed so hard that we had to stop paddling to catch our breaths.

Later in the day, when fatigue finally caught up with us, we established a rotating schedule of cat-naps. Every hour, one of us slept for a timed ten-minute lapse while the other held the helm and maintained momentum. We only maintained momentum as a courtesy to the River anyway. It seemed happy to carry us along whether we helped or not.

The shore landscape gradually dried, and the river became milky white as sediment-loaded tributaries joined us for the ride. We weaved a careful path through sandy braided channels, until suddenly, we hit ground.

The unexpected stop shook me awake from a cat-nap with no clear indication of which world I was awaking to. I had just been dreaming that I was kayaking the Yukon River, and according to Mike, was still paddling in my sleep. Mike jumped out of the boat and pushed us back into the current while I readjusted to the current version of reality.

Once freed from the sandy channels, the river meandered through steep rocky banks. The large, flat rock faces were perfect blank screens for our wild imaginings, and the gallery of cartoon characters carved in the rocks was more intricate than a sailor's full sleeve tattoo.

Not only were Mike and I seeing the same scenes, – the same monkey with cymbals, wrapped in a dragon's tail, the fire of which grazed the top of the princess's hair – but I was seeing the same scene twice myself, superimposed in the present moment.

The overwhelming sense of simultaneous déjà-vu was uncanny, but only at the superficial level of my consciousness. Below this layer, I still felt present and grounded. Through the perceptual oddities, I was still savoring the beauty of the pristine Yukon wilderness and relishing my current place in it.

We were so close to Dawson by then – a few hours away at most – that I almost could taste the ice cream of victory waiting for us a few blocks from the finish line. But, suddenly and without a transitional stop, the kayak reversed direction and climbed back up-river, stern first.

"What's happening?" Mike would know of strange eddies in this part of the river, I was sure of it.

"What do you mean?"

"Look at the trees!"

The trees on the shore were gliding towards the stern of the kayak from my point of reference, the converging lines at the bow pointed forward as they had the entire trip, and the fizzle from the silt grazing the hull traveled from me to Mike, but my brain interpreted this information as evidence that *we* were going backwards. All five of my human senses told me that we were going backwards, but Mike disagreed with all of them, and I trusted him more.

My only recourse was to cut all sensory input and keep on paddling. I closed my eyes and retreated to a safe place by focusing my attention on the marching ants. The ants went marching one by one, hurrah, hurrah. Two-by-two. Three-by-three. I occasionally fell asleep, but continued paddling and counting in my dreams. The line between my awake and sleeping states was barely perceptible. Behind the song and the closed eyes, I was vaguely aware of a sad feeling in my heart for all the breathtaking scenery I was missing, but I felt too close to that line between altered perception and insanity to let go of the ants.

The army of thirty-eight marching ants had just tumbled down to the ground to get out of the rain, when I suddenly felt the kayak switch back to a forward motion.

With a sigh of relief, I reopened my eyes to a wide bicolor Yukon River – blue to the right, brown to the left. What new optical trickery was this?

"We just passed the confluence with the Klondike." Mike said, "We're in Dawson!"

Three days later, sitting outside the ice cream parlor one last time before heading out of Dawson on our next adventure, Mike and I silently nodded to the Yukon River in gratitude. That we finished last in our category despite being a stronger team was puzzling and yet completely irrelevant. We had visited Dawson as the tourists that we were. We had slept, eaten, enjoyed French Cancan in an old west saloon and drank whiskey in which floated a frost-bitten toe, but always we returned to the river, drawn back to the strange world we had been privileged to navigate.

As we drove away, big tears rolled down my cheeks, the kinds I had historically reserved for Mt. Baker and Death Valley. I had met myself on the Yukon River – that synchronized, fine-tuned version of Melissa exactly in character in her own story -, and I wished to never be anything less than she was.

07/03/2011
Sourtoe Cocktail Certificate
  "In recognition that Melissa Wyld, in the presence of witnesses, drank an authentic Sourtoe Cocktail, thereby following in the wayward – even staggering – footsteps of Capt. River Rat, and has proven to be a person capable of almost anything, and is therefore fully entitled to bear this certificate with such rights & privileges as may at any drunken moment be decided upon. In witness whereof I have hereunto set my hand (or my seal, or made my mark, or whatever I was capable of at the time). Capt. Dick Capt. River Rat"

Part 4

QUANTUM LEAP

Absolute Freedom requires Absolute Trust

- Excerpt from my journal 05/31/2011 -

CHAPTER 20

On September 6th, 2011, the day before my forty-first birthday, I drove all day from Black Rock City, a surreal ephemeral town of sixty-five thousand people gathered in the desert to celebrate freedom and art in the spirit of Burning Man, to Vancouver in British Columbia, where I was to start my PhD program in Geophysics.

So abrupt was the switch that I still had desert dirt in my hair when I first walked into what was to be my office for at least the next four years.

I once had been ecstatic at the prospect of this PhD program. My project involved exploring remote desert areas of Chile and Peru and using an array of geophysical methods to determine the potential of harvesting geothermal energy from these areas. I could not have dreamt a better project for me.

03/08/2011
Email to a few friends, sent from Minneapolis.
Titled: "Can you see me? Am I standing in a pool of light?"
    I told my future advisor that I would not be able to start the PhD program in the fall of 2011 because I will be walking the PCT next year. He asked how long I needed. I told him six months. He said that my plan can totally be accommodated.

So, I'll start this fall in Vancouver (stay close to Bellingham friends and mountains, check), then from January to March 2012 I will be off to Chile and Peru to gather data (awesome geology fieldwork in foreign countries, check), then in mid-April I start the PCT and walk until September (amazing journey, check), and come back to the university in late September to finish off that semester (ward-off post-trail blues with interesting project, check). Oh, and the University awarded me a $20k/yr entrance scholarship for three years, in addition to the NSF funding I still have (pay for all my crazy adventures, check).
Anybody knows God's address? I'd like to send a thank-you note.
Love to all!!!
XOX – Mel.

By the time I arrived in Vancouver, however, my priorities had changed. The original intent I had placed with the Universe to become a Geophysicist had been fueled by such passion that everything I had wished for had been granted. Yet, like an obsolete gift, I found no joy in it when it arrived.

My life path had bifurcated. If I followed the path to the right, I became a Geophysicist – an explorer of the world through academic study, with ample funding for my adventures, surrounded by intelligent, educated, science-minded colleagues, and with the option to make a difference in the world through teaching and research. If I followed the path to the left, I stepped into the unknown. The slate was blank and any experience or outcome a possibility, including the one where I slipped hopelessly in misfortune. I could feel the tug of the left path on my heart, but could not fathom why.

At first, I assumed that my unease was a form of mourning for the loss of my care-free summer days, and devised a daily routine of positive affirmations to expedite the recovery process. I reminded myself every morning of how incredibly fortunate I was – and I really was – and took walks in the lush green forests of my new home to counteract the hours I spent sitting at a desk.

The lush green leaves turned to vibrant yellows and reds, and still, I felt miserable. I meditated and practiced yoga, learned fascinating facts about volcanic fields, gravitometry, magnetic resonance and the wonders of geothermal energy, and still, I struggled just to feel content.

Sofia visited me often and lent a friendly ear to my woes. While I had been enjoying the perks of playing Melissa-the-explorer towards the end of the summer, she had transcended her earthly personality and had no woes of her own. She lived in a state of joy, a feeling of being in love with no object. She embraced every situation with equanimity and detached interest. Even when I told her, "You know, I'm happy for you that you're enlightened and all, but frankly, hanging out with you without your personality is really boring," she simply laughed and continued to love me without judgment.

I was in the throes of the other side of that coin; my only claim to fairness was that I judged everything and everybody with equal disdain. The bus was too slow, the town too noisy, my colleagues too practical, my advisor too friendly, and everyone lived small silly lives, me especially.

I often considered quitting the PhD, but I needed enough funds to finance my PCT thru-hike. That adventure was non-negotiable. I had some investments left from my days in a cubicle, but not enough to finance a full year of adventures. Quitting the PhD also meant walking half a year in the wilderness with no health insurance. Although my Higher Self assured me that all my needs would be met, I still didn't believe that such a promise could come without a deductible, so I purposely excluded my investments from any calculations of assets. I could see no way around it: I had to work. But no job I could imagine getting could be better than being paid to study geothermal energy in exotic locations, so clearly, I couldn't quit.

What a dilemma! I agonized about it. I wrote confused and angry notes to my Higher Self in my journal, but received the same non-judgmental detached support I was getting from Sofia: "There is no wrong answer, the choice is yours, follow your heart."

Follow my heart, follow my heart … what if my heart had lost its mind? What if my heart was leading me to a path of ruin? What if my heart couldn't appreciate what had already been given? My brain now, it knew what was right, reasonable and profitable. It could see plainly that my heart was blind. I had learned so much in such a short time about Soul, trust, faith and the spiritual ways of the world, and yet I still feared taking the leap into the unknown.

The vibrant yellow and red leaves faded to dull rusty browns, then were gone, defeated by the advancing grey and its daily drizzles. My anguish turned to depression.

I hid from the world in hot baths. By the side of the steaming tub, I carefully placed my reading glasses and a small pile of professional geophysics papers related to my project. I even occasionally pretended to read them, only to realize three pages deep that I had not retained a word I had read. I ate odd food combinations – couscous with vanilla yogurt and a side of tuna – because I could not be bothered to go grocery shopping. I was bored with meditation, yoga and movies. I was bored with my boredom.

And yet, through it all, I was fully aware of my own depression. I watched it evolve like a curious little caged animal, wondering how long I would choose to feed it and keep it as a pet. I recognized that my woes had all the hallmarks of a pain-body, an energetic disturbance obscuring the perfectly joyous being I was meant to be. I understood that pain led to healing from lessons I had received on the benches of the Intense Sunday School for the Rebellious.

"Acceptance of experiences as they are leads to healing," my Higher Self had written.

"Pain is the breaking of the shell that encloses understanding," Sofia reminded me, quoting one of her favorite Khalil Gibran poem.

Apparently, in this case, awareness and acceptance of the experience of pain were not sufficient to dissipate it.

I wallowed in self-pity for several weeks before deciding to lean into it. If acceptance was ineffective, I was willing to try exaggeration. I crafted a music playlist of the most depressing songs I could gather, dimmed the lights low and sat in the middle of my one-bedroom rug. I let the music slowly envelop and infiltrate me, down my throat, to my chest and my heart. Once there, it started to squeeze, extracting any tears I had not yet cried. There was poetry in the depth of my sadness and I meant to let myself be as sad as I possibly could. I wailed, sobbed, and let tears soak my sleeves and snot cover my face. When the playlist ended, I crawled into bed and cried myself to sleep, something I had not done since I was a child.

When I woke up the next morning, the angst was gone. My shoulders were relaxed and my face was soft, albeit still a little red and puffy. The thought of how dramatic – tragic even – the previous night's scene had been made me giggle. What an experience! I had no idea what had been healed, or how, but I knew that I was done with the fuss, the worry, and the fear. I leaned over the edge of the bed to inspect the state of the outside world through my window and found it as grey and wet as it had been for weeks. Yes, I was definitely done with this. It was time to leap.

CHAPTER 21

I sat in the parking lot outside of the Earth Science building, fascinated by my decision to quit the PhD program for at least half an hour. Then I called Jack.

"Hey, so, I have a question," I said, skipping the pleasantries, "if I were to do something really stupid, and fall flat on my face, would you rescue me?"

He knew I meant financially. One of the reasons our divorce had been amicable was that neither of us had asked anything of the other in the separation. Jack was much wealthier than I was, but his friendship meant more to me than money. He had said that if I ever needed anything I could call on him, and here I was.

"Are you quitting your PhD?"

"Yep." I was.

"Is it sucking your soul?" This was a rather out-of-character question – I had not known Jack to speak of souls before – but I heard the truth as I spoke my answer, "Yes, it is."

"Then, sure. How much would you need?"

We briefly discussed the cost of a PCT thru-hike, and agreed that if I were to borrow the money, I would repay it within a year of completing my hike.

Feeling fully backed, I confidently walked to my advisor's office.

There, I discovered a second supporter. I was not the first student to quit a PhD program, and at least, I was quitting before any data had been gathered, so the project was intact to attract another candidate with big dreams of becoming a Geophysicist. My advisor met the news of my departure with understanding but suggested I complete the semester to avoid having to reimburse the portion of the scholarship that had already been disbursed. He further assured me that I was making the right choice: if my heart wasn't in the project after a few months, I was unlikely to survive the three-year PhD blues, when most students quit.

I walked back across the parking lot as though I were floating above it. My heart was buoyant, free and filled with glee. The unknown that had so worried me suddenly looked like a golden field of infinite possibilities.

My exuberant joy was short lived, however, drowned within a week by the harsh reality of looking for work in a college town. I answered every Bellingham job advertisement for which I was even remotely qualified and did not receive one call back.

Meanwhile, my advisor had been investigating other project opportunities within the Earth Science department. If volcanology did not inspire me to pursue a PhD, maybe glaciology would. It is sometimes difficult for people who are passionate about their field to understand why one would want out of it, especially when said one once displayed equal passion for the field. He called me in his office a week after our talk – a week I had spent in utter despair at the job market – and presented me with an alternate plan. I could, if I chose, transfer to the glaciology department and study vast glacial valleys in the Yukon using a Ground Penetrating Radar. I could even be involved in the design and building of a Ground Penetrating Radar. I could still walk the PCT and keep all my scholarships. Very little paperwork would be required for this transfer. I had a week to decide.

I walked back out and across the parking lot feeling I had just been shot. Seriously! I had followed my heart and quit a perfect project, and here, I was offered an even *more* perfect project. What was my Higher Self doing?

If I thought I had agonized over the decision to quit the first time, I stood corrected: this was agony. For a few days I paced in my room muttering to myself, until I finally sat down with my journal and called for help.

11/11/2011
Excerpt from my journal
<u>Me</u>: *Dear God,*

You might just be my Higher Self, but it is more comforting to me right now to think of you as some omnipresent loving parent, friend and guide. I would love some guidance.

I understand that you cannot tell me what to do because 1) it would defeat the purpose of free will and 2) I would likely not listen if the answer is not to my liking. But still, just out of curiosity, what do you think I should do about the PhD offer?

<u>Him</u>: *You already know the answer. What is the answer?*

<u>Me</u>: *That I don't want to sit in an office and study glaciers right now. [I answered without thought and was surprised to discover that I knew indeed]. But a few days ago, I seemed to think it was the right choice. I was excited about it. Money and a medical card came in the mail today to remind me of what I would be giving up.*

<u>Him</u>: *Or to remind you to take care of business before you bail.*

<u>Me</u>: *So you think bailing is the proper path for me?*

<u>Him</u>: *Yes, if bailing is what you are doing then it is obviously the proper path for you.*

Me: Can you speculate about what would happen if I stayed? Wouldn't I find joy eventually?

Him: You have chosen to seek spiritual awareness. It started with your intent to go to Death Valley and it has been your repeated prayer ever since: "I want to be awake". You can be a scientist, or an adventurer, or anything. Your personality's attributes are relevant to your quest only in the form of the seeking, not in the substance of the seeking. You could stay here, where it is safe, but you already know it isn't right. The drive in you to find what you seek is stronger than any reason your mind can construct. Yes, you would get to the same place eventually. Growth in awareness is inevitable, but if the form of the learning does not suit your current personality, your progress will be impaired by resistance to what is.

So, this was it. I wiped the fog off my hindsight goggles and scrutinized the events of the past year with new clarity. I realized for the first time that Melissa the Geophysicist was no longer. I had deviated from that path many months prior but had been carried forward by the momentum of my former intents.

Whereas Sofia had gracefully transcended her personality, I felt temporarily lost and rudderless without mine. I was still very attached to my self-image as a scientific explorer. I had only seen glimpses of the free-spirited woman I had claimed for myself in Death Valley. I didn't own it yet. I didn't feel I deserved it yet. I knew in the year to come I would own the "PCT thru-hiker" label, but that time hadn't arrived yet, and in the interim I needed to gather funds to make it a reality. Although I was grateful for the safety net provided by Jack's promise, I fully intended to finance my own thru-hike and survive the year by my own means.

11/11/2011

Excerpt from my journal

Him: You don't need to decide anything further, Melissa. Let it flow now. See what surfaces. The PCT will not be taken away from you. I promise [I was skeptical]. I absolutely promise.

*I hear your fears. You are 41, you have no job and you will be out
wandering for a year. These are your fears? They are very unMelissa-like.
A year out for somebody as loved and supported as you are is nothing. The
inspiration to yourself and others — priceless! [He was quite amused by
this]*
<u>Me</u>: *I don't know how much inspiration I will be. I'm mostly going to
appear like a crazy woman in the midst of a mid-life crisis.*
<u>Him</u>: *The glow you will acquire will be your justification in the eyes of
those who care.*
<u>Me</u>: *Thank you [crying]. I needed to hear that.*
<u>Him</u>: *You will be scared again occasionally. It's alright. Just come back to
yourself, your presence, your faith and trust. Yoga will help. Being in the
woods will help.*
<u>Me</u>: *Why make me go through the whole quitting process again? I had
already taken the leap to quit.*
<u>Him</u>: *You had quit and you didn't know why. Now you do.*

I wrote two term papers as a PhD student — one on the
volcanic history of Mt. Shasta, a mountain around which I
would be walking as a PCT hiker, and one on the ecological
impact of geothermal energy harvesting, to dispel the last
qualms I had about quitting. I once had cared so much about
my grades that I would have considered an 'A-' a failure, but
the new Melissa, not yet fully emerged from her chrysalis, was
indifferent to grades and all things academic.

I finished the semester, but not very gracefully. The cold
drizzle of the Pacific Northwest winter sapped any drive I
might have had to step outside, whether to get to my office at
school or for a walk in the neighborhood. Instead, I wrote my
term papers in my sad little room and only braved the outside
world to get to a yoga studio a few blocks away. My job search
remained unfruitful, and the long wait at the Canadian-US
border dissuaded me from visiting Bellingham friends. I felt
tucked away in the corner of the world, stagnant and
uninspired, yet I never again second-guessed my decision to
quit. Something was coming. I just didn't know what, or when.

CHAPTER 22

ജ · ഐ

Quantum Leap – *n.* The scientifically unsubstantiated (but occasionally experienced) idea that entities in the world of form, such as people, can jump from one reality (parallel universe) to the next instantaneously without going through the intermediate space and time, as quantum particles do.

ജ · ഐ

I no longer recall what random Google search led me to the Tribe Yoga website, but I believe the quantum leap happened when I first set eyes on the school's welcome page. My heart suddenly pumped faster and harder. An indistinct buzzing surrounded my head. In that instant, I knew I was going to India to become a yoga instructor as surely as I knew I was walking the PCT. The program started in early January, two weeks after the end of the semester, and concluded in mid-March, two weeks before my scheduled start date for the trail. The cost of the flight, accommodations and tuition were not out of my budget, because I had *no* budget.

The leaps of faith I had taken by quitting the PhD program twice suddenly revealed themselves to be merely the bounding steps preceding the actual jump. Did I have enough faith in my new worldview to forgo any chance of earning an income before the trail, compound my debts with an irresponsible trip to distant lands, and still trust that all my needs would be met?

I remembered the softly spoken words of my grandfather in Death Valley, reminding me that I was the Explorer. I remembered that outward labels may come and go, but the intrinsic chosen personality remains – it is the part I play in the machine, my unique experience of reality, one of the infinite lenses through which the Soul experiences itself. Here was my chance to apply what I had learned on the benches of the Intensive Sunday School for the Rebellious.

I charged the deposit for the tuition and the cost of the flight on a credit card and committed to wandering uncharted territories, to whatever end.

A few days later, walking in my favorite park along Bellingham Bay, I discovered that a new statue had appeared on a protruding rock in the bay. An anonymous artist had snuck into the park at night, swum to the rock, drilled a hole, filled it with epoxy and placed the metal statue for all to see. He or she then slipped a letter under the local newspaper's office's door explaining that the statue was a gift to the people of Bellingham and that it would be removed as covertly as it was placed as soon as it started to rust. Thus, for about a year, a graceful metal statue of a yogini woman in dancer pose graced the shores of Bellingham Bay and I, narcissistically, knew this was a sign of approval and encouragement from my Higher Self for the path I had chosen, the path of yoga, the path to India – the path of trust and surrender.

CHAPTER 23

02/10/2012
First Facebook status update from Rishikesh, India
I just rode across Ram Jhula, a pedestrian-only bridge suspended sixty feet over the sacred Ganges River, on the back of an old scooter driven by a man I paid 400 rupees for the ride to a hotel because I had to get out of the taxi I took from Haridwar because the taxi driver had enough English to repeatedly insist "You, me, Rishikesh, Love? (Suggestive look)" to which I answered without fault, "No. You, drive. Me, Rishikesh." And that's just the last couple of hours. This one hour internet cafe I fear is NOT going to hack it for my storytelling needs!

Jack always said that I attracted adventures. For the thirteen years we were together, we joyfully embraced a semi-nomadic life. We lived overseas for months at a time and assuaged our common case of wanderlust with shorter trips to exotic destinations whenever we settled back in the United States.

Traveling with Jack always began as a precise endeavor. Before we left, we knew where we were going and how we would get there. Hotels were booked or at least ear-marked in the travel guide, and sufficient funds were always available. Once in the country, however, things rarely followed the plan. I simply talked to people, and all plans evaporated. We were invited in locals' homes and taken on lesser-traveled paths and unforeseen adventures. My contribution to our travels was exhilaration and predicaments; Jack's was appreciation and rescuing.

Without Jack, proper prior planning didn't even cross my mind. The night before I was to set for India, I still barely knew where Rishikesh was or how I might get there. I just knew that my Higher Self would facilitate a safe passage to my destination.

02/10/2012
Excerpt from my travel blog

To celebrate my departure, Sofia and I went out for Indian food at Chutney's, a restaurant that delivers consistently amazingly delicious food, and Tuesday was no exception. When the restaurant's owner discovered that I was going to India, alone, with neither plan nor reservations, it was all he could do to not faint. A few phone calls later, I was no longer landing alone with neither plan nor reservations. Two of his life-long friends picked me up at the airport at one in the morning, took me home, made me tea, changed my money, and got me all booked and loaded on the "completely full, no more seats" train to Haridwar that same morning. I know how it works, that business of believing in miracles which makes them come true, but still, I get awed at my own good luck sometimes.

The six-hour train ride to Haridwar was a good introduction to the Europeanized side of India. In business class, where I sat, well-dressed English-speaking train attendants served teas and crisp little cakes to a subdued background of classical music. My traveling neighbor was a physics professor born and raised in Rishikesh. He knew that Rishikesh was the birth place of yoga, but had never had any inclination to practice yoga himself. We discussed science education and the socio-economic realities of the non-educated in India in polite tones until we both fell asleep. This gave me an opportunity to recover my strength from the long flight before plunging into the colors and noise of Haridwar.

I stepped off the train into another world. The stream of cars, rickshaws, scooters and motorbikes was incessant, horns full on at all times. There were monkeys screeching, cows mooing, drums playing, music blasting, people shouting draped in bright oranges, yellows and blues, and vendors touting their glittery jewelry, bright fabrics and fried delicious treats.

I shouldered my backpack and weaved a path through the crowd to the market. I felt so "me", the epitome of the great explorer I always dreamt I could be. I greeted every passerby with a wide smile, even that man in the orange robes who gave me a dirty look and blew me a raspberry.

A taxi was available right away to take me to Rishikesh, but I soon began to doubt I would make it to my destination alive. Driving on backcountry roads in India is an efficient path to spiritual awakening, as every one-lane bridge and blind curve is an opportunity for a near-death experience.

I did not close my eyes. Instead, I crawled over the backrest into the front seat to meet my demise head on and greeted each miraculous crossing with uninhibited laughter. The driver seemed fascinated by my reaction to his driving and promptly introduced himself, shook my hand and suggested in rudimentary English that we get to know each other "better" once in Rishikesh. This would have been the part where Jack rolled his eyes and braced for a change of plan.

Because I am not as naïve as I might appear to the casual observer, I asked the taxi driver to drop me off far from my hotel, then proceeded to get lost through the city, which made me laugh as well. But serendipity had my back, and soon I was flying across Ram Juhla, precariously loaded on the back of an old scooter. Women in bright saris jumped aside as we sped toward a magnificent orange temple nestled in the lush green vegetation of the northern shore. Once on shore, we took a sharp right through the market and slalomed around monks, yogis and monkeys to a narrow back alley that led to the footsteps of the hotel I was to call home for the next six weeks. I walked into the hotel's lobby in a state of blissful dishevelment under the curious eye of the man at the reception desk.

I recognized the stamp of my own creation on that grand entrance. Whether God or my Higher Self, whoever crafted that day knew me well.

02/10/2012
Excerpt from my journal
Dearest Love,
Thank you, thank you, THANK YOU, for the wonderful gift of adventures you have arranged for me. Thank you for the guidance and opportunities that have led me here. It was perfect!

CHAPTER 24

I fell in love with Rishikesh immediately. Not because of its exotic temples, breathtaking Himalayan foothill landscape or friendly street vendors, but because it vibrated at such a high frequency. I felt I had reached the heart of the city at the end of the Rabbit Hole – the Zion or Mad Tea Party of my personal journey. The feeling was akin to standing on the summit of a high peak after a challenging climb, a mixture of humbled satisfaction and incredulous excitement.

02/25/2012
Excerpt from my travel blog
Imagine, if you don't already believe or know this, that the lives that ninety percent of humans live, with their daily drama, interactions, needs, desires, worries and other normalities is but a story we tell ourselves, a dream we have about our life. Then imagine that the other ten percent, through luck, good karma, dedicated seeking or whatever, suddenly wake up to the truth beyond the story we all tell. But maybe not quite fully. They are like Neo the first time he meets Morpheus, contemplating whether he should take the red or blue pill. Well, ninety percent of people

in Rishikesh (and I feel quite a few cows too) are like Neo, either right
before, during, or after the taking of the pill.
You can go to the cafe and enjoy your chai tea while discussing the One
Soul. This is completely normal, maybe even expected. People whom the
sleeping-dreaming world would call enlightened — though I prefer the term
awake — come here and sometimes live here. Miracles are common place.
There is a man down the street that has been teaching yoga for eighty four
years. He is now one hundred and four, and doesn't look a day over
ninety. There is a Brazilian man who can fill a room with entranced
devotees. His mere presence makes you feel warm and fuzzy, and the
chanting that greets his daily talks can bring up emotions you didn't know
you had. There are sages who have not eaten for years because they can
extract essential nutrients directly from the sun. There are some who can
levitate, or transport themselves to other places instantaneously. There are
people dressed in white (yoga teachers mostly) who cast an aura of strength
that is palpable within a hundred feet, and some you would call beggars or
homeless who hold the joy of gleeful children in their eyes.
But that is not the most amazing part of Rishikesh. Gurus, masters and
sages — that's fine — it's the regular people, the hotel staff, the cooks, the
shop keepers, the cane-juice makers, the construction workers, etc. that
truly make you feel that you have strayed into Shangri-la. Sure, they like
their pop-music, cell-phones and such, but when they work, you will hear
them sing "Om Namah Shivaya" (Adoration to Shiva). Spirituality is a
way of life here, not a side-track for hippies disillusioned with the
mainstream worldview. This is the Rome of spirituality. All spiritual
roads lead here.

The day before the start of the Yoga Teacher Training, I
spent the whole day exploring Rishikesh, its little markets,
vegetarian restaurants and sacred river shores. I was in love
with everything and everyone, and because I radiated such a
positive energy, the town welcomed me with open arms.

It was in this state of Universal Love that I met Rory.

Many foreigners wander the streets of Rishikesh, but I
instinctually knew Rory was one of the Tribe Yoga teachers
when I saw him walk towards me in the market. I introduced
myself and struggled to understand his name through a thick

Scottish accent. We quickly covered the usual small talk of "how was your flight?" and "where are you from?" and dove into the heart of our mutual spiritual interest.

"To every monk there is a path." Rory said, "One path to enlightenment is through yoga, which guarantees results if one is disciplined. Another path is simply through Love."

"Yes, Love is my path." I answered without hesitation.

If I had listened to myself at that moment, I might have followed my bliss to trekking the Himalayas, visiting the home of the Dalai Lama in Dharamshala or exploring the sunny beaches of Goa for six weeks. But sometimes loops are necessary before a journey can continue – and these are actually not loops but upward spirals. So, instead of wandering off into the wild immediately, I committed myself for the next six weeks to the path of yoga, the path of discipline.

ဆ · ‌ဗ

<u>Discipline</u> – *n.* A dirty word in my vocabulary – the (potentially) erroneous idea that forcing oneself to perform a rigid set of tasks neatly organized in a schedule, instead of embracing random fanciful whims as they arise, can lead to personal growth and Greater Good.

ဆ · ‌ဗ

Within a week, the daily training schedule had become routine. Our day started in the dark, at 5:30 am, with the kriyas (purifications) – scraping of the tongue, cleansing of the gums with salt, clearing of sinuses with salt water, and vomiting in a bucket to inspect the bile for health information. By 6:00 am, my tribe of fellow students and I sat in a circle in a beautiful wooden shala (yoga room) on the top floor of the hotel for an hour of pranayama (breathing) and meditation, followed by three hours of asanas (postures). At 10 am, our first meal was taken in silence and always included a delicious green smoothie. The rest of the morning and afternoon were dedicated to lectures and teaching practicum, with a one hour lunch break, until about 6 pm. Some evenings, we concluded the day with an additional hour of chanting.

The thought of such a schedule beforehand would have

horrified me, but in the state of excitement with which I started the training, nothing bothered me – not even the ritual of the morning bucket.

I found a new and different kind of freedom in the rigidity of a fixed schedule, the freedom from having to make decisions about what to do next or even from having to pay attention to arising fanciful whims.

The breathing and meditation hours with the gentle Sequoia were the most difficult for me, because they required stillness – a clear indication that there lay my greatest growth potential. But the hours spent in asanas and lectures with Rory, Scarlett and Fabiano always seemed to shrink to a mere few minutes. With each asana I gained strength and an intimate knowledge of my body. Each sentence of each lecture was a pearl of wisdom, and I feared missing any of it. I absorbed all topics indiscriminately, postponing any siphoning or critical evaluation of the ingested information until later. After all, I would likely need something to occupy my mind for 2,660 miles on the PCT.

My Higher Self had chosen the yoga school well. While other schools focused their curriculum on the asanas, which are only one of eight limbs of the yogic philosophy, the Tribe teachers adhered to the foundational text by revered Master Patanjali, including rules of ethical restraints and abstentions applied to the outer and inner world – all of which involved some form of discipline – postures (asanas), breathing techniques (pranayama), and four levels of meditation towards complete Oneness (Samadhi).

This was not my first excursion into the world of Yoga Teacher Training. I had been an intermittently avid yogini since my early twenties without ever attending a class. I learned yoga from books and videos and concocted my own style of yoga. I was thirty-five years old exactly – it was my birthday – when I first joined an actual class. That class released so much inner joy that I thought I had found my calling. I then had not yet discovered the lure of Geophysics but was nearing the end of a six-year career as a photographer. I temporarily funneled all my passion and drive into creating a livelihood from yoga. But a few weeks into the Yoga Teacher Training, the teacher gracefully suggested I seek training elsewhere. When I pressed her for a reason, she admitted that, in her opinion, I was "too stuck in my ways" to be a good yoga teacher.

This was an accurate assessment. I was then only interested in the asanas, the active part of yoga. I had no patience for any chakra occult nonsense.

What a difference seven years make. My thirst for knowledge about the concepts I had formerly denigrated was insatiable. I had once believed that chakras were a lovely tale for imaginative but uneducated people, with neither scientific nor natural foundation whatsoever. After a full summer of lessons from the Beyond on the Soul and how it relates to energy, learning about chakras seemed as elemental as Quantum Physics 101.

I understood that Prana (the Life Force) was none else but energy, expressed in the body – and in all things – as the vibration of subatomic particles. Organs, such as the heart, were but the grossest manifestation of a particular energetic signature associated with an energy receptor or chakra.

Yoga was so much more than a set of movements to achieve a strong lean body; it was the key to understanding and managing myself as the energetic entity I was.

I could stand in warrior pose and feel the energy flow into my right hand – a warm sensation – and out of my left – a cold sensation. I could focus my attention on one chakra at a time and perceive the energy of a situation expressed as different emotions, and I could sublimate these emotions through postures and breathing. Anger in my navel could be "sucked up" and transmuted to willpower in my solar plexus or love in my heart. This was not theoretical; the upflow of energy was physically detectable.

Much of Sequoia's lessons, on the other hand, were specifically designed to interrupt the storytelling, the investigation, the learning, and instead to just *be*.

During one of the meditation exercises, on a sandy beach

by the Ganges River, I strayed into absolute stillness, a place where my body, the beach and river, my fellow students, the loud city and the rest of the world disappeared.

During the morning meditation hours, I struggled to remain motionless for more than a few minutes at a time, an indication that I was not in stillness. True stillness I learned dwells in a timeless space.

When our teachers gently called our awareness back to the sandy beach by the Ganges, I felt I returned through a long dark blue tunnel of which the outlet was my physical form.

I didn't know how long I had been gone or from whence I returned, but for the rest of that evening, I remained evenly and contentedly pacified, even as I walked the exciting streets of Rishikesh with my joyful tribe.

CHAPTER 25

I had embraced the yogic path so fully during the Yoga Teacher Training that I didn't notice the first signs of a nascent internal rebellion right away. It began as a subtle general malaise, easy to overlook in the loving, nurturing and fun company of my tribe and teachers.

I believed that the road map drawn by Master Patanjali revealed a straight path to everlasting bliss, and since that was my destination, I had gladly turned off my own guidance system to join the well-trodden path.

But as the end of the Teaching Training approached, I began to study less and question more. I abandoned the scraping of the tongue and vomiting in a bucket, skipped the meditation hour to sleep in, and designed my practice classes at the last minute in a corner of my journal. Despite the shala's beautiful setting, I longed for wilderness and often disappeared into the hills around Rishikesh instead of joining the tribe's study sessions.

03/04/2012
Excerpt from my travel blog
Title: "Sat Chit Ananda" (Beingness Consciousness Bliss)
   Now in the last stretch of the Yoga Teacher Training, I came to India very much feeling in line with my Higher Self. I mean, there are always corners to explore and growth to embrace, but overall I was feeling pretty damn blissful. What happened here was a little bit like meeting a mapmaker and hearing him insist that the road from point A to point B goes through this town and that town and that other town, whereas I had been pretty sure that I could just climb up through the woods and get there just the same. Last week I went through an oppressing feeling: Oh no, I'm not going through the towns on the map, maybe I can't get "there" (Sat Chit Ananda) by going through the woods. But, then something happened in the sharing circle.

A week before the end of the training, tribe and teachers gathered in the shala for our last sharing circle. This was a familiar setup, reminiscent of the days with my desert sisters in Death Valley, a safe environment in which to express concerns, fears, gratitude, or any other feeling needing to be heard.

I meant to share how challenging incorporating the yogic discipline into the free-spirited lifestyle I had chosen was. I had some idea about how to eloquently convey this to the circle, but when my turn came to speak, words burst forth defiantly and without my consent.

"I just don't want to believe that the path to enlightenment precludes eating roast chicken or requires waking up at O-dark thirty every day!"

The circle was stunned silent for a moment, myself included. Nobody feels *that* strongly about roast chicken. Slowly, I released the tension in my clenched fists and lifted my eyes from the knot in the shala's wood floor I had used as a mental anchor. My gaze met that of my tribe, and there I found nothing but support. The last of the tension escaped from me in the form of a short and sudden laugh. My laugh was met with the same non-judgmental support as my outburst had been. I felt loved in that circle, as I was, roast chicken quirks and all. Nobody ever mentioned the incident again, except for my friend Angus, who joyfully tormented me about it for days afterwards. I likely would have thought less of him, if he hadn't.

But the seed was planted. I could read between the lines of my silly yet profound outburst. I had to get to everlasting bliss my own way. Rory's favorite quote, "To every monk there is a path", finally trickled down from my brain to my heart, where true understanding takes place.

Yes, yoga was an efficient way to reach enlightenment, but after following that reliable, well-lit path for six weeks, I still chose cutting through the woods, at the risk of getting lost. I accepted that it would likely take longer, but I was in no hurry. I preferred meandering journeys through uncharted territories anyway; they made the best stories.

I had enjoyed playing the role of a disciplined-yoga-teacher-in-training very much, but it was time to absorb it, ingest it, and let it nourish me while I returned to my whimsical ways. I suddenly could see all the subtle ways in which yoga did not fit me.

I had been puzzled during lectures about the yogic philosophy's emphasis on ending the cycle of pain and suffering in order to transcend the physical form. Maybe I was missing something, but I truly loved the physical plane. I loved not only my own life, but the entire world with all its faults, flaws, inequalities and injustices. I had no suffering to escape, no better place to get to, and I sure hoped for the opportunity to be reincarnated as many times as I could get away with. I was even willing to delay enlightenment for a chance to play again.

Of Master Patanjali's rules of ethical restraints and abstentions, I adopted those that already felt natural to me – nonviolence, honesty, and contentment with what is. Others I filed away for consideration at a later date – cleanliness, study of scriptures, and surrender to God. And in the far far back, I tucked spiritual austerities, a concept I then misinterpreted to mean commitment to discipline for its own sake.

Although yoga as a path to enlightenment did not fit me, teaching yoga still appealed to me. I liked the image of myself as a yoga teacher, bringing a little bit of quiet introspection and nurturing self-care to the overworked west. I therefore approached the final practical exam, a seventy-five minute yoga class of our design, with the reverence due to important career moves.

On the morning of the final exam, I was nervous. Our teachers had invited random people on the streets of Rishikesh to be our students. These impromptu students were lured by the promise of a free yoga class but were unaware that our teaching styles and techniques were being evaluated.

I led a good class, but not a great one. I stepped on and off my mat too often, demonstrated only half of the transitions and corrected positions from awkward angles – oh, so sorry about grabbing you there. I caught my mistakes immediately and flowed to the next sequence of movements with apparent ease. My students for the day praised me for a flawless sequence, but my evaluators were not fooled.

"You have charisma and presence when you lead a class. Your passion for the art is evident." Scarlett said, "But if you are to ever become a great yoga teacher, you will also have to acquire some discipline."

Scarlett's words struck straight at the hub of my rebellion. There was that "discipline" word again! As I looked up to Scarlett, however, I realized that she embodied what she preached perfectly. Discipline was a key component in the strength and equanimity with which she embraced a fulfilling life of worldwide yoga teaching and adventures. Her life seemed to me like a dream.

Even wandering through the woods, which I took to be my forte, Scarlett hiked faster, sang songs louder, jumped naked in hidden streams more inhibitedly, and navigated precarious rock ledges more gracefully than I did. She, more so than Patanjali, was my teacher. And my teacher thought I needed more discipline. I could appreciate the Universe's craftiness in delivering this last minute punch line. I thanked my teachers and stepped out of the shala for the last time with a quandary under my arm.

I then did something rather out of character for that time: I let it go. Instead of analyzing, pondering or asking, I simply offered the problem to my Higher Self. I trusted that all would be solved in its appointed time, and with a clear mind and a joyous heart, I walked to town to meet Angus for a celebratory "Hello to the Queen" – a massive ice cream dessert.

For my last few days in India, I joined three other students on a trek to the Himalayas. During the Yoga Teacher Training, I had enjoyed perfect health despite violating every tourist rule in the book – I drank the water, ate meals from street vendors and restaurants of suspicious hygiene, and carried no disinfectant gel with me. But it finally all caught up. As soon as we set foot on the trail, I strayed into a land of rotten-egg burps and explosive diarrhea.

During one particularly unpleasant episode, the thought crossed my mind that of all the people on the planet, having all the experiences in the spectrum possible, I had been handpicked for this task. There was no one else, right then, being as sick as I was, on this particular trail, with this breathtaking view of snow-capped Himalayan peaks, and this group of friends making inappropriate jokes I found hilarious despite my miserable state. It was my job to be exactly me, then, and at all times.

It was only a flash of a thought between bouts of diarrhea, but by the time I returned to Rishikesh – several pounds lighter – my quandary was solved. I understood that people perfectly on their paths, like Scarlett, are our teachers, but the lesson was not to follow in their footsteps, it was to follow their example in leaving fresh footsteps. So all I had to do was to find some untrampled wilderness in which to roam.

CHAPTER 26

"Where were you traveling?" the customs officer asked, as though the bright orange jacket with Indian embroidery, Om bracelet, and small touch of paint between my brows weren't a dead giveaway.

"India."

"What was the purpose of your visit and how long were you there?"

I told him that I had been in Rishikesh for a six-week Yoga Teacher Training.

"Is that your profession?"

I was annoyed by the officer's tone and attitude. I guessed that I had been singled out because of my backpack and dirty hippy appearance. I was most likely smuggling some sort of drugs to corrupt the good citizens of America, and his duty was to nip that possibility in the bud. I also sensed my own annoyance and noted how easily I had been thrown off balance from my yogic state of contented bliss.

"Well, it might be my profession now, if I find a studio in which to teach. That's the whole point of getting trained."

I spoke clearly and slowly, as to a child, matching his testy attitude. His jaw clenched. I was pushing my luck and I knew it.

While he scribbled some words I couldn't see on a form, I decided to change my perspective. This man, likely unaware of his true nature as an eternal multidimensional energetic entity, was playing the role of a customs officer. In fact, this was the best customs officer performance I had ever seen.

I chose to see it as such.

"What do you do then?"

"I'm unemployed."

I thought I saw a fleeting spark of triumph in his eyes. He had me pegged right. I *was* a dirty hippy. Suddenly, I was feeling rather fond of this customs officer. I was even happy about the triumph I imagined he felt. I also knew without a doubt that this encounter would end soon, and that it would end well. My task was simply to relax and enjoy the game.

"Well then, and where did you get the money to travel to India?"

Now, that was a good question. Check.

I considered answering, "I manifested it," in jest, but decided to play it safe. Instead, I told him that I had quit a PhD in Geophysics and had some money saved from my scholarships. Checkmate.

Although I believed I was lying to the officer – I had saved no money from my scholarships – for the sake of a customs game, I was actually the one fooled. I had indeed manifested the money. I just didn't know that I had yet.

What I did know was that my answer solved my customs predicament. Regardless of what else I had said, the word "PhD" transmogrified me from dirty hippy to eccentric scholar in the officer's mind. He instantly closed his forms book, nodded towards the doors to freedom and simply walked away.

I repacked my backpack and walked out without haste, leaving none of my mind behind to linger in the customs area.

As I did so, unbeknownst to me, $10,000 sat in my bank account like a fat cat on the sofa waiting for my return.

From a nonlinear perspective, the manifestation that led to this miracle was simple and elegant, the hallmark of Higher Magic. In that precise moment, by the Mississippi River, when I gratefully spoke the words: "I am walking the PCT. I am taking six months off next year and walking from Mexico to Canada." I created a bubble of intent that unfolded a set of well orchestrated events, some dating years prior and well into the future of that particular Now.

As it appeared to my limited linear perception, before I knew anything of the trail, intents, timelessness or Higher Selves, I was granted a National Science Foundation (NSF) fellowship for my Mt. Baker project. The tenure for the fellowship was three years, but I used only two years of funding for my master's degree. So, by the time I graduated, I had one year of funding left.

When I started the PhD in Vancouver, my Higher Self and

I had a small disagreement about how to use this money. Using the third year right away made no sense to me. I had a scholarship from the university in Vancouver for three years, but my PhD would likely take four years, so why not keep the NSF funding for that last unfunded year? In addition, I would be taking a leave of absence to walk the PCT and lose half a year of funding, whereas if I waited, I could use it in its entirety.

But my Higher Self insisted that I use it all right away.

"You walk in the valley, but I see the landscape from the top of the peak. Trust me that I know the way." He said.

Before leaving for India, I filed a termination of tenure with the NSF. I was grateful that the money I had not used would likely be reinvested in some young, bright scientist with a passion for his or her field and a desire to make the world a better place. I was grateful to have chosen to play instead.

The salary checks stopped immediately, but the tuition fee – $10,000 – had already been disbursed directly to my bank account. I expected a letter asking for the return of at least the unused portion of the tuition fee, if not all, but it never came.

My final report and tenure resignation were accepted and I was suddenly out of the system. All expenses for my travels to India and the entirety of my PCT walk were miraculously funded by a grant reserved for passionate exploring scientists, of which I still counted myself.

CHAPTER 27

"Sofia!" I reached around her trendy coat with both arms for a much-welcomed reunion hug.

"What a nice orange jacket you have." She stepped back to appreciate the embroidery.

"I know …" I began telling her the story of how I had wished for an orange jacket and how my steps had led me through the market and across Lakshman Jhula – another suspended bridge – to the perfect shop, ran by a friendly man, where I had found the jacket. The Storyteller was ignited. I was still storytelling when we drove away from the airport, and when we stopped at the grocery store for roast chicken, and when finally I dropped my backpack in Sofia's living room.

I let myself collapse on her sofa and took a long sigh of contentment. I was home.

Although Sofia and I had exchanged a few emails while I was in India, much had happened that we had not shared with each other. Yet, as always, our lessons from opposite side of the earth fit together like pieces of a puzzle.

On the day when I left for India, Sofia met a man – a tall, handsome man, perfectly crafted to destabilize her from her former ego-less equanimity. The relationship had lasted six weeks, exactly the amount of time I spent in India.

From the first step we took together down the Rabbit Hole, I considered Sofia to be my guiding light. Our learning was symbiotic, but while I questioned, strayed and stumbled; she trusted, flowed and thrived. I was the explorer, the earth lover; she was the philosopher, guided by Angels. Sofia's trust had always inspired me to believe.

Falling in love, however, had tickled her lower chakras – those governing survival, sexuality and self-esteem -, while six weeks of yoga, chanting and meditation had kindled my higher chakras – the seats of universal love, higher communication and wisdom.

Suddenly, the distinctions I had always imagined between us did not seem so contrasted anymore, nor the hierarchy so apparent. Looking across the sofa where we both sat for a late night tea, I, for the first time, saw Sofia as my spiritual equal.

Of course, Sofia was my equal. Our chosen personalities were so different. I could have never followed a path that suited her. I would not have wanted to. We could each create fresh footsteps to our common destination. I could walk through deserts and forests and she could take high-heel friendly walkways. The substance of our seeking was the same, so we could attend to the same healing in vastly different forms and both benefit from the expanded field of perspective.

What a gift!

I felt my heart swell with gratitude for the presence of Sofia in my life. A traveling companion was so much more valuable to me than a guide.

I was also grateful for the peace and joy I had brought back from India, especially in contrast to Sofia's relationship-induced disorientation. I had finally reached that state of equanimity Sofia experienced while I struggled to leap out of my former Vancouver life. Rather than transcend my earth personality, I had embraced it more fully, with the same result: at last, I, too, could live in a state of love with no object, freed from woes and blinding desires.

Sofia and I walked such perfectly parallel paths; I should have anticipated that my own destabilization was just around the corner.

CHAPTER 28

On my last night in Rishikesh, sensing the occasion was propitious for the complete release of any remnant of my previous life, I bought a lotus flower prayer candle from an older woman on the beach. I stepped knee deep into the sacred Ganges River and infused the candle with my prayer.

"I pray that any karmic ties between Logan and me be now released. Thank you." I gently deposited the lit candle on the river and incredulously watched it float *up*-river.

I turned to Angus still standing on the beach.

"Is it supposed to do that?"

He stepped in the river and stood by my side as we watched the candle head towards a rocky outcrop.

"I don't know." he said, "Maybe it's caught in an eddy. It will turn around probably just there and then join the flow."

In the center of the river, several lit candles bravely carried prayers past mine, in the proper direction. But when my candle finally reached the rocks, a wave toppled it over, and it promptly went under. I felt my mind's processing circuit heat up for the strain but said nothing. I didn't need to. Angus gently took my arm and pulled me towards shore.

"Bah, it's just a candle … Come on, let's go get ourselves a fantastic meal."

A week later, walking downtown Bellingham towards another fantastic meal, one involving raw fish, I suddenly felt a distortion in my energetic field, as though the air on the street was suddenly thicker and more tumultuous.

Logan. That energy felt like Logan. My heart beat a little faster as I stopped to inspect the street as far as I could see on both sides of the road. I could not see him.

It had been almost a year since I had driven away from Logan's house without an explanation, a year since I had faithfully repeated the words "I pray to never see Logan again." I had then written in my journal a set of logical steps to set myself free. The love was in me. Logan was only a trigger, a catalyst. My heart had nodded yes then, leading me to believe it agreed, yet it surreptitiously escaped to rosy revised pasts and fantasized futures of happily-ever-afters anytime my guard was down. Despite my Higher Self's unwavering assurance that the relationship was over, I carried Logan in my heart's side pocket that entire summer, to the Yukon, to Vancouver, to India, and even to the wish-granting waves of the Ganges River, only to see my plea for freedom sunk and denied.

I walked another hundred feet, with all five senses on full alert, and turned right at the street corner. There he stood, in front of the sushi restaurant, my destination, staring at the street corner intently as though it were an occupied dragon's lair.

Our eyes met. He shook his head, in defeat rather than triumph, and turned to the tall man by his side. "I knew it!"

He stomped past me towards the street I had just left.

In a flash, I noted the new blue fleece jacket – electric blue, my favorite color – the strong gait, the approach climbing shoes, the downcast green eyes, and the alpinist logo on his cap.

"Can I ask …" I called to him. I had just learned, in an instant, that he was healthy, working, climbing and still in love with me. What was left to ask?

"No!" He threw his arms up and turned the corner out of sight. The world was gone, except for that corner and my heart beating a deafening dance of bewilderment, fear, hope and disappointment.

Through the internal drumming I barely heard the tall man, who had, it seemed, just lost his lunch partner with no explanation, ask me, "Do you know Logan?"

"Yes I do." I opened the door to the restaurant without a glance back at the man. "He's the love of my life."

Wait! Who said that? I entered the restaurant, feeling as confused as I imagined the tall man now alone on the sidewalk must have felt.

Of course, I spoke about this with my Higher Self, who assured me: "Don't worry. You will not return to Logan."

That night, however, I sat on the edge of my bed holding my phone like a crack addict — I'll be gone on the trail in a week. I can sublimate my emotions now. I can manage my own energy. It will be fine.

I incredulously watched my fingers dial Logan's number and was relieved when he didn't answer. Instead, a few minutes later, he knocked at the door.

I felt faint.

"We need to talk." He spoke efficiently, truck keys in hand, as though he meant to expedite this inconvenient business and move on to more important matters. Without a word, I led him to one of the upstairs bedrooms, where we could converse without disturbing Rose. I climbed the stairs two by two to match his long legs, painfully aware of his eyes on me, and let myself sink on the floor with my back against the futon. He sat directly facing me just beyond arms reach.

"Why did you call?" His tone was firm, but not aggressive. His eyes lowered to my hands, and I worried he would notice that I was shaking. Looking back into my eyes, he softened his tone. "What do you want from me?"

What did I want? I wanted what I always wanted, a healthy, harmonious relationship with this man whose green eyes made me lose all wits, even if I had to get enlightened to earn it. I didn't need to answer. He had once told me to only call him if I wanted him back, and I had called.

Although it seemed neither of us had moved, he was suddenly sitting so close that my far-sighted eyes could no longer see him clearly. The rest of my senses, however, were drinking his presence with big gulps.

"Did you tell my friend that I'm the love of your life?"

"Yes." I had heard the words as well. I just wasn't sure who had spoken them.

"Look," he said, finally, "This makes no sense, but the bottom line is that I want you back too. So, do you want to come home with me?"

"Absolutely." The butterflies in my stomach clapped their wings in unison to the news – I'll be gone on the trail in a week. I can sublimate my emotions now. I can manage my own energy. It will be fine.

I had no doubt that this was the right decision.

A few minutes later, we were driving away, stealing dubious glances of each other as though we had just discovered that the entrance to the dragon's lair was actually a portal to another planet, one populated by pink unicorns.

04/09/2012
Excerpt from my journal [Edited for length]
Him: I told you that you would not return to Logan, and you will not return to Logan.
Me: But!! But I already have! I am with him right now, as much in a "relationship" as any human couple can get. We are physically together, emotionally involved and we have this big relentless love.
Him: The love is real, but incarnation is more complex than I can explain to you right now. In your space-time Now, your energies are not mingled. "You" and "Logan" are energy fields. The physical form is part of this energy field, like a suit or a cloak, with its own vibrational frequency. You are nothing. Movements in the void. What you think of as Melissa is here

and everywhere. In several of her "everywhere" her energy IS mingled with that of Logan. Residual imprints carry through in your current physical reality, but your contract here is done.

Me: I don't understand.

Him: I know my love, but someday you will.

Me: What about my anger outburst? Is that residual too?

Him: Anger is just an energy form, like everything else. Let anger pass through your physical form as it carries toxic false beliefs out. You are upset about your own anger because you are attached to your self-image as a calm and well-balanced person. That is an important trait in a pack society. The moment you decide to leave the global consciousness, or rather unconsciousness, to become awake, you automatically forgo your claim to "normality". That is quite alright. Normal is overrated. Let the anger wash over you, if that is what you are experiencing.

Me: Ugh. Couldn't I bring myself to the light in a less dramatic fashion?

Him: What, and run the risk of being boring? [He was amused]

Me: I'm serious.

Him: I know. That is your main problem, actually. Lighten up! This is your journey, make it enjoyable. Don't resist the heaviness, or the craziness, or anything else. Just experience it, accept it and move on.

Despite my Higher Self's continued and confusing reassurance that I had not returned to Logan's arms, in my own reality, I had. And if this was residual energy, it was potent residual energy.

By the end of the week, Logan's bedroom wall was disgraced by a fist-size hole, his driveway was marred by the rubber of my screeching departing tires, I had a sizeable bruise on my leg and our friends and roommates were shaking their heads in disbelief. Yet, when Sofia drove up to take me to the airport, she found us interlaced in loving, sorrowful goodbyes.

"Have fun. Be free. Walk strong." he said as Sofia pulled out of Rose's driveway.

I nodded silently and watched him get smaller in my rear view mirror.

"How are you doing?" Sofia finally asked, encouraging me to release the knot in my throat.

"I don't know yet." I still couldn't believe the surreal week I had just experienced. Had I been tested again? Had I been shown lacking in self-awareness and common sense?

During the week I spent with Logan, I learned that I could step outside of our common drama to the vantage point of an observer. From that place, I could manage my own energy and sublimate my negative emotions, albeit sometimes with a delay – a sufficient delay to leave tire rubber in the driveway. Yet, for all my life-altering experiences and leaps in personal growth, I still could neither resist nor release this man. I could see the "intense couple" game we played and the roles we adopted, but my awareness wasn't sustainable. I secretly wanted to get lost in the story as soon as I stepped in my role. I assumed it inevitably led to a happy ending. Otherwise, what would be the point of all this love?

As the plane left the ground, I breathed out a sigh of relief and breathed in the sight of my beloved Pacific Northwest through the small window – the green forests, the bays and lakes and in the distance, the snow-capped Cascades mountains, several of which I knew on a first name basis. There was a sight of beauty to inspire me to walk 2,660 miles home.

"I'll be right where you left me when you come back." Logan had said. From this height the plot of our story was clearer. There was love, yes, but no happy ending in sight.

Like clouds dissipating in the sun, my thoughts of Logan gradually faded and the excitement for the adventure ahead reclaimed its rightful place in the forefront of my mind – the Pacific Crest Trail, at last. I would be walking home, but, for the second time, I knew that the current version of myself would not return.

.

Part 3

2,660 MILES TO FREEDOM

Oh! The places you'll go!
You'll be on your way up!
You'll be seeing great sights!
You'll join the high fliers, who soar to high heights.
You won't lag behind because you'll have all the speed.
You'll pass the whole gang and you'll soon take the lead.
Wherever you fly, you'll be the best of the best
Wherever you go, you'll top all the rest

Except when you don't
Because, sometimes, you won't.

- Dr. Seuss –
(*Oh! The Places You'll Go*)

CHAPTER 29

I kicked my shoes off under the only tree – the only shade – for miles up the slopes of a parched Anza Borrego hill, stepped barefoot on the rocky trail, unfurled my superhero cape into the wind and launched into one of the most joyous harmonica solos I have ever played.

I played a song of gratitude, a composition of my own, to the hundred-degree day that guaranteed me solitude for a few hours – none of my trail family would leave the Scissors Crossing water cache in this heat. I played to celebrate the beauty of the flowering ocotillos and cacti along the trail and to serenade my trail-mates, the lizards, hummingbirds and rattlesnakes. But mostly, I played because I had so much joy pushing outward on my rib cage that I feared my heart would burst if I didn't open safety valves. So, I danced, sang, howled, laughed, cried, wrote poems and invented songs I then played on my harmonica, alone in the desert.

I had been on the trail for less than a week, but anything that preceded my first steps away from the Campo Pacific Crest Trail monument might as well have belonged to another lifetime.

I had often fantasized about the emotional first steps I would take away from the Mexican border, but on the first day, after a few photos at the monument, I simply shouldered my pack and joined the trail with a confident gait – nothing extraordinary, a stroll through my living room, as natural as breathing. I didn't even sign the start register.

The trail began as a dusty descent towards the town of Campo. With each step, little puffs of dirt covered my purple trail-runners and legs, blurring the once sharp transition between me and the trail. I was absorbed, acquired and welcomed. The realization of my current place in the world slowly seeped into my awareness. This ribbon of dirt – brown, narrow, soft, dusty, safe and infinite – was a visual timeline linking all the adventures I was yet to have, the landscapes I was yet to discover and the new friends I was just about to meet.

Mile marker "1" appeared around the corner, and a sudden swell of love for the trail overtook me. I laughed and cried simultaneously, then wiped my face with already dirty hands. With dirt on my feet and dirt on my face, I already looked like a thru-hiker. The assimilation process had begun.

On that first day, I only walked eight miles before night found me. I had started late and walked the first few miles with the directional focus of a two-year-old. I greeted every bug and flower and resisted the urge to collect all the sparkly rocks on the way. I felt I had just barely started walking when the sun sunk below the horizon. My body still pulsated with such excitement that I likely would have walked all night if I didn't fear missing important trail vistas in the dark.

When a slightly convex granite boulder exactly the size of my body serendipitously appeared by the side of the trail shortly after dusk, I assumed it was my cue to stop.

I spread a cheap poncho directly on the rock and unrolled my brand new sleeping pad and sleeping bag on top of it.

My rock was an island in a sea of low brushes. Who knew what lived in those brushes – lizards, spiders, beetles, scorpions? I almost worried, but then I remembered a time when I was parked behind a seedy bar in Nebraska. I felt infinitely safer in the wild.

I was much too excited to sleep, so I lay flat on my back on the boulder and explored the immensity of the night sky one corner at a time, starting with the slender sliver of the moon and outward to each bright star. The moon had almost migrated across the entire sky when at last I allowed my eyelids to close. The scratching, thumping, scurrying and pitter-pattering of my small – I hoped – roommates lulled me the rest of the way to peaceful dreams.

I was still smiling when, only a few hours later, I reopened my eyes to a full panorama of a pink and orange sunrise over the desert. This was not the barren desert I had envisioned before the trail. I had longed for the stark beauty of a desiccated landscape but was greeted instead by a fragrant and colorful desert in full bloom.

I sat upright on the granite boulder, still cocooned in my bag, and breathed in the silence of the morning as though it were precious cactus nectar. The night creatures, it seemed, had not yet awoken.

"I'M ON THE PCT!" with both arms out of bag, I greeted my first full day on the trail with full volume.

I had planned to begin each day with a yoga session to keep myself centered and avoid the repetitive stress injuries common to thru-hikers, but faced with such beauty and potential for adventures, I could not have delayed walking by even one second. I rolled my poncho and sleeping bag, poured cereal into a Ziploc bag to eat as I walked and headed on down the trail with a bounce in my step.

Less than twenty steps away from my boulder, I came upon a clean, crisp folded twenty dollar bill. It was held upright by two blades of grass, right on the side of the trail, as though it had been placed there especially for me. This was the trail's first act of magic. I bowed and said "Thank you, trail." and bounded on as though nothing unusual had happened.

"I'm on the PCT!" For the first couple of days, I repeated the words often, out loud, just to hear them. My presence at each switchback, each hilltop or creek crossing begged to be documented. I feared that I would later doubt I really walked the trail or forget how beautiful each plant, creature or panorama was, if I didn't photograph every inch of it.

"Hey there! Are you a thru-hiker?"

I heard the first hiker I met on the trail before I saw him. I had just left the convenience store near Lake Morena with an ice cream cone and had temporarily diverted my attention to its fast melting goodness. His call startled me.

Was I a thru-hiker? I briefly pondered if it were fair of me to claim the title after walking such a small fraction of the total trail. I was disheveled, covered in dirt, had slept on a rock and hiked all day with all my belongings on my back to get this ice cream cone. I believed I had met most of the requirements.

"I AM!" I jumped for joy at the realization and joined my new friend in the shade.

Columbia was his trail name. He was a tall man with a small pack. He leaned to the side to inspect mine. I expected a question about my pack's brand and giddily anticipated his surprise when I told him that I had made it. The frown on his face, however, wiped my giddiness.

"How much weight are you carrying? ... Thirty three pounds! That's a heavy pack – and you're so small! I don't think you'll make it to Canada with that much weight on your back. Trust me on that. This is my seventh attempt at completing the trail."

Columbia's words flew around me like wind around a granite boulder. I was as impervious to grim prognostics about my chances of success as I was to dreadful water reports, news of forest fires or warnings about injuries, water-borne illnesses and poisonous plants.

"Well, that's all good to know. Thank you for your advice and warnings. I'm actually not worried ... I'm the Bobcat."

I enunciated the last sentence with a wide smile, as though it were self-evident that the Bobcat was immune to trail calamities. He smiled in return, though I could not assess whether in appreciation of my confidence or anticipation for the trail lessons awaiting me.

I bid him good luck and skipped on down the trail solo, as any bobcat would have.

⁝ · ⁞

Bobcat – *n. Lynx Rufus*. Bobcats range from northern Mexico to southern Canada. They can travel surprisingly long distances despite their short legs. They are territorial and solitary roamers, except during mating season. Their prey selection depends on location, habitat, season and abundance. As the most adaptable of all the big cats, they are equally at home in arid deserts as they are in alpine settings.

⁝ · ⁞

I had been "The Bobcat" for two years before the trail. It all started as a joke, on me: Logan was nine and a half years younger than I was, and I was not yet forty when I met him, which – my geologist friends had agreed – made me not quite a cougar, but more of a bobcat.

Did the name endure because it matched my personality beyond the joke or was I infused with its essence until I fully represented it?

I did find myself equally at home in a hundred-degree desert as I did on alpine glaciers, and I was driven to walk forth by feline-like curiosity, more so than by the need to achieve mileage goals or reach destinations.

Like the rest of my kin, I roamed solo from dawn to dusk, with no need for a time schedule of any sort. I carried a watch, but only used it to thwart my stomach's attempts at getting a snack every ten minutes. Time-keeping on the trail seemed pointless as minutes and hours were secondary to the terrain. I never walked on purpose for twelve hours or thirty miles, but at times surpassed both just to see what was over the next hill.

The only limiting factor to ultimate freedom from any schedule was my stomach. A simple math problem, really: If the distance between two resupply towns is 150 miles, and the Bobcat needs 3 lbs of food per day but can carry only 20 lbs of food. How many miles a day must the Bobcat walk to avoid starvation before the next resupply town? The math didn't always translate to the real world, and for many of the initial miles, I alternated between carrying too much and too little food.

"Prey" selection was often limited in resupply towns. For six weeks, in Rishikesh, I had mindfully feasted on blessed and wholesome meals of fruits, legumes and vegetables. My first resupply on the trail, at a small convenience store near Mt. Laguna, consisted of Spam, Bacon Bits, Oreo cookies and Ramen noodles. Luckily, bobcats are the most adaptable of all the big cats, so I ate what I had and giggled at each meal for the next sixty miles.

Although I preferred to roam solo, the hiking pack had not yet dispersed in the desert section of Southern California. I met other hikers or trail families – as groups of hikers are known – several times a day, especially around water holes. All hikers I met were delightful, but I remained politely aloof. This was not just any old trail; this was the PCT – a mystical land accessible only to true adventurers – and I meant to not miss any of it to human distraction.

Even alone, I berated myself if I became lost in thoughts, if I emerged from an auto-pilot trance to discover I had missed part of the trail.

"Please pardon my absent-mindedness." I told the trail as I stretched my vision to include as much of the missed section as possible. I only walked in one direction, so I had only one chance to experience each step.

There were no conversations with my Higher Self either. None were necessary. I had no overarching quest, no dragons to tame, no philosophical concepts to explore, heartbreaks to overcome or mistaken beliefs to release. There were no lessons, just the experience of walking the trail. There was no role for Melissa but that of the Bobcat.

Like a lusty lover whose identity is suddenly solely defined in the eyes of the beloved, for a little while, I became the Bobcat at the exclusion of all else.

PCT 2012. Mile 109.
Excerpt from The Roaming Bobcat's blog
Titled "Expectations – Reality – Honeymoon"
    I love this. I mean, I LOVE LOVE LOVE this! I love every step, every day, every person I've met, every plant, every star over my sleeping bag at night, every friggin' molecule, second and ounce of this trail. And I love who I am on it.
Trail wisdom claims that one finds his or her true self fast on the trail. Wow. Is this me? The Bobcat is something else. I recognize myself, but barely. I have soooo much energy and joy here. Social filters are extraneous on the trail. I can be as quirky as happens naturally, and the depth of my quirkiness is surprising even me. Among other trademarks, I have been wearing a superhero cape from 10 am to 5 pm every day. In just a few days this has become completely normal. Nobody cares. Quirks are encouraged and often matched. This is freedom of being as I have not known it before. This is the magical world I always suspected existed.

Chapter 30

PCT Day 5 – mile 56
Excerpt from my trail journal [edited for length]
Amazing sunrise! Not even photographable. Range of low hills, each one a shade darker than the preceding. Desert shrubs silhouetted in the foreground. Right at the horizon, a progression of intensely bright colors from orange to yellow to blue to deep blue. A few stars sprinkled in the deep blue, which still covers most of the sky. A gentle breeze. Birds chirping. The ants are already at work. All is perfect.
I just woke up from a dream. There was a council sitting in a circle, showing me on a white board how guidance is applied in the subtlest of choices. We can always choose, they said, we have free will, but some paths are more obvious than others. If we are wise and open (i.e. if we pay attention), the path to the most joy, the most learning, the most natural progression is always revealed. It was then decreed that I should go on a date with an unseen entity named "The White Rabbit" to see the movie "Wizards of the PCT," which I haven't seen yet.
What does it meeeeeaaaan?

I closed my journal and shifted inside my warm bag to properly greet the ants by my side.

I loved these ants. They were the reason why I slept in this perfectly level and flat sandy ledge overlooking the desert. The map showed only a few suitable sleeping surfaces in the area. I had arrived late and last but was the first to consider ants a bonus instead of a nuisance.

I had spent hours during the fast in Death Valley observing ants at work. I had learned that they listen if spoken to but carry on immediately, out of busyness more than oblivion. The pause in their movement was almost imperceptible yet sufficient for me to believe that communication was possible.

I sat next to the anthill when I arrived to feel whether I was welcomed or not. I saw no sign of aggression, so I unrolled my poncho next to the anthill, placed one of my poles — named "This" to match its brother "That" — between us, lined the pole with a row of little rocks on the ants' side, and spoke to the ants.

"Hi ants. I would like to sleep here, please. You stay on that side, and I'll stay on my side. You don't bite me, and I promise I won't crush you. I'm here only for one night. I mean you no harm, and I thank you in advance for accommodating me."

I was certain this would work and fell into a deep restful sleep peppered with important dreams.

The ants stayed on their side. They were still sluggish at six in the morning, but they were already working.

Hikers nearby were also already awake. I could see three of them silhouetted against the sunrise — Two were dressed alike, a father and son it seemed, and one had a glorious red beard. If I wanted to walk alone, I had better pack up while they were still busy photographing wild flowers in the sunrise's golden light.

In just a few minutes, my poncho, sleeping pad and sleeping bag were rolled and secured. I shouldered my pack, slipped This and That's straps around my wrists and was about to start the great adventure of that day, when the red bearded man greeted me.

"Hi, I'm LB."

I thought he said MelB, which was my nickname when I still had my maiden name, so I replied: "Oh cool! That's my name too!" and we were both confused about our trail names until the snake incident – which I will get to.

LB asked if I was going to the Kickoff, the annual hiker reunion about to take place. I was not. The estimated attendance for that year's Kickoff was seven hundred hikers – Seven hundred smelly, hungry hikers in line for free burritos in a camp with only a few toilets. No, thank you.

"You should come. They're going to play 'Wizard of the PCT' on Friday night."

My jaw dropped. I had just been instructed about this.

"*You* are the White Rabbit I'm supposed to go on a date with!"

"Yes!" He could not have known about my dream, but I guessed from his grin that it did not matter; he liked where the conversation was going.

"Well, I guess I'm going to the Kickoff with you then. I prefer to hike alone though, so let's meet in Warner Springs, and we can hitchhike together to the Kickoff."

"Sure. I get you." He smiled and turned back towards his friends, the father and son amongst the wild flowers. "Hike your own hike. I'll see you in Warner Springs."

This was my first encounter with this classic mantra of thru-hiking – "Hike your own hike" – so when LB simply walked away, I was grateful, but also surprised, and maybe a little disappointed.

A few hours later, I was sitting on top of a wrecking ball abandoned in a pasture near a water tank where I had just refilled my water bottles when a rowdy trail family arrived at the water tank. They asked if I had seen LB – you know, Last on the Bus, red beard, white hat, orange-eyed skulls on his gaiters. The description matched the White Rabbit, who had passed the water tank while I was filling my water bottles. I told them he was ahead.

"Oh good, I'll chill here for an hour and maybe it'll take me a full eight minutes to catch up to him."

That was Legion. I later described him in my journal as a "handsome, witty pain in the ass – I'll probably like him." The rest of the gang laughed, but I sensed no mockery, just playful fondness.

They lounged in the shade of the water tank and bantered amongst themselves. I listened quietly from the top of the wrecking ball under the shade of my cape.

I liked the energy of the group. Although I wouldn't have admitted it then, I secretly wished I could have a trail family like this one. But to remain true to my intent for solitude, I slid down the wrecking ball and rejoined the trail.

"Hey, nice cape! What's your name?" Legion called out before I could disappear.

"I'm the Bobcat."

"We'll catch you too, Bobcat." They all laughed, and I laughed with them. They looked much too comfortable to catch up to anyone.

Sometime over eight minutes later, I spotted LB walking in the distance above the low shrubs of the desert. I was faster than he was, so I had to pace myself in order to keep a bubble of personal space. I didn't mind the slower pace; the desert was warm and fragrant, and there was so much to see at each step.

Suddenly, about ten feet ahead, a snake slithered out of the low shrubs and raced towards me on the straight line of the trail. I instinctively planted This and That and jumped both legs up, suspended on my poles. The snake slid right under me, between the poles. I landed back on my feet and turned around just in time to see it slither back into the low shrubs, about ten feet behind.

That was incredible! Such a story deserved an immediate audience. I quickened my pace to a trot to catch up to LB.

"Hey, hold up! You won't believe what just happened."

Thus ended my illusions of a completely solo hike. I could have hiked on; I was faster. But every time I gained any distance, LB asked a fascinating question or shared a hilarious observation, and I slowed back down to hike with him. After a few miles, I saw the futility of my attempts and decided that snakes don't randomly race under people's feet. The timing was too precise. That snake meant for me to hike with LB. It probably was sent by the council of – not so subtle – guidance.

LB was a chill cat from Minnesota with aspirations of becoming an astrophysicist. He was also a veteran thru-hiker, who had not only completed the Appalachian Trail, but also ridden his bicycle from Florida to the start of the PCT.

With his shuffle steps and booming laugh, he stole most of my attention away from the trail. We had so much to discuss, from the difference between quarks and neutrinos to the effects of daily Ramen noodles on stool color and consistency – and yes, there was a correlation.

I occasionally swept the desert with my eyes to imprint some of the trail in my memory. I didn't miss all of it. In fact, I found that often LB noticed details I might have missed – like a bee in a cactus flower – if I had walked by at my usual pace.

I would have also missed getting to know a patch of grass under a ten by ten tarp, and the trail family hiding from the hundred-degree day under it. There were just a few hikers under the tarp when we arrived, but soon, the motley crew from the water tank caught up, for a total of twelve hikers.

We discussed no age, occupation, social status or home location. These off-trail considerations were completely irrelevant. Only Chili, the thirteen-year-old veteran thru-hiker in our midst, revealed his age, but only to alleviate his dad's concerns about topic appropriateness, which seemed unrestricted to me anyway.

By nightfall, we hadn't moved at all, and my cheeks were sore from so much laughing. I remarked to LB that we had only hiked twelve miles. Many more still separated us from Warner Springs if we were to get to the Kickoff for our movie date on time.

"Relax MelB. Success on the trail is measured in smiles, not in miles."

"Yes, but you're 'Last on the Bus' for a reason. I'm not sure your philosophy will get me to Canada."

"I'm 'Last on the Bus', not 'Late for the Bus'. I still get on the bus."

He leaned over and handed me a handful of M&Ms. He was right. This was the life, complete with magnificent vistas, inconsequential candies and instant best friends. Why would I rush through this dream of an existence?

That night, as I lay under the stars, kept awake by the concert of my new friends' snores, gratitude overtook my heart.

"Alright, you win. Maybe I don't want to hike the whole trail alone. Maybe I can make room for a few humans. Thank you for being more stubborn than I am and for sending me a snake."

I didn't know if I was speaking to myself, the council, the trail or my Higher Self, or whether there was any difference.

CHAPTER 31

"Wizards of the PCT" was never shown, and to LB's chagrin, there was no official "date." It was, however, not from his lack of trying.

As soon I set my tent on the designated lawn at the Kickoff, LB matched his tarp's entrance to mine, so that I had to crawl past his pillow to get out. He also kept me awake at night with jokes of questionable taste, cheered my yoga practice on the lawn as though it were a spectator sport and lured me into the shade of a large oak tree for a mid-afternoon whiskey break, which rendered the rest of the day utterly unproductive.

Despite these minor inconveniences, LB was a true asset for me early in the hike, and not only because he made me laugh. There is trail wisdom that can only be gleaned through experience, and LB was generous with his.

He taught me how to properly pierce and drain a blister to prevent further damage when stopping wasn't an option, to seek the cover of a tree at night to avoid getting drenched in meadow dew, and to tighten a tarp obliquely to withstand strong unidirectional wind. He shared with me his trail recipes and ways to extract more heat from my three-ounce alcohol stove. And, maybe more importantly, he inspired me to completely rethink my gear system.

At thirty-three pounds of base weight, my pack was ridiculously light compared to those I had carried on Mt. Baker, but still, within the first hundred miles of the trail, I realized that I was using only a fraction of what I carried.

"People carry their fears." LB said, "First aid kits, bear canisters, spare socks, even tents — it all can be traced to fear, even if it's fear of discomfort. It doesn't mean that you shouldn't carry it; just be mindful of what you pack."

I didn't want to carry my fears, so I spread the entire content of my pack on the lawn and carefully considered each item.

I immediately discarded the tent. I had slept in it only once and felt isolated the whole night. Even the thinnest of silicone-coated nylon wall was too much separation between me and the trail. Toast Cousin, one of my new trail friends, had hoped to purchase exactly the tent I no longer wished to carry, so within a minute, it was sold. Toast Cousin was concerned, however, that I was left without shelter. He offered me the use of his ultra-light bivy bag until I found a better solution.

I never found a better solution. At less than a pound, his bivy bag barely fit my sleeping bag, offered very little protection against the elements and allowed only minimal body movement if the bug netting was zippered shut. I loved it. In that bag, I was sheltered from no experience the trail offered.

I shipped all spare clothes, including all underwear and socks but two pairs each, and all my rain gear to my friend Margaret, who had volunteered as my resupply person and liaison to the off-trail world. For the rest of the trail, I washed underwear and socks in creeks, my cape doubled as a stylish wrap-shirt for town and the poncho protected both me and my pack from the rain.

I threw the mascara and deodorant in the box, puzzled that

I had even packed them.

The UV pen I had used to sterilize potentially contaminated water also went home. I had grown weary of its incessant "dead batteries" warnings. I had, at the time, no backup plan to treat water, but was open to guidance on the topic.

Finally, my entire first aid kit joined the homebound gear. I only kept the tweezers inside my tiny utility knife and a needle to puncture blisters – not because I still believed the Bobcat impervious to trail calamities, but because the range of potential calamities was so vast that I could not adequately prepare for all eventualities. Trusting that I could prevent injuries with preemptive awareness and creatively overcome those I couldn't prevent lightened my pack by over half a pound.

At the last minute, reluctantly, I placed my hoop earrings in the box. I didn't really need them.

In hindsight, the earrings were the only items I regretted shipping home. They made me feel beautiful beyond the grime and dirt and, as such, were well worth the couple extra ounces. Luckily, a set of fabulous blue dangling earrings appeared on my path in Idyllwild, a mere fifty miles later.

I repacked the items I had chosen to keep and shouldered my pack for a test. It was so light that I could have flown. I removed it from my back and hugged it. I knew that I carried exactly what I needed and not an once more. I felt an intimate bond with each item and complete trust in my system as a whole. I carried no fear, but I still had questions.

"So, what if I need something I haven't even thought of yet and I'm days out from a resupply town?"

"The trail provides. Don't you worry, MelB."

I remembered the twenty dollars I found on my first day, the snake that guided me to a trail family, the free pies in Julian, the water cashes in the desert from anonymous, generous Trail Angels, and myriad other small acts of magic. I knew what LB meant. If all my needs were covered in the off-trail world, I likely could expect extraordinary abundance while on this magical trail. This was the experiential phase of the

Intensive Sunday School for the Rebellious, and I believed that, as long as I upheld blind trust and faith, I could neither get lost nor hurt.

CHAPTER 32

On day 17, at mile 183, I had a prancing accident.

I had many reasons to prance: I was on the PCT, it was a cool, sunny day, I had just stood at the top of windy San Jacinto peak, and Trail Angels Ziggy and the Bear's famous fresh green salad lay within a day's walk.

Suddenly, by mechanics that still elude my comprehension, This – my left hand pole – lodged itself firmly in my left armpit with my hand still in its strap. On the next step, instead of moving forward as expected, my whole body pivoted around That like a barn door on a hinge, until my foot was over the steep edge, off the trail. I remained in suspension just long enough to appreciate the oddity of the movement before crashing down on a folded ankle.

The trail disappeared in a swirl of pain. Instant tears flooded my eyes. I slowly regained my breath and crawled back up to the trail. I sat motionless, still tangled in my poles, for what seemed like an eternity and giggled within the pain at the intensity of the sensation.

When the biting edge of the pain finally dissipated, I slowly stood and tested a step. Nothing seemed broken, just a little tender. I walked carefully at first, but by the time I reached the top of Fuller Ridge, a few miles later, I could almost walk evenly if I kept a slow pace.

The descent from Fuller Ridge is one of those landmarks about which thru-hikers like reminiscing. The term "ridiculous" is most often associated with it. The trail's switchbacks take over fifteen miles for a three mile descent. Each switchback contours the entire mountain, drops a foot and contours the mountain the other way. Signs warn hikers of penalty for cutting switchbacks. Ridiculous! I could have jumped to the lower portion of the trail.

Except, right then, I couldn't jump because my ankle was throbbing with pain. I couldn't stop either because there was not a drop of water to be found for fifteen miles and I only had a few ounces left. In all the excitement at the top of the ridge, I had forgotten to refill my water bottles.

When the sun reached the edge of the desert, I was still high above the valley floor, far from Ziggy's salad, and yet, there was no place on earth I would have preferred.

The hills exploded with colors. The scrubby chaparral and each flower's outline glowed in the golden sunset. Lizards of all hues grew formidable by the addition of exaggerated shadows. And just when I thought the sky had reached the apogee of breathtaking beauty, a large and almost full orange moon rose over the San Gorgiono Mountains directly across the valley from my vantage point.

I was completely out of water, my parched throat grated with each attempt at a full breath, and both my ankles throbbed in unison – one because I had sprained it, the other because I had overcompensated to avoid walking on the injured one. It did not matter; my heart soared with bliss and gratitude for the moon, the stars, the lizards, flowers, and the ridiculously long set of switchbacks that had allowed me to greet them all.

I unrolled my sleeping bag on a small level platform just off the trail, under a fragrant bush and in direct sight of the large orange moon.

No pain could endure in the midst of such beauty. In the morning, there would be water and my ankles would support me strongly again. I was certain of it. To confirm that I understood the process of the medicine, I shouted up to the sky: "I LOVE YOU, MOON," then whispered intimately, "I love you, trail."

Around noon the next day, I hobbled into Ziggy and the Bear's yard after a sweltering crossing of the sandy valley floor. I was parched, hungry, overheated and still unwaveringly happy.

I had planned only a quick stop of a few hours at most, but as soon as I walked under the shade of the hikers' tent, Ziggy took my pack, offered me a chair and placed my feet in a hot water bath. Before I could argue, she pointed towards the back of the tent.

"There's watermelon in the cooler and some nuts and candy bars in the box next to it. The computer on the table has internet access and the password is on the post-it next to it. Help yourself to anything."

She returned to her kitchen, leaving me unattended in this sudden self-service paradise.

I looked at the computer and wondered ... I had only spoken with Sofia and Margaret since the start of the trail. I had no interest in contacting anyone else. The trail fulfilled all my social needs, and I was much happier without the world's drama, whether personalized or generalized.

I ate a few snacks, massaged my sore ankles in the warm water, and still, that computer taunted me.

A loud and talkative hiker came in and was treated to a hot foot bath in the chair directly across from mine. I feigned interest in the quasi-monologue of a conversation we began, but my mind was a single-track laser-beam on that computer and any potential email from Logan it might have held.

In the middle of one of my new friend's endless speeches, the need to know finally won. I jumped to my feet, started the computer, and fidgeted with a nearby pencil for the interminable thirty seconds it took the internet and my emails to load.

PCT Day 19 — mile 219 — Whitewater Preserve
Excerpt from my trail journal.

Logan answered the email I sent him the night before I started the trail, the one where I say I don't know what we are and I don't know how to deal with the events right before I left, for which I still have a bruise on my leg. I told him that although I love him, a line was crossed that should have never been crossed and I just don't know what to do about it.

He answered:
"I figured that was the consensus.
We are what we are.
I love you.
Hike strong and keep me in the loop.
Refer back to line 3."

I read and reread Logan's email, each time finding new meaning in the few simple lines, yet still missing the essence of it. The voice of the hiker behind me, who was still talking, oblivious to my lack of response, slowly faded to another world, and I was left alone with Logan in my mind.

Like a genie out of a bottle, his energy suddenly occupied the whole hikers' tent, and not for the first time. I turned back to the row of chairs and piles of buckets awaiting feet in various states of damage. Which of these chairs had been his, exactly ten years prior, during his own thru-hike of the PCT?

Logan had hiked every mile of my beloved trail and described with precise accuracy the rib-bursting joy, the sense of freedom and the instant connections with hikers who become life-long friends. He had also hiked the Continental Divide Trail and the Appalachian Trail in full and learned firsthand that thru-hikers don't return, and that thru-hiking is often fatal to off-trail relationships.

But, we were what we were – and back to line 3 – and we had survived so much already. Wouldn't we survive a bruise on a leg? Wouldn't we survive the trail? The combination seemed lethal to me, but I had learned not to underestimate the potency of the catnip-kryptonite.

As the shadow of the hikers' tent grew long, more hikers arrived until each chair was occupied and the splashing sound of feet in hot water rivaled in volume the humming of conversations and laughter.

I would have typically enjoyed the scene, but I was precariously balanced with one foot in hiker world and one foot wrapped around Logan in my mind. I figured what I needed most was quiet trail medicine.

The moon that night was a super-moon, bigger by fourteen percent and brighter by thirty percent than a regular full moon. Super-moons were blamed for all sorts of natural disasters, howling dogs and mental disorders. Hiking alone at night in unknown mountains without a headlamp in my state of Logan destabilization seemed like lunacy – Perfect!

When I left Ziggy and the Bear's, the moon was still orange, right at the horizon, behind an alien landscape of wind turbines. As the night deepened, it rose to its full blinding white majesty, illuminating each of the millions of mica flakes in the sand as though from within. The trail became a luminous path through the pitch-black gullies and canyons. In the distance, silhouetted wind turbines watched my progress and pointed the way with their long arms like ghostly semaphores, making it impossible for me to stray.

The decibel level dropped to almost nothing. Stillness was only disturbed by the faint songs of the crickets and the intrusive crunching under my steps and poles.

But through the ethereal beauty of the night, where was the Bobcat? She was lost in her own story, following a luminous path blindly and underestimating the profundity of the crickets' songs. I even forgot the pain in my ankles.

Instead, I replayed scenes from the past in my mind, changing one element at a time to evaluate where I might have gone wrong. I imagined heart-felt conversations and grandiose emotional reunions just as vividly as I imagined tracing a line in the luminous sand and never looking back over it.

By the time I reached the Whitewater Preserve, I was limping so severely that I could no longer concentrate on my internal drama. I collapsed on a picnic table and winced at any further movement.

The next day, I could not even walk to the bathroom. Luckily, the Whitewater Preserve was a small enclave of creek-fed cold water pools and shaded picnic areas. I painfully wobbled to the creek with my journal, my harmonica and some snacks and spent the entire day in convalescence with both ankles in cold water.

My mind was once again inundated with Logan drama.

I tried meditating on the sun's dancing reflection on the water surface to return to stillness, but to no avail. I stood in the middle of the creek, about knee deep, and tried to match the rhythm of the sun's reflection pattern with notes on my harmonica. A slow, plaintive blues melody gradually emerged. I had never played so soulfully, though I had always aspired to. I wailed my love and its pain, impervious to the occasional hiking onlooker or to the heat of the noon sun.

Gratitude returned to my heart. What a privilege it was to love someone so deeply as to feel so hurt. Maybe I didn't mind the pain so much. If it was time for Logan's energy to join my hike, then I would carry it. If it was time for me to walk on swollen ankles, then I would embrace it.

Oh, how easy it was to resolve to persevere when I still had both feet in a cool little pool.

CHAPTER 33

I was still in the creek in the late afternoon, when a familiar shade of red appeared around the corner.

'LB!" I jumped to my feet out of the water and improvised a wobbly celebratory dance of joy. "Yay for sprained ankles. You caught up to me."

The last time I had seen LB, he was nursing a hangover in the shade of a tall oak tree at the Kickoff. He had rejoined the trail a day behind me, but, according to a fast hiker, was last seen napping under another tree a mere mile past Warner Springs. Honestly, I had doubted I'd ever see him again.

LB laughed at my wobbly dance and gave me a big bear hug. He then leaned over to inspect my private pool in the creek and must have liked what he saw, because he immediately dropped his pack and removed his shoes.

His feet were covered in dime- to quarter-sized blisters.

"Holy smokes, LB! Your feet are all chewed up."

"What, these? I always have blisters when I hike. It's part of the trail for me. It's alright. I pack some vitamin I (Ibuprofen) and walk it off."

"Well, that's perfect. I can't walk either. Let's hobble on together tomorrow. We can distract each other from our woes."

The next section of the trail, along Mission Creek, was so hot and desiccated that for once I was glad to be distracted. The low shrubs were nothing but dried gnarled twigs, and although the Mission Creek Preserve was known for its rich riparian habitat and abundance of birds, the only wildlife we encountered consisted of spiders and rattlers.

"MelB, don't be so stubborn. Take some Ibuprofen."

LB shook the canister in my direction, and I shook my head in response. I didn't want to take any pain-masking substance and risk injuring myself further by putting more pressure on my ankles than they could handle. But on the other hand, I was walking so slowly that even chill-cat LB was getting bored waiting for me.

"The trail is a place of healing. The pain will pass. I just need to trust more and relax into the sensation."

"Right. The trail *is* a place of healing, and it sent me to deliver some Ibuprofen. Don't refuse trail magic."

LB didn't even believe in magic – it had been one of our most heated topics of debate – but he knew how to speak to a stubborn Bobcat. I took one Ibuprofen pill, and, magically, the pain dissipated enough for us to hike on.

For the next fifty miles, as the desert slowly transitioned from Sonoran to Mojave, LB and I talked the miles away.

Somewhere along Mission Creek, I gave LB a disclaimer. I warned him that I might flirt with him, leave notes for him on the trail, and crawl under his tarp in case of adverse weather, but that under no circumstance should he read into these any romantic interest on my part – nothing personal.

He agreed with a laugh and I believed we had a deal.

"So, why aren't you available?"

"His name is Logan."

Stories of Logan began bubbling up, discreetly at first, but

LB was such an attentive audience that the storytelling quickly became rampant.

Despite the moments of blissful romance and the sense of belonging Logan and I shared, only the most gruesome parts wanted to be told – the classic tragedy of impossible love, the lies, the deceit, the heartbreaks, the volatility and the violence. The stories were one-sided, but the storytelling was therapeutic. This was no rehashing for the purpose of vilifying the man I loved but an act of release. I was offering my most painful stories to the trail, watching them float up and out into the wild where they could dissipate in dilution, like a tear in the ocean.

I presumed that LB was astute enough to understand the one-sidedness and therapeutic nature of my Logan storytelling. But as I exposed the rawest bits of my heart to my best trail friend, as I cried by his side and regained my strength through our shared laughter, a depth of connection was created between us that could have fooled any man into hoping for more, even a smart, forewarned one.

By the time we reached highway 18, outside of Big Bear City, the top tier of my Logan stories had been released into the wild, and I was just getting out of my self-absorbed trance to realize I had complications in another relationship to navigate as well.

While I had been lost in storytelling, LB had approached his sleeping pad a little closer every night. It seemed convenient; we always talked well past dark. We also shared meals, walked in step and took naps together. By the time I noticed the changes, it was too late: we were a trail couple in the eyes of the community.

I knew that with LB straight forward honesty was the best policy, but Powah Nap and Young Geyser had joined us at highway 18 to share both a ride and a hotel room. I decided to delay the "friends only – part two" talk until we could be alone.

Big Bear City, however, had other plans for me, starting with another email from Logan.

PCT Day 22 – Mile 266 – Big Bear City
Excerpt from my trail journal.
I got an email from Logan. A three-page long email! He is usually a man of such few efficient words. This must have been the longest email he has ever written in his life. In it, he surprisingly owned his half of our dysfunction. He said he has cancelled all his summer adventures to climb the hardest trail, that of personal growth. He then thanked me for being who I am. He wrote:
"Be free. Fly free. Be your most amazing self, and show the world what we, passionate people, can do when we are not impaired by limiting relationships."

I read such kindness and raw authenticity in his email, as though he were standing naked in front of me for the first time, that in that instant, I loved Logan more acutely than I ever had before. But, what did he mean by "Fly free?" Fly free by my side because I now understand that your wingspan is as wide as mine or fly free away from me to other skies because I am moving on myself?

I rested my fingers on the keyboard of the hotel's computer seeking the words to express to Logan my simultaneous gratitude, love and confusion.

Across from me, on the large common room's back wall was a painting of a Bobcat walking through snow. His eyes seemed fixed on mine with a pointed look. I imagined his disapproval, but disapproval of what?

I typed "I love you." It was a good start, but before I could write anything further, an older man on crutches walked in the room and began talking to me.

He only had a month to live, according to the doctors. Although he had discovered that he had cancer only a month prior, his was the kind that couldn't be survived. There was no cure, so he had come to Big Bear City to end in a nice place. He was looking forward to the end of the pain.

I didn't know what to say. I wished him good luck, and he walked back through the door from whence he came, which I didn't believe was actually part of the hotel.

After such a surreal encounter, I had even less words available to type. The timing of that man walking in was too precise to be accidental. Maybe I wasn't meant to answer Logan's email. Before I could over-think it any further, I hit the "send" button. "I love you." was all my email said. And before I could send another, I closed the computer and returned to our hotel room.

Although the boys had gone to town, probably for second or third breakfast, the room smelled like fifteen hikers were currently washing their socks in the sink. I hadn't showered or washed any laundry in over a hundred miles myself and felt I needed a good cleaning – both a body scrubbing and a mind clearing.

I emptied the contents of my pack on the bed and sorted through items to be washed. I had acquired a good half an inch of dirt and twigs at the bottom of my pack while walking through the desert. I opened the big trash can in the room and shook my pack upside down above it.

I had just about shaken everything out when my little utility knife went racing down after the dirt and twigs and landed somewhere in the trash. Luckily, that knife was so small that I had expected I might lose it and had tied it to my pack with a string. I followed the string through the trash and found my knife comfortably resting on a big wad of cash – a $185 wad of cash, to be exact.

When the boys returned from their meals and errands, each in turn claimed the cash, but none of them could accurately guess the amount.

"Now, that's some trail magic! Good for you, Bobcat. Now, don't forget the little people." Powah Nap said as he checked the other trash cans in the room, just in case.

I stashed the cash in a special pocket in my pants and spent the rest of the day spreading magic to other thru-hikers. Anyone could get a grant from the trash can fund to buy a meal, duct-tape, alcohol to fuel a stove, or anything else. I only kept the last few dollars as a fee for passing on the magic.

LB, Powah Nap and I returned to the trail the next day. In

less than twenty four hours, I had met a dying man, possibly said goodbye to Logan, found $185 in a trash can, and been mistaken for LB's trail bride by all new hikers we had met. My processing systems were on overload, and I was eager to return to the simplicity of the trail, even with two swollen ankles.

First, however, and especially with my relationship status in sudden limbo, I had a potential trail romance to squash.

"I don't want to be your friend. Don't put me in the 'friend' bucket." LB stopped hiking and turned to face me. How could he not want to be my friend? That's what we were. "Once you are in the 'friend' bucket, you can never get out of it."

We stood facing each other in silence for a moment. I had not anticipated any resistance. LB was not just my friend; he was my *best* friend on the trail, which meant a lot to me.

"Friendship is all I have to offer." I shrugged in apology. I hoped it was enough.

"Then, I'm not interested." He stepped to the side of the trail, gently gestured for me to go by, and said nothing more. My heart sunk. Friendship really was all I had to offer, and I couldn't imagine it would change.

We continued walking in step for about a mile, but silently. Then, despite the swollen ankles, I quicken my pace. The gap between us grew until we were completely out of sight. I would not see LB again for ninety six miles – ninety six painful miles.

CHAPTER 34

PCT 2012. Mile 370
Excerpt from The Roaming Bobcat's blog
Titled: "Teaching the Bobcat to walk"

 My relationship to the trail has entered a new phase. It is testing me. "So, you claim to love me so much", it said, "but what about now? Do you still love me when both of your ankles are so swollen that every step sends shooting pain up to your mid-calf? Now that I have lined up both sides of the trail with Poison Oak so you cannot get through without touching it? What if I remove shade and raise the temperature to over a

*hundred degrees and cook your brains out? Scorpions? Tarantulas?" and
I said "Yes, trail, yes. I still love you, unconditionally."
And so it said "Good. Then I shall teach you to walk."*

My apprenticeship began immediately. If my ankles rolled outwardly ever so slightly, shooting pain climbed up the side of my shin bones. If they rolled inwardly ever so slightly, the massive blisters on my heels straightened my gait. These were not ordinary blisters, but deep little cushions of pain under a layer of callus too thick to pierce with a needle. So for the first time in my life, with the help of my trusty poles, This and That, I walked perfectly balanced on the central axis of my feet.

Walking monopolized my attention, but luckily the terrain past Big Bear City was uncomplicated. The trail turned sandy and soft, brown, beige and dusty. It meandered through the charred ghosts of burnt forests and sparse low brushes with dusty leaves. I was grateful for every sandy step. I could learn to walk without additional obstacles. I was slow, but at least I was steady.

I walked from before dawn to well past dark to compensate for my reduced pace and still maintain a twenty mile per day average, which I knew was sufficient to stay ahead of LB and Powah Nap and get to Wrightwood in six days, before depletion of my food bag and right on time for Logan's birthday.

The trail watched my progress like a patient lover and, as a reward when I did well, surprised me with fields of purple lupines. It showed its support subtly but frequently. One lonely flower in a mile of sandy fields covered in fallen, blackened branches was enough to light up the whole trail. An occasional couple of steps without pain revealed the immense joy still at my core and fueling my walk.

"Pain is the breaking of the shell that encloses understanding" The phrase played in my head in Sofia's voice like a song earworm.

What understanding was I lacking? That I was not the cape-wearing superhero I had fancied myself to be? Oh, but I was.

Superheroes were not forged on lounge chairs but in the fire of discomfort. That I was overconfident in my ability to complete a thru-hike? No, I was still walking to Canada. It was decreed and non-negotiable. That I was mistaken when I claimed to have neither pain to escape nor suffering to transcend? No, that wasn't it either.

I intuitively knew that the pain was an intrinsic part of my thru-hike, and strangely, as such, I became fond of it. It didn't even occur to me to wish it gone. The trail provided neither pointless nor accidental experiences, so the pain, like everything else, must have existed for my benefit.

Then, one day, as I was contouring the scintillating shores of aptly named Lake Silverwood, after two and a half weeks of walking on ankles swollen to the girth of my calves, I became curious. What was pain anyway? What precise sensation in the body was the experience of this breaking of the shell that encloses understanding?

I continued walking with a soft focus on the path ahead but turned my conscious gaze to the physical location I associated with the pain. I could not locate it. If I looked at my ankles, I felt the pain where I looked, but if I looked away, the pain was evasive. It was not sharp. It didn't itch, burn or sting. In fact, no adequate word for pain accurately described it. It was ... blue, a dull metallic slightly teal blue with occasional flashes of crimson red, and it tasted earthy, like blood and dirt, and it sounded like a low pitch hum with a steady drum line and no melody. What was I supposed to do with this fascinating information?

As the sparkles on the lake turned from silver to gold in the late evening, I shuffled my indefinable pain to a picnic table overlooking the entire lake, and claimed it as a home for the night. There were silver linings in my hike everywhere – like this flat level sleeping surface, by a lake, with actual flush toilets nearby.

I fell asleep with both sore ankles wrapped in the bottom of my sleeping bag and with a smile on my face, once again expecting the pain to be gone in the morning. Hadn't my

Higher Self once written that acceptance of experiences is all that was needed for healing?

I was, therefore, not surprised when I first opened my eyes at dawn the next morning to find that the pain was gone. Until I moved. Then it all came back. I sat up on the picnic table and stared at the lake. Of course! The pain was in my ankles, but the suffering was in my heart, because the heart was the source of everything.

The shell broke, understanding came, and still, I chose to hike faster than the pain dictated to call Logan on his birthday. I chose the pain over the release, and I was aware that I was choosing, and grateful for the ability to choose.

Meanwhile, my world was shifting. The forerunners of the pack of hikers that had left campo right after the Kickoff were catching up to me. I called them "the fast ones."

Every day brought new friends for a few miles or an entire day depending on the balance between their speed and my desire to explore the new connection.

Brightcloud's unconventional interpretation of human nature kept me at full speed for over twenty five miles.

"There's evidence in human DNA for splicing between Neanderthal and Alien chromosomes. The X chromosome is ape-like, but the Y isn't at all. The Y is actually unlike any other creature on earth. So humans are hybrids. We have both cosmic and earth origins."

When I asked him how he knew so much about it, he said "I read a lot ... and I eat mushrooms."

I was still pondering Brightcloud's conclusions and their strange congruence to the yogic concept of the human body as a conduit for both cosmic and telluric energy, when I met Billy Goat.

I had hoped to meet Billy Goat. At seventy-three years of age and approaching forty thousand miles on foot, he was the most accomplished and well-known thru-hiker of whom I had heard, and I must admit that I was a little star-struck when I first spotted him in the shade by the creek.

"Are you the famous Billy Goat?"

"I don't know. Are you the famous Bobcat?" He laughed at my surprise, and then admitted that some of my trail family members had just left the creek.

"I suspected you'd be worth the wait." He winked and laughed again. His laugh was at least fifty years younger than his body.

I forgot all about my ankles and our hybrid origins for a few tens of miles as Billy Goat and I reminisced about trail hikes in which I had not partaken.

"Logan? Yeah, rowdy kid from the south, ten years ago. I remember him. He was a wild one. So, he's your boyfriend?"

"Hmm. I don't really know at the moment."

"That's good enough for me!"

I was still giggling at the memory of Billy Goat's laugh when I met Andrew.

Andrew and I leap-frogged for a few days and camped together for a few nights. I enjoyed his company and likely would have continued walking with him if I had had the chance, but he couldn't linger. His wife was expecting their first son, and he had promised her that he'd get to Canada before delivery. We parted a day before Wrightwood with hugs and words of good luck. Before setting off at a pace I couldn't match, he gave me his spare snacks and tiger balm for my ankles. I hobbled in the same direction for the last push to Wrightwood.

After twenty-two miles on the most painful ankles I had yet experienced, I dropped my pack on the pavement of highway 2 at exactly five in the afternoon on Logan's birthday. Three minutes later, I had a ride to town. Five miles later, I met Shameless at the local pizza joint and followed him to a Trail Angel's house. The house wasn't mentioned in any guide or on any map, but a hiker had shown him the way there, and he was paying the favor forward.

By six in the afternoon, I was sitting on a soft bed in a vacant room on the top floor of a beautiful house in downtown Wrightwood. This was trail magic at its best. I had not yet had a room to myself on the trail.

187

I closed the door for privacy and dialed Logan's number, three times. The first time, his phone was off, so I left a birthday message. The second time, his phone rang, but he didn't pick up. Not to worry, I assumed he would hear my message and call back. When he didn't, I called again to find his phone was off.

I understood. He had not missed my call; he had chosen not to take it. He was letting me fly away.

I collapsed onto the bed, too exhausted to let the thought evoke an emotion and fell asleep fully dressed, instantly.

I slept for twenty hours and was surprised when I opened my eyes to the setting sun. I was sufficiently attuned to the shades of daylight and position of shadows by then to recognize it was evening before checking the time.

Logan was gone. The change in the quality of the energy of our connection was subtle but unambiguous. We would likely always love each other, but it was time for me to fly. As of that moment, I considered myself single.

I slipped out of bed and walked over to my pack, where I rummaged for snacks. I was famished. I walked back to the bed with a spread of assorted Ziploc bags of nuts, seeds and dried fruit, and only then realized that I had felt no pain in my ankles since I opened my eyes. I jumped out of bed, stepped forward and jumped up a few times. The pain was gone, completely gone. What an interesting coincidence.

I then opened the door to find that LB and Powah Nap had just found their way to the same Trail Angel's house. What interesting timing.

I said hello politely but casually, as I would have addressed somebody I have met but don't claim to know well, and proceeded down the stairs.

"Hey, MelB?" LB called before I could reach the bottom of the stairs.

"Yes?"

"I'd like to be your friend again."

"Just friend?"

"Sure." He shrugged, but not even the bushy red beard

could conceal the mischief in his smile. "But I'll still try to seduce you, if that's alright."

"That seems fair, but don't hold your breath, you might pass out." It felt good to laugh with LB again.

By the time Powah Nap got out of the shower, LB and I were rolling with laughter on his cot.

"Powah Nap! It's not what it looks like." I yelled with glee.

"Oh, it's *exactly* what it looks like." LB corrected.

I left Wrightwood alone the next morning, but I knew that LB's and my path would cross again and joyously so.

With all pain gone, I could have flown across the desert, if I had chosen to, but I loved that section of the desert so much that, instead, I purposely slowed down to relish it longer. For the next three hundred and thirty three miles to Kennedy Meadows, LB caught up to me continually. We neither tried to walk alone nor together; we let the desert dictate our reunions.

Past Wrightwood, the desert really unveiled its vastness and magnificence. It crossed basins so flat that climbing on a concrete block offered an unobstructed view to the miles ahead. It followed metal aqueducts and meandered through forests of intermingled windmills and Joshua trees. Every day was bright, sunny and hot, and the wind flew my superhero cape to unprecedented heights.

In spite of its expansiveness, the section between Wrightwood and Kennedy Meadows was also one of the most social sections of the PCT. Most of us, thru-hikers, migrated through it like the native fauna, napping in the shade during the noon heat and gathering around water holes in the evenings.

Some well-established Trail Angels' houses through this section were the ultimate water holes. At Hiker Heaven, in Agua Dulce, fifty new friends and all members of my trail family gathered for showers, laundry, resupply and relaxation.

We all met again twenty five miles later, on the haphazard sofas of Casa de Luna, the aptly self-proclaimed "Hippy Day Care."

These were mandatory stops for a complete thru-hiking

experience. Nowhere in the world, I imagine, could one be spoiled with so much free food, beer, care and love. Nowhere else would fifty grown-ups spend days painting rocks, swinging under trees and cheering for their champion chocolate wrestler. The only hardship we faced was extricating ourselves from this gauntlet of goodness to return to the trail.

But, onward we hiked, and as soon as we did, the trail felt like home again, leaving us to wonder how we could have been seduced away from it for so many zeros (zero-mile days).

Eventually, to the delight of some, but to my dismay, green hills appeared in the distance, harbinger of the Sierra Nevada looming ahead.

Two miles short of Kennedy Meadows, I climbed on the tallest granite boulder I could find by a small well-vegetated creek and I cried. When the tears were insufficient, I played my sadness on the harmonica – the same farewell song on replay for at least an hour.

"What are you doing up there?" LB had caught up to me one last time.

"I'm crying."

The desert was hard on LB's freckled fair skin and Minnesotan heat tolerance, and I knew that he likely was looking to the Sierra ahead as a Promised Land of reprieve.

"I don't want the desert to end." I began crying again.

"Okay. It doesn't have to end yet. We still have two miles. If you want we'll camp right here. We'll only go on when you feel you're ready."

And so we did. We camped on the sand and ate our last packets of Ramen noodles only two miles from Kennedy Meadows, its camp, showers, burgers and ice cream.

Several trail families walked right by our camp, and Brightcloud stopped and camped with us. We laughed and talked well into the night – which by thru-hiker standards meant about nine pm – and finally fell silent under the wide desert sky.

"Thanks, LB"

"Anytime, MelB. Anytime."

CHAPTER 35

I left Kennedy Meadows without LB. We had a disagreement about the status of our relationship. I was upset that he registered us for the "couples only" trailer, and he couldn't understand why. We slept side by side in the dirt; why couldn't we sleep side by side on a bed in a private trailer?

"Come on MelB, don't be blue. It's just a matter of time before you come my way. I know I'm growing on you like a fungus."

It wasn't the awkward fungus line's fault. It wasn't anything LB had said or done. I just finally understood the depth of persistence with which he meant to seduce me. Although I won't deny that I enjoyed the attention, the desert was over. A new phase of my journey had begun and with it endless possibilities for which I meant to leave an open door. Or, more accurately, there was another on the trail who had caught my eye and for whom I wished to leave the door open.

PCT Day 50 – Mile 705
Excerpt from my trail journal [edited for length]
    Here it is – <u>The beginning of phase II.</u>
It starts in a similar fashion to phase I – Alone, late afternoon start with a heavy pack and a set of new gear I need to adjust to – most of which I found for free in the hiker box! I start with eager anticipation and joy in my heart, but maybe a little less exuberance. The trail is now my "normal" life, so I don't get so exuberant about it.
I start this new journal today. I don't know what the new phase will bring, but I'll be recording it as it happens.
I wonder who the new cast of characters will be. I wonder if I'll still hike with LB – growing on me like a fungus. I hope that Hobbes catches up. The thought of him makes me blush – and that is weird enough to investigate.

I only walked three miles from Kennedy Meadows before stopping for the night on the sandy shore of the Kern River.

I dropped the new Osprey backpack against a log. I had

traded my home-made eleven ounce pack for a four pound one, mail-ordered hastily to accommodate the mandatory bear canister and extra layers of warm clothes for the Sierra. My, that pack was heavy! I called it "the Red Beast."

My superhero cape was reassigned to cushion my hips under the heavily-loaded hip-belt. Instead of the cape, I wore a classic beige hiking shirt I found in the free hiker box in front of Trail Angel Tom's trailer.

I also found a pair of brand new hiking shoes with extra cushioned insoles in exactly my size, a lighter poncho and a polycro ground sheet in the free hiker box. Mountain Buddha had given me his spare journal and Margaret had slipped a new harmonica and my iPod in my resupply box. So, even camped only three miles from Kennedy Meadows, I felt like a different Bobcat.

I began my first full day in the Sierra by hiking slowly along the Kern River. I had to adapt to the new heavy pack and the new hiking shoes, or so I told myself.

In retrospect, I think I was purposely lingering.

By mid-morning, I returned from the woods after attending to some bodily business to find Hobbes inspecting the Red Beast I had left on the trail.

"Oh. It's you! I didn't recognize your pack."

"Hobbes, this is the Red Beast; Red Beast, this is my friend Hobbes."

The first time I met Hobbes, I was sitting on my superhero cape in the shade of a brand new fire station around mile 400, eating sardines on pita bread.

He appeared over the hill with a confident stride, swinging a water bottle in one hand, and quickly covered the distance to the fire station. His strong gait with a slight lateral sway, flamboyant long hair and bushy red beard were familiar to me. I didn't think we had met though; everyone on the trail looked oddly familiar.

"Hey, you're a new one. You must be one of the fast ones." I called to him.

He stopped suddenly as though my greeting had startled

him and stared at me without a word.

"I'm the Bobcat. What's your name?"

"I'm Hobbes."

His name amused me. In my younger, secular years, I often joked about creating a religion based on the teachings of the comic strip "Calvin and Hobbes", and here was Hobbes, complete with orange hair and whiskers in his beard. Any man named after a wise imaginary tiger was automatically my friend.

"Welcome then, Hobbes!"

He sat in the shade of the fire station among the small company of thru-hikers waiting for the noon heat to abate and introduced himself to each in turn.

"Bobcat! Next time, you should introduce yourself as Robert Feline," Legion suggested. "'Hi, I'm Robert Feline, you can call me Bob Cat for short'".

My head rolled back in laughter. That was brilliant!

I jumped to my feet, tied my cape back into superhero mode and paced in front of the small group to set up the scene. I then extended my hand to an invisible, unsuspecting victim and solemnly announced, "Hi! Robert Feline, pleased to meet you."

I jumped up in glee. Hobbes whiskers curled up in laughter.

"Oh boy, oh boy, I can't *wait* to meet somebody new!"

I was so excited by the prospect that I left the gang in the shade and hiked on in the noon sun. Before turning away on the trail's next switchback, I glanced back. That new hiker was intriguing, and he was still looking at me. We both smiled and I disappeared around the corner.

The second time I met Hobbes, I was standing in bees.

The trail had opened up to a dirt road, the entire width of which was covered in small holes of perfectly equal diameter and shape, as though somebody had taken a drill to the ground. Around each hole, golf-ball sized clumps of bees rolled on the ground in wrestling melees. I had never seen anything like it, so I carefully stepped right in their midst to see the action up close. Bees swirled around my entire body and wrestling clumps surrounded my feet.

I had already been standing in the swirl for several minutes when Hobbes and The Captain appeared over the hill.

"You're standing in bees!" Hobbes yelled from a safe distance.

"I know! I love bees. They're such amazing creatures. Come see this!"

Neither Hobbes nor The Captain came to see. Instead, they gave the bees a wide berth and waited for me on the trail, past the road. Hobbes whiskers were still curled up when I finally joined them.

From the bees, the trail meandered through the remnant of a massive forest fire. Vibrant colors already masked much of the devastation of only a few years prior as pioneer species of wild flowers and fragrant shrubs had reclaimed the vacant space and now covered the hillsides.

Unfortunately, the fragrant shrubs were Poodle Dog Bush – a fierce poisonous plant known to cause itchy rashes and oozy wounds on contact.

"I wonder how long Poodle Dog Bush lives." Hobbes danced around the violet flowers of a particularly tall specimen right on the trail.

"You should ask it." It was easier for me to clear the plant, because I was smaller. "Plants do answer, you know. It's just that we don't listen, so we think they're quiet."

There were the whiskers again; Hobbes seemed either fascinated or amused by anything I said.

"I'm not afraid of plants." The Captain chimed in as he brushed the Poodle Dog Bush dangerously close.

"No? What are you afraid of? What's your greatest fear?"

"To end up alone, with no one to love me." He answered quickly, as though the answer had just been on his mind. "The thought of loneliness in old age terrifies me."

I observed myself judging him – "Mmmh. Clingy. Better keep my distances."

"What about you, Hobbes? What's your greatest fear?"

"That's a hard one. I don't know that I could articulate just one fear."

He walked a few long strides pensively.

"Lack of inner or outer freedom. Entrapment. Though human language I feel is too limited to represent the broader concept of 'entrapment' as I mean it."

Fear of entrapment and lack of freedom – That orange tiger had my attention.

"Yes. Fear of entrapment for me too – being trapped in a small mundane life with no possibilities of grand adventures, ever." I shuddered a little at the thought.

Although I walked in the front and the Captain hiked between us, I distinctively felt Hobbes's presence, as though our energy fields were mingled and engaged in a wordless dialog.

I kept a fast pace over the crest of the hill and down to a small vegetated stream. Water had been sparse and we all needed to resupply to last to the next water source. I leaned over the spring's outlet and scooped a liter of water in my water bottle.

"You don't treat your water?" The Captain was unrolling the tubes of his filter's pump, which both men planned to use.

"Sure I do, like this ..." I hugged the bottle to my heart and gathered the immense love and gratitude I felt for the trail into a laser beam focused directly into the water in the bottle. "I love you. Please don't make me sick. Thank you!" I loaded each word enunciated carefully with intent.

"And that works?"

"It works if you mean it and believe that it does. I usually also thank the stream or spring where I take the water, for good measure. So far, it's working. I've drank out of some pretty scary looking water sources without a problem."

Hobbes nodded as though he had expected my answer.

"Does it work with other things or just water?"

"It works with everything. I don't carry sunscreen or bug-spray. I tell the sun 'I love you. Please don't burn me. Thank you.' It's a little trickier with the bugs. Sometimes they listen, but sometimes they bite. I also thank the places where I sleep for accommodating me, the landscapes for being beautiful, the flowers, the moon, the stars, the plants ... so, yeah, pretty much everything."

"I like your system." Hobbes stepped to the stream and scooped a Nalgene-full of water, held it to his heart, and repeated my mantra. "I love you. Please don't make me sick. Thank you." He then took a big swig from the bottle.

"Nice!" I thought I had just made my first convert.

"Actually," he said "I only filter in some portions of the desert. Once we get to the Sierra, I'm a lot more comfortable with the quality of the water."

With a full resupply of fresh water, we climbed back up the hill and followed an exposed ridge crest in the sweltering noon sun, and then back down on the other side towards a paved road, finally out of the Poodle Dog Bush. A KOA campground lay just on the other side of that road.

I quickened my pace. The promise of imminent swimming pools and ice cream coolers would have sufficed as a lure, but mostly, I was eager to drop the Red Beast in the shade of a tree and spend a leisurely relaxing afternoon chatting with Hobbes, alone.

Suddenly, although the KOA was not yet in sight, I left the trail to make a random bee-line across a field.

"Have you been here before? How did you know this was a shortcut?" Not only had Hobbes hiked the trail twice already, but he also often volunteered as trail crew and knew this section well; I had never hiked it before.

"I didn't know it was a shortcut. I guess I just had an intuition to go this way and I trust my intuition."

"That's what I thought. You're a textbook case."

"A textbook case of what?"

"You flow with what it is. You trust. You enjoy fun for its own sake. You probably can manifest your own reality, can't you? I suspected from the first time I heard you laugh that you, somehow, were not bound to the Old World Paradigm."

ଅ · ଓ

The Old World Paradigm – *n.* That time/space section in one's personal evolution during which fear and external impositions are the primary driving factors in one's destiny, rather than love and joy.

ଅ · ଓ

It seemed like quite a compliment, but I felt the praise undeserved. I wasn't doing anything. The trail was taking care of all my needs; I had no reason *not* to be joyous. I had no need to manifest anything. And as for flowing, my only task each day was to follow a beautiful ribbon of dirt, which required neither decision nor will-power, just gratitude.

I believed that I was no more of a textbook case than the next thru-hiker, but I loved that Hobbes thought me special. My heart quietly glowed at the compliment, and some of it spilled over to my cheeks. Luckily, I was still walking in front.

CHAPTER 36

"Hello Red Beast. Could I hike with you and the Bobcat today?"

The last and only section of trail Hobbes and I had hiked together was the few miles leading to the KOA campground, 465 miles before Kennedy Meadows. We had practiced yoga on the campground's lawn, eaten dinner in the shade of a large tree and photographed a partial eclipse of the sun, but always with a small group of hikers. The next morning, Hobbes's tent had been gone before sunrise. Our paths had crossed again at Hiker Heaven, Casa de Luna, and Trail Angel Tom's in Kennedy Meadows, but never had we been alone until that exact moment when Hobbes spoke to the Red Beast.

Without waiting for the Beast's explicit consent, I fell in step behind Hobbes. The lateral sway of his long gait made the straps on his pack dance across the trail rhythmically. I matched my steps to their cadence, and we immediately launched in a day-long conversation.

By then, I perceived thru-hikers as a natural extension of the landscape, no more distracting than a leaf on a branch. In my consciousness, Hobbes pack, red hair and strong calves blended perfectly with the expansive grassy meadows and conifer forests of the lower Sierra; and the song of the wind and birds harmonized perfectly with his unusual life story.

Hobbes's life was a song of freedom unlike any I had heard. He had first joined the trail-world as a teenager, and had simply never reintegrated into the confines of society. He had no address, no phone, no bank account and no driver's license. He had never driven. His possessions fit in his pack. He worked with stones for the pleasure of sharing his art, and if a gift of money appeared, he accepted it, but never expected it. He had escaped traditional education to pursue the development of his natural talents and ever deepening levels of self-discovery.

Through this unconventional path, Hobbes had learned much the same curriculum I had on the benches of the Intensive Sunday School for the Rebellious. We just pursued different majors. For example, while Hobbes did not communicate with his Higher Self as consciously as I did, he was an experienced astral traveler.

Hobbes was very curious about my divine conversations – how I started, the sort of questions I asked, and the process by which I let my mind become sufficiently blank to hear answers.

Unfortunately, the process was so organic for me that I didn't have a set of clear steps to share with him. My conversations were casual and happened when I needed them. Hobbes was surprised to learn that sometimes my Higher Self cursed or told bad jokes, that I argued back with Him and often ignored His directives.

Hobbes, on the other hand, had explored the steps to full OBEs – Out of Body Experiences – with full intellectualization once he realized he had a natural ability to "get out." He could retrace the process precisely from the initial precursory sleep paralysis to full astral projection.

" … Again, human language isn't really suited to these topics. It's not so much a 'getting out' that occurs during an

OBE; it's more that consciousness extends to the next layer of the onion of our true self. The first layer of illusion of limitation – the space-time physical realm – is removed. Once physicality is transcended, the thought-creation process is instantaneous, so you can go anywhere."

"Oh, that makes sense. It's probably the same with my conversations. I'm not really speaking with a separate, "Higher" part of myself, and no entity is coming down to earth' to speak with me; I'm just expanding my conscious perception to that next layer of the 'Self' onion beyond the five senses."

While we were talking, the trail left the meadows and forests to quickly ascend to its cruising altitude of 10,000 feet, to the land of grandiose vistas – the High Sierra. The vibrant Indian paintbrushes by the side of the steep trail acted as little visual anchors to remind me of my physical place in the world while the conversation with Hobbes soared to ever more esoteric realms.

My interest in OBEs was then purely academic; with so much granite beauty surrounding me, I had no desire to leave the physical plane.

"I love being incarnated. It's such a treat to be able to roam the earth, and especially this trail. I get why we choose to create physical reality – it's so delicious. I just wonder why we make it so dense. I mean, if the thought-creation process can be instantaneous, why give ourselves the illusion of limitation?"

"I think for the experience of the process. We basically give ourselves amnesia for the fun of solving riddles to bring us back to Consciousness. And in doing so, Consciousness gets to experience Itself in full-sensory details in the space-time realm."

Of course, Hobbes was right; it was always about the journey. I could fly to Canada from San Diego if I chose to, but I much preferred walking and sleeping under the stars for six months.

The sun was still floating high above the hills when Hobbes

and I crested the first pass of the High Sierra. Although the day still held several hours of walking before nightfall, the top of the pass was perfectly flat and level, with expansive views to the valley below, so we decided to stop for an early camp.

I watched Hobbes set up his tent with experienced, precise movements from the comfort of my instant bivy-bag in the dirt. We cooked and ate our meals together, then ventured to the edge of the rocks to watch the orange sun slide behind the Sierra's jagged ridgeline.

Every sunset on the trail was spectacular, but that evening, the sky turned surreal. Beams of crepuscular rays cast upward through the haze, a progressively more vibrant fan of shadows and orange light straight to the heavens, until finally the blue velvet of darkness absorbed it into quietness.

The last of the day's heat was absorbed with the last of the light, and Hobbes and I hurried back to camp and to the warmth of our sleeping bags.

I zipped mine completely and cinched the hood around my face so that no night chill could get in. Only my eyes were left exposed to see the stars. The fog of my breath escaped upward through the opening in the hood.

"Good night, Bobcat." Hobbes called from his tent.

"Thank you for today." I called back.

What a day indeed! My mind still swirled from the conversation with Hobbes, too expanded to be confined. If I had wanted to, right then, I believe I could have effortlessly left my physical body for an astral journey.

But, I didn't.

Was I scared? Maybe. Probably. I understood the theory – there was no "leaving", just expansion of consciousness. But still, I imagined my disembodied spirit swirling upward like the fog of my breath. What if I couldn't return? It was not worth the risk. I felt the heat of my body inside my bag, the support of the earth under my back, and inhaled a deep, cold pine- and dirt-scented breath. I was so grateful for my own physicality; I couldn't imagine astral projection providing me with greater bliss.

CHAPTER 37

The next morning, Hobbes and I walked through fields of hearts. They were everywhere – heart-shaped rocks, heart-shaped leaves, curved branches into heart shapes, even heart-shaped clouds.

"Look, here's another one! The trail must love us this morning." I pointed to a knot in a tree.

"I think they're all for you. You see them. I only see them when you point them out."

I was fairly certain the hearts were in celebration of Hobbes's and my connection but thought better than to insist so to a man whose greatest fear was entrapment.

"Well, if the trail loves me, I love it back!"

I kept an eye out for hearts while Hobbes and I resumed our spiritual musings of the day prior. I expected another day-long dialog, but we had barely opened the subject of our dual nature as cosmic and earth beings when I suddenly left the conversation and the trail mid-sentence.

A tall and magnificent piece of granite with strategically placed handholds at the edge of a cliff had appeared by the side of the trail.

"Let's climb it!" I had already dropped my pack and started up the face of the boulder.

"No, I don't climb. I'm not comfortable with heights. But you have fun with it. I promised some friends I would hike to the summit of Mt. Whitney with them, so I'm going to hike on. It's been a real pleasure hiking and camping with the Bobcat. I hope we see each other again."

I stopped climbing about six feet off the ground and hesitated. Down on the ground was a man with a fascinating, unconventional worldview; up on the boulder was a hawk's eye view of the trail and valley below. Hobbes's curled whiskers encouraged me to climb on without a word.

By the time I reached the top of the boulder, he had already walked out of sight. I lay in the sun with both feet dangling off the edge. Hobbes was fast, but if I climbed back down right then and hurried, I could still catch up to him. It was a nice thought, but it was too late. I was already held hostage by the delight of warm sun on my closed eyelids.

I relaxed into the idea that Hobbes was likely meant to hike on. Some days I needed mind-bending spiritual conversations; other days, I needed grass-stains on my knees and sunshine on my eyelids. The trail knew exactly what to provide.

And the trail was never wrong. That day, after Hobbes left, I swam naked in Chicken Spring Lake, climbed a few more boulders, serenaded a family of marmots in a grassy meadow, and wrote in my journal in the shade of a twisted Juniper tree. When the alpenglow finally painted the top of the serrated peaks, I tucked myself in before the chill of the night could find me.

"Good night Hobbes. I hope you have a great hike. I have no doubt that I'll see you again. And thank you, trail for yet another perfect day."

Each day in the Sierra was more beautiful than the preceding, and I understood why, in a timeless realm, the trail and I had purposely created Hobbes's departure – that section required my undivided attention.

To an endless string of jewel-like ponds and lakes, the trail added pegmatite granites with inch-wide crystals, forests of sequoias and meandering creeks, and finally the crown jewel, Mt. Whitney.

By the time I reached Crab Tree Meadows, at the foot of Mt. Whitney, I had been walking in beauty of such magnitude that I had ceased all futile attempts at capturing it with my camera or with words in my journal.

Waves of gratitude rose and fell through my heart and pulsated in my mind throughout the day. The feeling was akin to the rib-expanding joy I had felt in the desert but deeper, thicker, rounder, more unctuous. It had left the confines of my rib-cage and extended outward like a glow around my body.

I was surprised when I reached Crab Tree Meadows that none of the thru-hikers gathered at camp commented on my glow. The feeling was so palpable to me that I expected others to detect it. But each hiker attended to their own needs, in their own private world – napping, eating, washing socks in the river, playing cards with friends. I did as well and wondered how many others hummed internally with subtle ecstasy behind mundane gestures.

I climbed Mt. Whitney in the dark to reach the 14,500-foot summit right at sunrise. The steep trail landed on a pink granite moonscape with cliffs on all sides; my jaw dropped in awe. On the edge of a pinnacle rock, I rotated in a three-hundred and sixty degree pastel dream.

I could have looked at that landscape all day and never tire of it, but the frozen wind set limits to how much beauty was allotted each hiker. Soon, we all gathered our blown minds and frigid bodies into the relative warmth of a rock shelter. We huddled in groups, wrapped ourselves in sleeping bags and down jackets, shared snacks and met new friends.

From the huddle, I noticed the Violinist sitting on another pinnacle rock at the edge of a multi-thousand-foot drop. I didn't really know the Violinist, we had met only briefly at Kennedy Meadows, but he looked cold, alone on his rock, so I walked towards him to keep him company.

With less than twenty feet to walk, I was suddenly struck by how handsome he looked. Even with the hood of his down jacket completely cinched around his face, the perfect curve of the wrinkles around his eyes tickled my heart. I giggled inside my raised collar and wondered if the altitude was affecting my brain. He watched every step of my approach as thought I were trail candy being delivered into his hands. I guessed the altitude affected his brain as well.

After a brief chat about the cold, the views and our unfortunate lack of hang-gliders, he wrapped his arm around me to fit us both in a summit photo. He held on much longer than the shutter required, and I let him. Maybe he simply needed warmth; I certainly enjoyed his.

Sunshine slowly covered the summit, and the Violinist and I naturally fell in step for the descent back to Crab Tree Meadows. Within a few hours, the morning chill dissipated, and the heat of windless, high-altitude days baked the bare granite. Down jackets, hats and gloves quickly returned to our packs. And yes, I did notice the Violinist's hard body when he switched shirts. He glimpsed up right before slipping on his hiking shirt. He knew that I noticed, and I knew that he had wanted me to notice.

This could have been all, a brief encounter between strangers, an ephemeral flash of chemistry. The Violinist suffered from shin-splints, a common ailment among "fast ones", and needed a few zeros to prevent further injury. I didn't carry enough food for a few zeros even if I had wanted to wait for him. And I saw no reason to wait. I still had a long trail to walk to Canada.

"I'll catch up to you when I'm healed."

I thought that he might but was not attached to it. Our meeting on Mt. Whitney was sufficiently special in my heart as a stand-alone event.

I left for the next pass with an extra bounce in my step despite the heavy Red Beast. I hiked twenty five miles that day, including the climb of Mt. Whitney, and I cried a few times.

By the combination of the climb, the views, the look of desire from a new friend, the clean air, the trail, this life, *my* life, and everything in it, I felt overwhelmed with gratitude. I opened through it, offering my raw emotions to the trail. I cried and yelled "Thank you!"

I laughed too, in disbelief.

The sounds, textures and vistas had become unbearable, and I was left breathless. I stood in absolute stillness at the apex of the Bighorn Plateau, right underneath the clouds, and surrendered to the surge of expanding love melting me into the landscape like a drop of rain on a parched plain.

"Trail High" is what LB called that feeling, or his version of it. The Violinist called it a "Serotonin rush", and Hobbes referred to it as that feeling when your Higher Self lovingly hugs you. I rode the crest of the wave of emotions without naming or describing it; my mind was well past words.

Fueled by this ecstasy, I flew over Forester Pass – at 13,200 feet the highest pass on the trail – Kearsarge Pass and down to Onion Valley in just one day. By the time I reached the Onion Valley trailhead, from which I hoped to get a ride to Bishop to resupply, my legs burned, and my Trail High had stabilized to sustainable, manageable happiness.

"Ah! *You're* the Bobcat. I know just what to do with you. Get in the car." Other hikers had been waiting for a ride to town for much longer than I had, but Trail Angel Sleeping Bare was insistent without an explanation. I sat in the front and three more hikers climbed into the back. But while the other hikers shouldered their packs in Independence, Sleeping Bare kept mine.

"Not you, Bobcat. You're going somewhere else."

Although the blind trust I had in the trail and the steady happiness in my heart prevented me from worrying, I did see a flash in my mind of the headlines about the kidnapped hiker I could become, especially when Sleeping Bare drove me back to his own RV.

"Hobbes!" I jumped and danced to celebrate our reunion. Sleeping Bare had been instructed to keep alert for a potential Bobcat sighting for a full day. My timing was impeccable. Hobbes's friend, Ranger Ryan from Bishop, was on his way to pick him up.

"I think you'll like Ranger Ryan. He was a park ranger in Death Valley. He always gets excited speaking about the Valley, like you do."

I did indeed like Ranger Ryan within two seconds of meeting him. His energy was playful and light, yet grounded, like a dust storm in Death Valley. Before we even reached Bishop, Ranger Ryan and I had agreed that a visit to *our* Valley was imperative, immediately.

"But …," Hobbes objected. "We have food to buy, laundry to do, showers to take, photos to download, cameras to recharge …"

Ranger Ryan and I smiled. After a good meal in town, we loaded coolers and packs in his truck and drove straight to the Saline Valley Hot Springs.

Less than forty eight hours after standing on the highest peak in the contiguous United States in my down jacket, hat and gloves, I was naked in hundred-degree Death Valley with Hobbes, suffering a serious relapse of Trail High.

How could I not let my heart grow even wider while held in Mother Earth's warm little pool under the infinity of stars? Death Valley – although the Saline Valley Hot Springs were located at the exact opposite end of the park from my sacred canyon, this was the place of my true birth. I once was those stars, tethered to the earth through a tiny body. I once was infinite here.

How glad I was to have reintegrated! No ethereal bliss could rival the soft caress of the desert wind on my bare skin, the taste of salty dust in my mouth, and the warmth of kind companionship.

"I think this is the happiest day in my life." Hobbes spoke the words first, but Ranger Ryan and I nodded in agreement.

Walking through the town of Bishop a few days later, Hobbes and I still carried the connective, peaceful energy of shared Paradise – a version of desert glow for two.

"We're for keeps, Hobbes, in whatever shape our relationship takes. I feel you and I are bound beyond the physical time-space realm."

Hobbes sat next to me in the shade on the steps of the closed library – neither of us had remembered that it was Sunday – but he didn't answer.

"I would like to hike with you from here, if you want."

"Yes, I was hoping we would as well."

"The only thing is … I mean, as our connection deepens … what if I were to become interested in someone else on the trail? Would you feel hurt?"

I was, of course, contemplating the ramifications of another encounter with the Violinist. He had sent me a message; his shins were healed and he was moving fast in my direction.

"I'm responsible for my own feelings. If I feel hurt, it wouldn't be your fault; it would be for me to work through. I think that's what love is, essentially, to support someone on their path and to see them thrive, even if their path takes them to connect with someone else. To see you be your truest self would mean more to me than any sense of possession."

I was speechless. A sense of truth flowed through my heart, the human connection equivalent of Trail High. A layer of illusion was removed – heart-based companionship remembered.

When I finally could speak again, I wiped a few tears from my eyes and held my hand to my heart.

"Thank you."

I thought he knew I meant "I love you."

CHAPTER 38

"I'm off now. I hope you have a great day and a great hike. If I don't see you again, please know that I feel honored to have had the opportunity to hike with the Bobcat."

Every day, right before dawn, Hobbes said his last goodbyes. This was a precaution born of years of trail experience.

"Sometimes," he said, "you leave ahead of someone at a water source by a few minutes and never see them again."

But, every day, either around four in the afternoon when he stopped for dinner or after dark if I lingered someplace beautiful, I found him again.

"You're here!" Hobbes celebrated each of my daily arrivals as a miraculous reunion and each evening spent together as a special occasion.

For hundreds of miles, we alternated hiking apart and together for that section of the trail that coincided with the John Muir Trail of the High Sierra. We climbed steep rocky steps and contoured emerald lakes. We descended into valleys along thunderous waterfalls only to ascend back to another pass. In total we climbed seven passes above 11,000 feet, and still maintained a daily average of twenty miles, heavy Red Beast and all.

Hobbes and I connected at the intersection of our personal rhythms. Hobbes walked steadily. He had routines and preferences of time and locations for meals and camps; I had none, and wanted none. I roamed the trail like a curious Bobcat. I followed my whims off-trail like I followed butterflies and easily lost track of time gazing lovingly in the eyes of Mother Nature.

I had lived on earth for forty-one years prior to the trail, yet never before had I noticed the elegance of fractal patterns in the veins of leafs, the variety of harmonics in the call of the Chickadees – which had always seemed repetitive – or the growth sequence of a thunder cloud from a mere wisp of vapor in an otherwise blue sky.

I once sat on a rock by the side of the trail and rolled my hiking shirt's sleeves up. "Have at it!" I called to the mosquitoes. Just for curiosity's sake, I wanted to fully experience being stung. Here was a readily abundant experience that we, humans, instantly refused. I opened all my senses of perception to receive the tickle of their skinny legs through the sun-bleached forest of my arm hair. I detected with acuity the exact moment of puncture through my skin and found it oddly pleasurable. I watched them fly off with crimson bellies full of my blood, and I was glad, grateful and wished them well.

Hobbes loved observing me observe nature. Whenever we hiked together, he patiently waited with curled whiskers until I returned my awareness to include his presence.

"This is the strangest interaction between a human and a bee I've ever witnessed." Hobbes stared at the top of my right index finger where a bee was collecting pollen-like Doritos dust leftover from my snack break. Through the extreme tickle and occasional spike of pain, I kept my finger perfectly still. The rest of my body, however, wriggled and contorted to compensate. The tactile sensations were so intense, and the risk of being stung so exhilarating, that I had no choice but to surrender to the sweet agony.

Hobbes also waited patiently for me whenever I ventured

close to cliffs' edges, climbed precarious boulders or jumped in frigid little creeks, not out of worry for my safety, but in eager anticipation of my full report when I returned.

I once disappeared right out of his sight, when the rock that held both my feet plunged into a cold pool underneath a waterfall, taking me along for the ten-foot drop. In spite of the surprise, I felt the gradual progression of the creek's wet fingers engulf my immersed body, from my bare arms to the deepest recess of my closed hiking shoes. I was there and aware when the icy liquid first entered my nostrils and when the image of my iPod in my pocket first appeared in my brain's front lobe.

I began laughing before I even returned to the surface.

"You're not upset? What about the electronics?"

Upset? This was the most thrilling experience of my entire day. Of course, I wasn't upset. I held the iPod close to my heart and sent it healing love.

"I love you. I'm sorry for your bath. Please don't die."

I sensed, or imagined, that my apology was accepted.

"It says it will be fine." And then it was.

"It is astonishing that you exist!"

Yes, truly, Hobbes appreciated my experience of the process. For every tree I hugged, every heart-shaped rock I collected, every serendipitous camp I uncovered, and every story of an experience I shared, Hobbes cooed. Occasionally, he even shared his feelings with human language.

"I appreciate you to the full extent of my current capacity."

But when night fell, the man, his appreciation and delicious whiskers zipped themselves into the tent, and I was left to explore the pangs of disappointment.

Not once had Hobbes invited me in his tent, not even when I suggested we might chat more comfortably inside. "If you come in, the mosquitoes will follow you, and then I'll have to kill them." He said.

Not once had Hobbes spontaneously wrapped his arms around me – not that time when I felt dizzy from the over-heated hot springs in Reds Meadow, and not that time when I shivered huddled against a rock at the top of Pinchot Pass.

I observed the gradual rise of my internal longing with the same fascination I held for outward experiences. I imagined the rough callused yet warm sensation of his hand on my skin, the tickle of rogue whisker hair on my face, the pungent intoxicating fragrance of unwashed, unmasked body odor.

Hobbes seemed immune to carnal impulses. I decided that he must be barely incarnated. I preferred this explanation to the alternative, that he simply did not find me physically attractive, that his interest in me was purely intellectual – I was such a fascinating textbook case.

"Barely incarnated ..." The words echoed in the background of my mind as I stared at Hobbes's strong calves climbing up the trail. I studied the interplay of muscles from his ankles to the back of his knees with each step and only spared a small portion of my conscious awareness to his current complaints about incarnation.

"I understand that pooping and brushing one's teeth are necessary; it's the lack of choice about body self-maintenance that I resent. I would just as well be free of physicality."

"Speaking of physicality ..." I heard the words escape my mouth and stopped walking abruptly.

"Yes?" Hobbes stopped walking as well, and slowly turned to face me.

"Well, I guess I started, I might as well go for it. It's just that I was wondering if you were planning on snuggling or kissing me any time before Canada."

I spoke very fast, to the rhythm of my palpitating heart.

"You're interested?" Hobbes, on the other hand, enunciated each word carefully.

"Yes, I thought I made it obvious."

"Oh!" And he walked on.

I stood rooted in confusion and watched him walk up the hill for a full minute. I guessed the answer was "no".

When I caught up to him again, we spoke of the vibrantly green moss on the granite, the expected below-freezing temperatures for that night and the approaching boundary of

Yosemite National Park, but not a word about physicality.

Hobbes was getting off-trail in Tuolumne meadows for four days to visit friends, so it was just as well. I likely would not see him again after the next day anyway.

As the night approached and cold air descended into the valley, frost gradually covered my bivy bag and rimmed the edge of my sleeping bag's hood.

"You can sleep in my tent, if you get too cold."

"I'm fine. Thank you. Good night." I resolved to brave the cold rather than further inconvenience Hobbes with my physical impulses.

But as the night progressed, the chattering of my teeth kept me awake. This was, by far, our coldest night yet. Finally, I quietly unzipped Hobbes's tent and crawled into the fit-to-measurement spot he had left for me.

I was still shivering when I wiggled my sleeping bag against his. I wrapped my arm around his body, and he tucked my frozen hand between his. His hands were as calloused and warm as I had dreamt.

Although our energies still felt mingled and connected, he made no attempt to express his appreciation in any physical manner beyond holding my hand.

We slept and awoke in exactly the same position.

CHAPTER 39

"Hobbes, I'm going to hike on. I'm not going to wait for you in Tuolumne Meadows. I mean, I understand that you 'appreciate me to the full extent of your current capacity', but it'll be awkward now that you know how I feel. And also, I miss being alone with the trail. I get too distracted by my physical longings when I'm with you."

"Why do you assume I don't have the same longings?"

"Well, I've had plenty of clues. You wouldn't let me sleep in your tent because of the mosquitoes, you haven't tried to hold me or kiss me or ..."

"No, no no! I wanted you to sleep in my tent. I was just warning you that I'd have to kill mosquitoes. I didn't want to upset you. I know how much you value them. And for the rest, I feel that all our interactions could have been interpreted as platonic, and I didn't want to be presumptuous."

"Are you saying that you're interested as well?"

"Yes, of course."

"Oh!" I kept walking and staring at the trail, as Hobbes had done the day prior, while the gears in my mind upgraded my perceived reality by placing each event in the light of a new perspective.

I had not yet fully absorbed the implications of our conversation by the time Hobbes and I reached Tuolumne Meadows, but the pack of thru-hikers loitering between the road and the burger joint welcomed us like long-lost family, and our privacy instantly vanished.

Amidst the group's stories, news and laughter, furtive glances laden with unfinished business kept us connected. The glancing continued as we deployed our hitchhiking thumbs in opposite direction along highway 120. Within a few minutes, two cars stopped at exactly the same moment and carried us away with no concrete plan of reunion.

Technically, I didn't wait for Hobbes; I just lingered.

I took two indulgent zeros in Mammoth Lakes, hitchhiked back to Tuolumne Meadows via Mono Lake and Tioga Pass, and rejoined the trail only two days ahead of Hobbes.

The granite walls, meadows and forests of Yosemite National Park supported and encouraged my lingering. Roaring waterfalls beckoned to be photographed, vanilla-scented ponderosas extended their cool shade over soft napping needle beds, and the trail basked in the heat, sun and bugs of long summer days – a time best honored with rest and play. Every couple of miles, I stopped to skip rocks on ponds and rivers, investigate shiny minerals with my geologist hand-lens or dangle my bare feet over steep ledges. I also wrote notes I left for Hobbes on the trail. Nothing too personal, I knew that all passing hikers would read them as well, but just enough to incite him to hike faster.

From Tuolumne Meadows to Sonora Pass, I barely averaged fifteen miles a day.

"Bobcat! I was wondering when you'd show up." Right across Highway 108 at Sonora Pass, Trail Angel Sleeping Bare – the same Sleeping Bare who had kidnapped me at Onion Valley – was relaxing in a camp chair in the shade surrounded by coolers of "magic" – cold beers, fresh fruit and salty snacks. I bounded across the freeway to hug him and join the small group of hikers trapped by the magic in the shade. I did not move for the rest of the day.

The next morning, only six miles past Sonora Pass, at the top of a volcanic rock spire, Hobbes caught up to me.

There was no doubt about anyone's interest in physicality after that day.

On the night of our reunion, we lay facing each other awkwardly in Hobbes's tent. My fingers traced a meandering line from the inside of his hand, along his arm, through the thicket of red whiskers and to his lips. I had never seen him up close. Suddenly, his details filled the entirety of my vision: the invisible hair on his upper cheek, the minute lines around his eyes, the subtle tremor at the corner of his lower lip as I drew even closer.

It had taken six hundred miles to get us to this point, so I assumed that our physical exploration would be measured and progressive. I was wrong; we reached full ignition the moment our lips met.

We still hiked our own hikes, but wherever our rhythms intersected, we melted into the intensity of our connection. We stroked embers with gentle cross-sleeping bag caresses before the sun rose, interrupted walking for long kisses, and returned our tired bodies to their natural intertwined position in the evening. We explored each other's skin like precious maps of undiscovered lands and inhaled and absorbed each other's scent as we had that of the trail dirt and sweet ponderosas. And yes, some mosquitoes did die because of this, but always respectfully and with apologies.

By the time we reached Lake Tahoe, our physical explorations had outgrown the confines of Hobbes's tent, so we agreed to share a hotel room for three nights and two town zeros.

This was our first public appearance. We walked down the streets of South Lake Tahoe hand in hand to retrieve my beloved home-made pack at the post office and ship the Red Beast home. We sat at a dining table together for the first time and ate with silverware at least three plates each of the all-you-can-eat Indian buffet. A few hours later we repeated the feat at a sushi restaurant. We showered, wore clean clothes, slept and made love on a real bed. The trail community nodded. Our relationship surprised no one.

Less than fifty miles later, we again left the trail, this time for four indulgent town zeros in Nevada City. The bed in that room was wider than the one in South Lake Tahoe, and we occupied it fully.

The trail, it seemed, supported Hobbes's and my connection. While we were together, the level of synchronicity – which we called "magic" – was extraordinary. We never waited more than a minute to catch a ride into or out of town. We were showered with free food, drinks and lodging wherever we went. On the trail, our thought-creation process appeared instantaneous. We merely mentioned a perfect level camp with unobstructed views and it materialized around the next switchback. A few minutes after I discovered the first sign of chaffing, a brand new bottle of Gold Bond baby powder lay in the middle of the trail. Hobbes even summoned a can of ravioli, out of nowhere. The daily miracles made us laugh.

My best manifestation, however, was five-foot-ten with a booming laugh and a glorious red beard.

"MelB! Nice kiss! I got a photo of it. I'll blackmail you with it when we get off-trail." Oh, I knew that laugh.

LB, Powah Nap and the beautiful Bloodbank had arrived quietly around a switchback while I had both hands inside Hobbes's shirt for maximum contact. I felt my cheeks flush and quickly removed my hands. I shouldn't have been surprised; just that morning, I had told Hobbes how much I missed LB and wished he'd catch up.

For a couple dreamy hundred miles through the shaded forests of northern California, I alternated hiking alone, with Hobbes and with LB.

"You look happy, MelB. Love suits you."

"Does that mean you won't flirt with me anymore?"

"No, that means I'll flirt with you even more."

We laughed. LB and I always laughed. Sometimes we laughed so hard that I had to stop walking to recover my breath. Loving Hobbes had in no way diminished my fondness for LB. In fact, I was certain that with each new connection, my heart grew larger. It could accommodate Logan, Hobbes, LB, my trail family, my off-trail friends, the trail itself – the whole world. When the family dismantled, when LB was held back by Giardia, when Hobbes and I eventually parted ways, it did not shrink back.

This was a new kind of romantic relationship – love within freedom – unlike any I had experienced prior to the trail.

"We are not a 'couple'." Hobbes and I told hikers who asked. "We are bound by love and appreciation, but not by any commitment or expectation."

This self-definition was important to us. It helped us alleviate any sense of entrapment in the "couple" label. But few understood, and even fewer believed us.

"You sure act like a couple. Don't you camp and walk together every day?"

We did, but not always of our own volition. We agreed to not walk together to accommodate our need for space almost daily. I left a day ahead from town with a good pace, then a fire right behind me led all hikers to be rerouted on a shorter path, and Hobbes and I landed at the same camp at the same time. He then hiked on ahead, and he naturally was faster than I was, until I remembered that the weekend was approaching and I needed to get to town before the post office closed to retrieve my resupply package, and we'd share a hotel room.

We actually hiked together more when we tried to not hike

together. We crunched in step through the red lava fields of Brown Mountain, hid from thunderstorms in each other's arms in the dewy, foggy forest of Sky Lakes Wilderness, and shared a tiny ledge overlooking the deep blue waters of Crater Lake and its surreal Wizard Island.

Until, one day, I left ahead of Hobbes at a water source by a few minutes and we never again hiked together on the PCT, except for a few miles on my birthday.

"Bobcat! I'm held up at Shelter Cove waiting for a package. I see there's one for you here. I'll be here til 4 pm, when the store closes, then hike on. Unless you're within striking distance. Text me if you want me to wait."

I just had enough battery life left to read the Violinist's text before my phone shut down.

This was incredible! The Violinist and I had been texting since Crab Tree Meadows but somehow had not been able to meet again. We had missed each other by less than an hour in Mammoth Lakes. We had been in South Lake Tahoe at the same time but in hotels on opposite sides of town. He had then hurried to catch me in Sierra City, but I had been off-trail in Nevada City. He had passed us then and had been ahead ever since. With each missed rendezvous, our texts had grown flirtier. They had amused Hobbes and delighted me.

So I had a choice. I could wait for Hobbes, use his battery-powered phone changer and text the Violinist to wait for me or I could walk ten miles in two hours.

Before my mind could even ponder each option, my feet had started down the trail towards Shelter Cove at a run. I flew over rocks, roots and streams, and giggled with each leap at the oddity of my decision.

"How did you get here so fast? Were you close? Did you run?"

I hadn't run the whole way, just most of it. I also had gotten lost, found a highway, hitched a ride in a temperamental RV driven by a leather-clad fairy on her way to Burning Man, caught another ride with a hunter and two dogs, to finally arrive at Shelter Cover before the store closed or the Violinist hiked on. There was definitely magic at hand in that reunion.

I retrieved my package from the store and marveled at the brand new pair of electric blue trail runners. My feet had ached for hundreds of miles, but I had grown so attached to my trail shoes that I had resisted switching them until just then. The pattern did not escape my attention – the last time I had donned new shoes was the day I bid LB goodbye in Kennedy Meadows and began walking with Hobbes.

I left Shelter Cover with the Violinist.

He still eyed me like trail candy, and I blushed and giggled accordingly. We talked and walked late into the night. I knew that Hobbes had likely already stopped – he disliked hiking in the dark.

The next day, the Violinist and I talked and walked all day. We talked about fishing, dancing and hiking gear. The topics didn't matter; I was fascinating, beautiful and irresistible – so irresistible that he moved his sleeping bag next to mine that night, crawled both hands inside my shirt and kissed me.

"Wow! You move fast."

"Over four miles an hour on a good day." He laughed, and then continued with a serious tone, "Just so you know, I carry only one condom. Do you have any?"

"No, I don't. I guess we'll have to save yours for a special occasion."

On our second full day together, the conversation had notably dried. I didn't analyze it. I still enjoyed the Violinist's company and was thrilled to follow him off trail for a burger at the Elk Lake Resort.

When we returned to the trail a few hours later, my eyes caught the imprints of Hobbes's trail runners. I knew his tracks and gait so well that I could see the movie of what happened. Hobbes had stopped where my tracks left the trail. He would have known these were my tracks – I was the only set of brand new Brook's Cascadia soles in a size seven. He would likely have also noticed the Violinist's tracks. The Violinist had distinctive soles, with a deep "V" in the middle of the print, which I had pointed out to Hobbes just past Nevada City.

Hobbes had taken a few hesitant steps before accelerating away from Elk Lake Resort.

He had understood, and he was giving us space.

Although I walked with the Violinist, I tracked Hobbes's steps for the rest of the afternoon through fields of flowers, forests and around ponds and lakes to the edge of the Wikiup plain.

Right there, at the edge of the plain, underneath the snow-capped majesty of the South Sister volcano, Hobbes tent glowed in the sunset gold. This was the best camp for miles, and the Violinist and I approached it with the intent to stay. I was riveted to the suspense of my own enfolding story.

"Hi, Hobbes. Is it okay with you if we camp here?"

"Of course … Are you two 'intimate'?" There was nothing but curiosity in his voice.

I meant to recount to Hobbes my experience so far, as I had done so many times, but the Violinist was approaching, so instead, I quickly grabbed Hobbes's hand and whispered in his ear.

"Not yet. I'm having an experience. I'll give you a full report later."

Hobbes's and my eyes locked for just a moment – four sets of smiling lines mirroring each other – before I walked away.

I followed the Violinist to the other side of a small grove of trees, probably less than forty feet away from Hobbes's tent. We unrolled our pads and sleeping bags next to each other's. As I fluffed my sleeping bag, I told the Violinist, "Just so you know, Hobbes and I were sort of a trail couple until I came to find you. I asked him, and he said he's fine with me being with you."

"Okay." He shrugged and asked no question.

The Violinist fell asleep quickly and facing away from me, and I was glad. His were not the arms in which I wanted to lay, but I sensed that I needed to complete this experience, for whatever reason, and to whatever end.

Two days later, I had returned to Hobbes's arms, our bodies interlaced in the sunshine streaming through the unzipped door of his tent, in a campground in Sisters, Oregon.

"So, tell me. What happened after I left?" Hobbes weaved his fingers between mine, expectantly.

"Well, ..." I spared Hobbes from neither graphic details nor embarrassing emotions. His eyes never left mine and his fingers held me safe throughout the story:

The Violinist and I had sex in the early morning in the meadow right below South Sister. I had chosen the man, the time and the place. I felt empowered for it – in the moment anyway. But once his one condom was used, my fascinating beauty and irresistibility vanished instantly. The Violinist walked on. The script was so predictable that it made me laugh. I caught up to him at a water source a few miles later, and we walked together through fields of lupines and obsidian flakes, around volcanoes and waterfalls. The landscape was much too spectacular to spare any mind for remorse. Besides, I was still fond of this man who knew what he wanted and had the confidence to get it. As the miles disappeared, the Violinist slowly relaxed, and conversation returned. I was like him, he said, made to enjoy but never to be owned. By the late afternoon, I had morphed from trail candy to trail buddy. As trail buddy, I could be privy to the classic moves he used in his game of seduction. He was a skilled player; I recognized the steps that had led me to run down to Shelter Cove. But I didn't feel wronged. How could I? It was a two-person game, and I had chosen to play.

The next day, the Violinist and I parted amicably and with wishes of good luck for the rest of the trail. The game was over. I hitched into Sisters where I found Hobbes waiting for me.

Hobbes was quiet for a few minutes as he absorbed the details of my story.

"Aren't you upset at all?"

"No." He leaned closer to kiss me. "I was mostly concerned that our connection might suffer, but the moment our eyes met at the edge of the Wikiup plain, I knew 'we' were intact. I did experience some insecurities and feelings of jealousy while you were gone. I was still happy for you. I just kept hope that we'd find each other again and both grow from the experience. I think we have."

I certainly had. Hobbes's theory of heart-based companionship spoken on the steps of the closed Bishop library, a thousand and two hundred miles prior, were from this point forth an experienced reality. I couldn't imagine ever returning to the pattern of possessive dependence I had once called 'love'.

I placed my hand on Hobbes's heart and let gratitude overtake me. We were quiet together in the sun. Finally, Hobbes took my hand between his and leaned back to look into my eyes.

"I'm getting off-trail here. I have an offer to housesit a yurt in Portland, and if I've learned anything from you, it's to follow my heart. This feels right."

Somehow, I already knew. "Yes, it does. My heart's telling me it's time to hike alone again. I'll be in the Cascades soon – I'll be home. Thank you so much, for everything."

"Thank *you*. How will I find you again?"

"You mean, besides our pan-dimensional psychic connection? Well, I guess you could get a phone."

CHAPTER 40

I waved to bus 106 departing from downtown Sisters with Hobbes on board. The two elderly ladies in the seat directly in front of his waved back. They had matching smiles – the sort of gentle smile with a tilted head people use when they feel your pain. I had spied them earlier. They had watched as we kissed in a hurry, as Hobbes grabbed his backpack and climbed on board, as we locked eyes when he sat down on my side of the street in the already moving bus. It must have looked so sad, this classic tale of two lovers separated by the increasing distance.

In our world, separation wasn't a sad event, but an opportunity to follow our hearts down different paths and learn twice as much about the overall terrain. Besides, our separation was only in the physical realm, our energies were still mingled beyond the space-time illusion, and soon, Hobbes would have a phone.

I walked in the same direction as the bus to rejoin the trail, but before I even left town, I had already acquired a new friend – a bright rainbow pinwheel with so much twirling joy that it ought to have weighed more than its few ounces.

It leaned out of my pack's side pocket, its foot held in the mesh that also kept my precious rocks, feathers and pieces of bark, and its colorful head peeking past me to capture the wind of motion.

It was such a sensitive friend. If I but paused to smell a tree, greet a bug or tie my shoe, it stopped twirling. It never overtly complained, but I sensed its disappointment, and immediately rescued it from stagnancy. Hikers I met called it "the Bobcat propeller". And propelled it did; through the rest of Oregon, I effortlessly covered thirty to thirty-five miles a day.

I tiptoed at high speed on prominent sharp edges through lava fields, jumped across gushing glacial streams pregnant with ashen sediments, and flew around familiar volcanoes of such beauty that the human mind cannot truly ever comprehend their existence.

Although the miles disappeared under the soles of my trail runners as fast as cookie crumbs in my food bag, I felt I missed nothing. Freed from self-induced relationship distractions, my mind opened outward like a casting web. I caught the details of the trail with renewed sharpness simply by walking through. I no longer purposely directed my attention; it all poured in indiscriminately – the subtle difference in fragrance between the pine and fir trees, the sensual dance of rivers around boulders, the paintbrushes, marigolds, and lupines bobbing their heads in my wake.

My walk became a cadenced meditation, anchored by the rhythmic crunch of my steps in the reddish-brown volcanic dirt. I was powered by super-human thru-hiking legs, and of course, the Bobcat propeller. The off-trail world receded to a faint wisp in the back of my awareness. I forgot to count days or hours and only marked the passing of the miles, sun and moon to the extent relevant to my walk. My mind lingered neither on memories nor on plans for the future. I didn't know what I would do after the trail, but "after-the-trail" didn't exist yet, so I didn't need to know.

Occasionally, random sentences floated through my mind. "I remember clearly the moment when I first lost my mind." was a big favorite through much of northern Oregon. I liked the sound of it and always enjoyed its visits. The stories I wrote on the Roaming Bobcat blog often bubbled up in the form of random sentences for a few days before I reached town, so I assumed the sentence belonged to a story. Only when "Mark, I think I'm going crazy. Do you think I'm going crazy?" appeared, shortly after the Washington border, did I realize the story was not a mere blog post. I was hearing the beginning of an extended story, maybe a book I might write some day in a direct linear future from my walk. But that day hadn't arrived yet, so I thanked the thoughts and let them float away.

My mind also occasionally invited friends over for a little fantasy. Logan was still a frequent guest, but without the judgments, emotions or analyses. His energy simply entered my field of awareness, and I always welcomed him and loved him, until he faded again. The same was true for Hobbes, LB, Margaret and Sofia.

I loved being disconnected, alone in my own bubble of a world, so it was with slight apprehension that I approached Mt. Hood.

I had spoken with Sofia from Sisters; she could meet me at the Timberline Lodge on Mt. Hood and whisk me away to Portland for a "real town" zero that coincided with her weekend.

Trail towns were still part of the trail. They were usually small enough to navigate on foot, remote enough to feel like the woods, and filled with other thru-hikers, concentrated in grocery stores, bars and restaurants. Portland, however, especially Sofia's Portland, intimidated me.

On the morning when I was to meet Sofia, I woke up with the sunrise and walked towards Mt. Hood at my usual pace. I watched its looming silhouette morph and grow through the trees all day as the trail approached its steep flanks, and finally ascended the last sandy mile to rejoin the Timberline Trail.

From the Timberline Trail, long steps descended towards the Lodge's parking lot, ever deeper into the crowd of international visitors. Tourists walked upward towards the views in waves of mixed perfumes —soap, shampoo, sunscreen, bug spray, cheap and expensive fragrances. The mountain sounds were drowned in the multilingual cacophony. There were people everywhere, and I felt dizzy from the sudden sensory assault.

For the last couple hundred feet to the parking lot, I anchored my mind on the rhythm of my steps and the sensations in my moving body, and hummed to drown the noise.

From the safety of my enclosed physical body, I could see the world as a holographic movie, separate from me. I could move through it, around it, outside of it.

Day-hikers stared and some smiled; I kept walking and humming until I saw Sofia walking towards me.

Although I had no concept of clock time, and Sofia had been delayed driving up the mountain, we reached the bottom steps of the trail, at the edge of the parking lot, at exactly the same moment.

She was a vision. I realized later that she likely had spent some time that morning selecting out of a closetful of tasteful outfits, the most casual, outdoorsy ensemble for the occasion. She had settled on simple yet elegant capris, a white tank top, a denim jacket and high-heel platform wedges – the name of which I learned that day. Her hair was clean, organized and softly held in place by strategically placed designer sunglasses.

To my feral eyes, however, she looked like a supermodel out of a magazine. I was awed by her beauty and elegance, and told her repeatedly. She laughed; she always looked fabulous, didn't I remember?

I was still staring at Sofia, the way I had stared at flowers on the trail, when we sat in her car. With exaggerated movements, she immediately rolled down her window. She had commented on none of my ratted hair, torn pants or dusty pack that sprinkled twigs and dirt over the seat of her car. But her scrunched nose, knitted brow and waved hand fanning air away from her face needed no translation.

"We need to get you cleaned up. You can't go out in public like this. Let's drop everything in the washing machine when we get to my Mom's house." Her tone was playful, but her words bothered me. I heard "You are non-conformable to society's standards, and we must rectify this situation."

Not only did I love my own body's trail aroma, my feet's quarter-inch dirt-encrusted black calluses, and the nascent dreadlocks at my hairline, but I had been treated like a superhero by all off-trail folks I had met for months – "You're hiking from where? Woah! Mexico – what? You're going how far? Canada! – That's amazing!"

I had become accustomed to the special attention, and maybe had come to expect it. I lived a self-reliant, no trace, off-grid ecstatic life in complete harmony with nature. I could sustain four miles an hour on foot, even uphill. I could communicate with insects, trees, water, the sun and the moon – and they answered. I could flow with what was and manifest magic without even trying. I was a thru-hiker. Didn't Sofia know? Couldn't she see?

After a long, hot shower and much resentful scrubbing, I slipped on a pair of jeans and a tee shirt of mine that Sofia had kept since I had left for the trail. They no longer fit; they were much too lose, and I didn't feel like myself in them.

"Ha! Much better. I'm taking you to one of my favorite restaurants downtown. The food is great, high quality, with wholesome ingredients, and I just love the ambience."

When our first delectable entrees arrived, I realized that Sofia had either not fully grasped or not believed my description of thru-hiker hunger, and the amount of food required to appease it. I could have eaten seven of whatever lived on my plate for about thirty seconds, but I certainly could not have afforded seven.

Sofia enjoyed her meal slowly and comfortably. She spoke of her office life and growing responsibilities with aging parents. These were her current experiences, and she was embracing whatever discomfort they occasioned with self-awareness, trust and faith. I listened carefully, but noted the disconnect. Sofia's life update was simply part of that holographic movie I was watching. The dialogs were engaging and well crafted, but irrelevant to my real life.

I spoke of the trail in return, of sleeping under the stars and cooking meals on a three ounce stove that looked like a cat food can. I spoke of my trail romances and of the characters I called family members. Sofia did not seem impressed.

By the time we returned to her mother's house, we had, it seemed, exhausted the conversation. This had never happened before. Sofia watched a movie; I fell asleep within five minutes of the intro. When the movie was over, Sofia lovingly folded my laundry and piled it on my clean pack, so that it was all set to go in the morning.

The next morning, we had breakfast at an outdoor French café that served authentic French quiches, croissants and cafés au lait, and then strolled through the shelves of a new age bookshop. We didn't speak much, and it was probably for the best. We still enjoyed each other's company, even if we were temporarily – I hoped – a little out of sync.

In the afternoon, Sofia dropped me near a coffee shop on Hawthorne Boulevard on her way back to Seattle. There were homeless hippies on Hawthorne that looked just like thru-hikers. I felt an instant kinship with them. I joined in the loitering and we chatted for a few minutes. By the time my friend Dacia picked me up, the hippies and I had established a quick friendship and parted with hugs and wishes of good luck.

Then, Hobbes joined us. This was the first merger of my trail and off-trail lives, the first time that Melissa met the PCT Bobcat, and I felt a little schizophrenic.

It would have been worse had Hobbes met Sofia. Dacia, at least, was an avid alpinist and a former wilderness guide. She understood the addiction to sleeping in the dirt and the delight in one's own mountain body odor. She also understood trail hunger.

That evening, Dacia and her husband treated us to a legendary four-course meal that included steaks, two different kinds of raw fish dishes, a monstrous salad, fresh homemade piña coladas, cakes, pies and cookies. Their four children were as astonished by the quantity of food Hobbes and I could ingest as they were fascinated by the stories of our adventures.

"Really? You walked from Mexico to here? And you sleep outside? How do you poop? What if there are bears? What if you get tired?"

Thank God for young inquisitive minds! – My ego sighed with relief. I could be a superhero again.

"The bears – you just let them know that you're coming and ask them to leave you alone – oh yes, they listen, but you want to use a loving gentle voice ... Now, to dig a proper poo-hole, first you need a stick ..." Hobbes disagreed; he himself was partial to the kick-dirt-with-your-shoe digging method.

From poo to the stars, the stories carried us through dinner and past the cakes, pies and cookies. There was much disgruntlement when bedtime caught us mid-flight. But Hobbes and I were still on trail time, and welcomed sleep as much as we welcomed food.

After a sweet night in Hobbes's arms, Dacia released me back to the wild, exactly where Sofia had found me.

I flew back up the stairs, lifted by the buoyancy in my heart. I was home, back on the trail. I had survived Portland, and I could still pretend for a little while that the trail was the only world that existed.

PCT 2012. Mile 2155
Excerpt from The Roaming Bobcat's blog
Titled "Reintroduction inoculation" [edited for length]

There are things about the trail I will miss so much when this is all over, like freedom, open skies, mind-boggling vistas, quirky instant random trail friendships, fresh water straight out of streams, the smell of dirt and pine trees and flowers, the comfort of knowing what today's task is (walking!). I will miss having my entire life in a pack and knowing I have all I need, nothing more, nothing less. I will miss peace.

Yesterday, I took the Eagle Creek alternate route, which features waterfalls every 5 minutes. At one of the waterfalls, I sat down for a snack. Since it's my birthday week, I treated myself to a resupply at Trader Joe's in Portland. My food bag is ri-di-cu-lous! It is unnecessarily heavy for a three-day section, which I ended up doing in two days anyway. I've got dried pineapples, pumpernickel pretzels, sugar lemon cookies, heavy Indian pre-cooked meals, and more. Mmmh mmmh mmmh. I sat with my ridiculous delicious food bag for a while and was amazed that I was even there. The green all around me was so vibrant, the water so clear and refreshing, the silence so pervasive. If there is an image of peace, I think I was sitting in it.

These are the moments on the trail that I will likely never adequately be able to share with you, not with words, nor with photos. They just need to be experienced.

I often feel a state of euphoric joy when I first leave town. I think it stems from a combination of proper nutrition and a sense of returning home. This time, the section was so short that it was carried over from Portland to Cascade Locks. I have it right now. It's like internal Heaven.

CHAPTER 41

In the morning of September 7th, 2012, I crossed the Bridge of the Gods, the passageway from Oregon to Washington. I leaned over the metal grids to watch the massive waters of the Columbia River directly underneath my feet while Hobbes documented my bridge crossing.

He had reached Cascades Locks by bus that morning

specifically to walk with me on my birthday, as I entered the last state of my journey.

The last state – I didn't even want to think about it.

"Hey, do you want salmon?" A man in an old rusted red pickup truck slowed down on the bridge and called to me.

" ... Sure." I was hesitant. It seemed like a joke, but the man handed me a ten-inch long piece of smoked salmon out the passenger side window, wished me "good day" and drove on.

I held the piece of salmon with both hands and turned to Hobbes to confirm that this really had just happened.

"Happy Birthday!" Hobbes laughed. "See, you're still a textbook case. You just manifested fish."

I smiled, but my heart wasn't light enough to laugh with him. How often would I manifest magic after the end of the trail? I gave the fish to Hobbes.

We walked past the "Welcome to Washington" sign and followed the trail off the road and into the lush evergreen forest. I walked in front, quietly, but could smell salmon just a few steps behind.

"From here, you have less than five hundred miles to go. You're so close. How do you feel?" Hobbes sounded excited.

My throat closed up so fast that I couldn't even sneak a small answer past it. Instead, I turned around and walked into his arms. I already had tears streaming down my face by the time I reached his chest.

"Oh! I'm sorry." He held me tightly and stroked my hair while I cried. I didn't say a word. When I finally stopped crying, I leaned back to look at him and laughed when I saw how wet his shirt was. I never answered his question. I just turned back to the trail and kept walking, my attention on the dirt and the leaves and the patches of blue sky up above through the trees.

Hobbes only walked a few miles with me; he had a bus to catch back to Portland. We stopped in a clearing in the sun, ate some snacks, kissed and held hands for a while.

Then, it was time. I shouldered my pack, kissed Hobbes

one more time and disappeared through the thick green underbrush.

As long as I walked solo in the woods, I could still pretend that Canada didn't exist, that the trail lived on forever.

And, in a way, I was correct.

As I meandered through forests of old friends, within sights of mountains I knew and loved, each step, each moment contained its own eternity. My hike through Washington was one long déjà-vu. I had hiked many trails and climbed all the volcanoes in the Washington portion of the Cascades, but never on the actual PCT, yet everything from the smallest speck of dirt to the entirety of the sky felt as familiar to me as my own body.

Physical boundaries blurred into soft gradations. Where did the trail start and the Bobcat stop, if the air in her lungs was pine scented? If the water contained in her cells also flowed through the veins of the earth underfoot? If her tongue was stained blue from frost-covered blueberries she picked with her mouth right off the bushes because using her hands seemed like a superfluous gesture?

I was no longer just the Bobcat; I was the trail. I saw myself in its symbols everywhere. I was the passion in the tinge of autumn reds at the edge of the leaves, the vigor of cold air rushing in my lungs in the morning, the wisdom in the deep roots of the trees and the frivolousness of the wind playing through needles and leaves.

I was also the blindness of the fog in the valley and the fragility of hundreds of daddy-long-legs crawling over my face in the darkness. I was the exhaustion of that odd orange beetle with dozens of baby beetles on its back that struggled to fly away from my evening meal in which it had landed, despite the spoon help I provided.

I asked Margaret to ship me a tent. I felt guilty about this. I had slept outside with the trail despite the scorpions, rain and snow, so why the sudden physical separation? The daddy-long-legs and cold nights were parts of the equation, but mostly, I was just tired. I wanted a safe haven, a chrysalis in which to disappear and rejuvenate at night, so that I could be strong enough for the steepness of the Cascades.

Somewhere on the grid of the Bridge of the Gods, probably in exchange for salmon, I turned in my thru-hiking superpowers. The trail off the clearing where I last kissed Hobbes climbed straight up to those patches of blue sky I had spied through the trees. I struggled to hike twenty three miles that day; they felt like thirty three.

If it were any other section of the trail, I simply would have slowed down. I would have carried more food and relished the slower pace through some of the best mountain vistas of the entire trail. I would have delayed getting to Canada to later in the fall, even if I had to cross the border on snowshoes.

But this was Washington. This was home before the trail. Throughout the state, friends turned Trail Angels were eager to meet me at trailheads with food resupply. I didn't spend a dime to fill my food bag for the last five hundred miles to Canada – a grand finale of trail magic, delivered by my own home clan.

I wasn't about to miss it, even if I suddenly had to push my pace to a fixed schedule that coincided with that of my Angels. I could line up my walking to the off-trail world's days off, but once the days off had been requested and granted, I could not deviate from the agreed schedule – Six days to White Pass to meet John, four days to Snoqualmie Pass to meet Margaret, three days to Stevens Pass to retrieve a resupply box overflowing with my favorite dark chocolate from Glen, and six days to Rainy Pass where Deborah would join me for the last stretch to Canada.

My short excursion to Portland had felt like a shock to my system, but my Washington Angel friends met me right on the trail, in my world. Some camped and some hiked with me. Only Margaret gently lured me into town with promises of spinach salad and roast chicken – the Bobcat's prey of choice.

I looked forward to the passes, and gradually relaxed into the idea that the trail would end, that Canada did exist, and that maybe it was actually for the best. There would be flush toilets again, and cooked meals beyond boiled water, and fresh veggies, and my truck – Oh, I couldn't wait to see my truck! And I would be able to finally rest.

PCT Day 158 – Mile 2458
Excerpt from my trail journal [edited for length and flow]
   So few days left now. 1 to Steven's Pass, 6 to Deborah, 4 to the border and Manning Park. 11 left. That's it.
The days go slowly and are gone in the blink of an eye simultaneously. I was so sad when I crossed the Bridge of the Gods, but it's different now. At the beginning I was thirsty for the experience of the trail, this freedom, this ability to walk without ever having to stop. I drank it all in like a parched person. But now, I've been drinking the deliciousness for five and a half months. I don't feel thirsty anymore. It doesn't make the trail any less amazing. I'm just satiated, and maybe I'm a little done. And yet I don't want it to end. I wonder if I'll ever feel the exuberance of my early days again.
Thank you, Love, for allowing this trail to be my life right now. I'm sorry if I sometimes take it for granted. I love you!
XOX – TheBobcat

CHAPTER 42

   I woke up below Mica Lake with a start, sat up straight in my sleeping bag and giggled. My, I had a lot of walking in me suddenly! I could feel the strength of my legs and the expanded capacity of my lungs. I had felt tired for days. What was the difference? I had slept from dusk to dawn, on the same pad, in the same tent, after eating a meal composed of instant noodles, nuts and dried fruit. Nothing unusual, except for a joyful exuberance in my heart, the like of which I had not felt since the early days in the California desert.

   The entrance of the tent framed Glacier Peak perfectly. It was so close that it occupied most of the sky. Behind it, the pastel pink of sunrise was just fading and opening the sky to a glorious sunny day.

   "It must be the energy of the mountain." I said out loud.

"Good morning Glacier Peak! Good morning trail! I still love you!"

In less than two minutes, I rolled my tent, pad and sleeping bag, set the Bobcat propeller in its pocket for maximum twirling, and bounded down the trail with a granola bar for breakfast on the go.

The trail dropped 1,500 feet, rose 3,000 feet, and back down 3,700 feet and back up another 4,000 feet, through spectacular high plateaus and across crystal clear rivers. By sunset, I had climbed the equivalent elevation of two Mt. Bakers from base camp to summit, gobbled over thirty PCT miles, and still I felt no fatigue.

The flat, level top of Suiattle Pass, where I stopped to watch the sunset and eat a handful of nuts and dried fruit, was an ideal camp with wide-open views towards Glacier Peak. While the mountain experimented with ever increasingly vivid shades of orange, I allowed the idea that I might camp at the pass float through my mind, but it never really settled.

Before I could decide, I noticed that only one cookie was left, in the form of crumbs, at the bottom of my food bag. I always ate a cookie after dinner, so, if saved it, I could camp at the pass, cook an actual meal, eat the cookie for dessert, and wake up with Glacier Peak once more. But if I ate it, I'd have to walk another ten miles – for a total of forty miles that day – to sleep within striking distance of the Stehekin Pastry Company.

Oh, I saw it happen. I saw the orange spoon dig to the bottom of the bag, and in one mouthful the cookie was gone. The sun was gone too, so I shouldered my pack and hiked on.

Bathed in the dusk's light, I could navigate boulder fields without a headlamp and play hide-and-seek with the moon shadows through the forest. My Trail High rose like the young moon over the clouds. The trees were awake and watching my passage, not with eyes or curiosity as humans would, but with exploratory energetic tendrils wrapped around my heart. I met them there with love and gratitude and also a hint of sadness.

As darkness deepened, an increasing sense of conclusion

weaved into the joy, love and gratitude. This felt like the last stand on the mountain, the final night of a five and a half month long vision quest.

Had I learned what I wished to learn? Had I become whom I needed to become? Was there meaning to my walk beyond the indulgent pleasure of an epic adventure?

I thought I might be granted a vision or a totem animal to represent my journey. I turned on my headlamp to ensure I could see it, if it appeared. Then I remembered that I was walking alone and in the dark, and asked kindly, out loud, that if a totem animal be presented, to not have it be anything large or scary.

Within a few steps, a golden salamander appeared in the halo of my headlamp. It looked exactly like my tattoo. A few steps further, a golden toad of the same size appeared in the halo. I didn't know what they meant but believed that omens and totems always come in three, so I began searching the trail for a third small, lovely, golden animal.

I was still searching when, right around midnight, I turned the corner of a switchback to traverse a steep part of the trail and found the way completely blocked by a fully spiked porcupine.

I stopped suddenly, heart pounding. The porcupine greeted me by thrashing its tail in my direction.

"Moon! What do I do?" I turned to look at its bright face. I really expected it to answer and simultaneously recognized how odd my behavior would seem to the off-trail world. But the moon did answer. I heard it in my heart; it sang a soft Harry Belafonte song, which I repeated to the porcupine.

" … But I'm sad to say, I'm on my way. Won't be back for many a day. My heart is down, my head is turning around. I had to leave a little girl in Kingston town."

The porcupine stopped thrashing but kept its quills fully spiked. The song also calmed me.

I extended This and That on each side of the porcupine and gently coaxed it forward on the trail. It lodged several quills deep into the rubber tip of my poles, and I was grateful for the safe reach they afforded. I continued guiding and singing for another fifteen minutes, until a slight widening in the trail allowed me to run by with a cry of joy.

A few miles later, the trail descended into the valley that led to Stehekin. It was relatively straight and gently sloping downhill – easy to walk – but a combination of too few snacks and too many miles by the fading light of my headlamp had rendered my legs wobbly and my head dizzy.

It was in this state that I came upon a wide and wild river. Large beams strewn across the river and massive concrete pillars on each shore suggested a bridge might have once existed, but the only way left across was a slippery log about a hundred feet downriver.

I stood on the edge of the log's overturned roots and peered into the dark waters.

"Right! So, I'm about to cross over a raging river, on a slippery log, in the dark, on unstable legs, and absolutely no one knows where I am right now."

I heard the words as I was speaking them and began laughing before the end of the sentence. I laughed uninhibitedly, like a mad person. I laughed so loudly that I likely would have slipped backwards if the roots hadn't held me. I already knew I was crossing, not because I was attached to hiking forty miles or believed a better camp awaited me further, but because crossing scared me.

I stepped over the roots and slowed my heart with three full yogic breaths before letting go. I stared straight at the other shore and carefully placed one foot in front of the other, using my poles for balance, until I was over land again.

I stepped off the log and onto the trail, then turned back to the river with my hands joined at my heart.

"Thank you, river, for the safe passage." A deep and centered calm enveloped me, yet I felt vibrantly alive.

This is how I played – I remembered – I played at the edge. I could step off the trail and back into the world. I had some playing to do there too. I knew I could navigate its pitfalls simply by letting the moon sing in my heart. I wasn't leaving the trail behind; it was part of me – and vice versa.

And yes, reintegration scared me. It tightened my chest and made me wish I could turn around and walk back to Campo. But once the log was crossed, it was crossed, and the only thing left to do was to walk to the bakery.

CHAPTER 43

"Wow. Look at you! You look ten years younger. Maybe a little tired, but all the stress is gone from your face. And you're so skinny. Your pants are hanging!"

Deborah would have known; we wore the same pants and the same hiking shirt, in the same size. The fit of our clothes had looked identical before I left, except for Deborah's few extra inches in height. We had looked forward to being trail twins since the day I announced I was hiking the trail and Deborah added "and I'm walking the end with you."

It was a matter of sanity, she said. As a full-time working single mother, she needed an outdoors adventure to remember who she was, and I expected I would need the fuel of her fresh enthusiasm for the last push to the finish.

"Oh my God! Look at this!" The trail had become such a part of me that I sometimes failed to still see it. Through Deborah's big blue eyes, I once again was held breathless by the vibrancy of the yellow larches of autumn and the majesty of the Cascades' peaks. "And you got to do this every day for five and half months? It must have been like a dream. I'd love to be able to hike a trail like this."

Deborah was a natural thru-hiker. Her ultra-marathoner's legs gobbled miles as fast and sustainably as mine, her appetite honored the stack of pastries that miraculously survived my three-hour stay at the Stehekin Pastry Company and subsequent twenty miles to Rainy Pass, and her spirit soared to her own version of Trail High as soon as we emerged above tree-line.

Deborah was my original trail family. Our mutual trust was

forged outdoors, caring for sensitive geologic instruments in epic weather. We had survived a sinking raft on a frozen lake, a sudden snow storm on an exposed ridge of Mt. Baker, an icy descent of Mt. Shuksan on skis, and most importantly our own well-matched fiery tempers. But in spite of our historical trust, without the experience of 2,600 miles of magic, Deborah was wary of my trail methods.

Whereas I walked until I felt like stopping, she wanted to consult the map to find camps and water to determine how far we had to go. She didn't worry about bears or freezing nights, but she did consider them. She checked the altitude, wind exposure and potential for wildlife encounters before she unrolled her bivy bag and was surprised that I didn't. I had before the trail. I had always carried the sanctified ten essentials and taken measures to protect myself from the dangers inherent to wandering in the wilderness.

"What do you mean; you don't carry a water filter?"

Water filters were so far removed from my consciousness that I had forgotten to warn Deborah to bring her own.

"I haven't the whole trail, but it's fine, really. Look, that's what I do."

I showed her – I filled my water bottle, held it to my heart and mindfully spoke the words I had repeated every day, several times a day, since California, "I love you, please don't make sick, thank you." Then, in one big gulp, I drank about a quarter of the bottle.

My cheeks were still filled with the sweet freshness of the mountain spring when Deborah pointed upstream with a raised eyebrow.

"Is that bear vomit, right there?"

No, it wasn't. It was a big pile of fresh bear poo directly in line with the little waterfall from which I had filled my water bottle. I spit whatever water was left in my cheeks across the stream.

Deborah laughed. "I guess we'll find out if your method works. I think I'm gonna wait 'til we get to camp and boil mine, but thanks for the suggestion."

She laughed about it for miles and told the story to all hikers we met from that point forth to Canada.

Deborah and the Bobcat — we were quite a vivacious pair. We argued daily, especially around five pm, right before dinner, but we also laughed all day. We enjoyed the hardship of freezing winds and steep ascents with the same glee and we stopped to the same views for minutes of silent awe.

In the evening we set our sleeping pads less than two feet away. The process was complicated because I slept in a tent and Deborah in a bivy bag. The fly of my tent had to extend over her bivy bag, and she had to be inside before I could stake the tent. It took a few tries, but eventually we perfected the method and were able to lay close enough to chat late into the night.

One by one, she updated me on the whereabouts of our common friends and others in Bellingham. What had the world been up to while I had disappeared in the wild? Not much it seemed. Most of our friends were reliably and steadily continuing on their chosen paths with neither major drama nor drastic change of perspective.

"What about Logan. Have you seen him?"

"Not since you left. Which is weird because I used to see him all the time. Almost every morning at the coffee shop. Maybe he quit drinking coffee." Deborah laughed. I could see how the thought of quitting coffee would be ludicrous to a single working mom.

"I don't know. Maybe he's moved out of Bellingham."

"Yeah. Maybe he has."

I knew that he hadn't, but I didn't know how I knew. His energy had grown stronger in my awareness since I entered the North Cascades, and some days it was so palpable that I expected an encounter at every switchback. I neither wished to see him, nor not. I knew that I was walking through his climbing territory. I felt his presence and walked with it.

By the time I re-emerged from my musings about Logan's omnipresent energy, Deborah was asleep. I smiled and closed my eyes too. We didn't speak of Logan again.

Deborah was such a strong hiker that we walked in two days the distance we had planned for three, and the border was suddenly less than half a day away. Neither of us wished to abbreviate our adventure, so we slowed down to bask in the beauty of the Cascades.

We lounged on a flat rock under the deep blue sky and played "name the peaks in sight" for a few hours. We sat at the edge of a valley and photographed the dappled forest of green hemlocks and yellow larches below. We reminisced about our past adventures and laughed at our former predicaments and old jokes. We also created new jokes and imagined ourselves reminiscing about them the next time we walked this section of the PCT together, which we agreed should be in the fall of the following year.

Knowing that we would return relieved the dread of the adventure's end, and at last, we shouldered our packs for the last long rocky traverse before the descent to the terminus.

I was contemplating the contrast between the heaviness in my heart and the playful bounce in Deborah's pony-tail in front of me when I caught it in the corner of my eye. If I had taken but a few steps forward while looking the other way, I would have missed it.

"Deborah! I see Mt. Baker!"

Only the very top of its glaciated summit and a little bit of steam from the fumaroles in Sherman Crater – my crater – peeked in our direction, but it was sufficient. We both jumped for joy and waved to the mountain. I didn't want to walk any further, and Deborah understood. We scrambled above the narrow trail and dug comfortable seats in direct sight of our common love.

Mt. Baker, at last. I had finally walked home. From here, the border was a mere a formality.

Staring in the fumes swirling up from the crater, I saw the whole trail unroll itself in my mind like the reel of a movie – the desert, the Sierra, the wild flowers and red lava fields of Oregon, the dense pine forests and jagged peaks of Washington. I heard LB's laugh on the soundtrack – that's when I began to cry. LB was at least two weeks behind. I knew I'd see him again but what about all the other ones? How many members of my trail family would I never see again? Large tears streaked the dirt on my face while Mt. Baker and Deborah sat by my side in silent support.

"Welcome back." the mountain said directly in my heart. "More adventures ahead" it assured me.

After a few minutes, Deborah reached over and offered me a cookie, which was a surprisingly astute gesture for a three-day section hiker. Snacks did have a way of improving one's mood on the trail instantly.

I looked at the cookie through my tears, wiped my nose on my sleeve and laughed. "Good call. Thanks. I think I'm good now. Let's go to Canada."

The terminus monument sat in a circular clearing in a dense pine forest. All the trees along the border had been cut, so the demarcation between the United States and Canada was a long, naked line through the forest and across the clearing with the monument.

Deborah and I were not alone at the monument. Shutterbug and Northstar, a lovely couple whom I had first met in the California desert had finished a few minutes ahead of us. Pounce, Nugio and Oregon arrived just a few minutes later. I stared at the monument scanning for any emotion it might trigger in my body, but none surfaced. I was much more fascinated by Pounce's finish-line purple sequin dress, Nugio's cigar and that naked line through the trees than I was by the monument or what it represented.

I used the last of my camera's batteries for a few snapshots of Deborah and me at the monument, and then signed the terminus register.

I simply wrote: "That was fun. Can I go again? – The Bobcat"

We only hiked four of the eight miles past the border to Manning Park before setting camp for the night. I saw no reason to hike further; we were in Canada.

PCT Day 169 – Mile 2664
Excerpt from my trail journal [last entry]
    Well. There you go. I walked from Mexico to Canada, then 4 miles
past that. It was a bit anti-climatic. I didn't feel any great emotion at the
monument, just the feeling of "Cool, I got here. Well, that was a nice
appetizer, now what?"
Yeah, now what? I don't know. Maybe move to a new place, maybe
Portland. Maybe teach yoga, or something else. Maybe write a book,
manifest enough money to live, keep up a life by intuition rather than fears
or expectations. Maybe go visit Hobbes, although I can't tell why exactly
when Deborah asks me. Maybe I just need to be held and loved for a bit.
That's what feels most right.
I do worry about being shown to be a fool in my beliefs. What if there is
no magic beyond the trail? Other times what we are is so obvious to me –
the meaning of Life, the Universe and Everything isn't 42 (that's the age
of the Bobcat), it is to have fun with the experiences provided by the
Higher Self, which is just the sentient part of our true, whole self.
So, the adventure continues, with a blank slate ahead. Who will I be?
How will I occupy my days? How will I live? I hope in joy and discovery.
I hope with Love. I hope with an open mind to see opportunities.
I am so so so SO grateful for the past two years, and in particular the time
on the trail, the people I met, the lessons, everything. You have truly
spoiled me beyond my expectations.
I LOVE YOU.

The next morning, the sun was already well above the
forest's canopy when Deborah and I crawled out of our tent
and bivy bag. Nearby campers had built a large breakfast
campfire. They called us to join them. We huddled to the
flames to warm our hands and ate anything left in our food
bags. Then, with much laughter and a few disagreements,
Deborah and I recounted our adventures of the past four days,
including the bear poo incident, to the group. The stories
continued until the fire was reduced to embers and the sun had
reached its zenith. It was time to go.

    I shouldered my pack one last time on the PCT and
consulted the map with Deborah. The last four miles to

Manning Park consisted of one long gradual descent. Perfect. That was the only walking I had left in me.

But the map lied.

I stopped at the bottom of a small hill – a really small hill, less than twenty feet in length and a few tens of feet in elevation, not a sufficient feature to appear on the map's contours – with a disproportionate sense of distress.

'No! Just no! I'm not walking uphill. I've walked to Canada. The map said it was all downhill. That's it. I'm done."

"You don't need to walk uphill." Deborah said, "That's why I came. I'm here to help you finish your walk."

Deborah placed both hands on my pack and pushed me all the way up the last hill before the final descent to Manning Park, where my friend John awaited to pick us up and return us to Bellingham, to the street where my truck was parked, only a block away from where Deborah lived, across the street from Boulevard Park and my favorite bay.

.

Part 6

ROAMING

All that is gold does not glitter,
not all those who wander are lost;
the old that is strong does not wither,
deep roots are not reached by the frost.

– J.R.R. Tolkien –
(*The Lord of the Rings*)

CHAPTER 44

There was my beloved Bellingham Bay!

I sipped on a mocha as I walked slowly along its shore, warming my hands on the paper cup. I welcomed the Puget Sound's misty kisses on my cheeks, and matched my own breath to its gentle, unconcerned ebb and flow.

There were the blue and grey waters, the familiar streets, the islands and mountains in the distance I had called home to anyone on the trail asking where I was from.

I had been off-trail and back in Bellingham for less than twenty-four hours, but I already knew that I wasn't staying.

Somewhere in the southern California desert, my friend Billy Goat had warned me about this. "The trail changes you," he said, "but you won't know it 'til you're done. It changes you slowly. Can't even tell it's happening. By the time you get to Manning Park, you might feel the same on the inside, but you're completely different to the rest of the world."

I sat on a mossy rock right at the water's edge and explained Billy Goat's philosophy out loud to Bellingham Bay. I didn't care if I was overheard or taken for crazy. I felt I owed my former playground an explanation, even though I knew it already understood.

"This is goodbye again. I know I just got here last night, but I must roam on. If I don't come back, please know that I love you and that you've been a wonderful home to me."

I checked to see if I was sad. I thought I might be – I had cried every time I had left Bellingham before – but found no sadness. My post-trail glow wouldn't allow it. The quiet of the trail still lived in my heart, and I still flowed in a world where all was exactly as it was meant to be.

To avoid complications or esoteric explanations, I contacted no one. I slipped in and out of Bellingham like a spirit of the land and was gone before the news of my return could spread.

On my way out of town, I stopped by my storage unit. With a blank canvas of open roads at my disposal and no concept of where I was going or how long I'd be gone, it seemed that I ought to pack *something*. When the sliding doors creaked open and the light of the corridor illuminated the stack of boxes – all labeled "Melissa's treasures" – and the jumbled assortment of gear and furniture, I stumbled back. I saw no comfort in my material possessions, just responsibilities. I had lived so well with my twenty pound pack, what could possibly have been so important to me that it warranted paying sixty dollars a month and occupying this stagnant space?

Luckily, I was wise enough to realize I couldn't trust myself then and resisted the urge to give everything away. I had just gotten off-trail; I had likely not yet even begun the reintegration process.

૪ ꞏ ૭

Reintegration. *n.* The act of abandoning magic for reality, freedom for responsibilities, and roaming for soulless work to pay off trail debts – believed by some to be a depressing yet inevitable post-trail transition phase.

૪ ꞏ ૭

I was about to slide the door closed without taking a single item out of storage, when my eyes caught fuzzy ears sticking out of a wooden crate. It was Timothy the Tiger, my 2011 adventure companion, and in good company – there were also an unnamed leopard and lion that I had adopted when I was

246

sixteen years old and Ddraig the red dragon, whom I had rescued from a small shop next to a Welsh castle. So, there were treasures worth saving after all.

After much consideration, I decided to take the dragon with me. The cats could hold the fort in my absence. I also packed my laptop, my yoga mat and a small blender to make green smoothies. I couldn't imagine needing anything else.

At my peak walking performance on the trail, I could sustain four miles an hour. Four miles an hour felt fast, so releasing the clutch of my truck into first gear for the first time in months was exhilarating, like being strapped to a rocket. I drove down the first narrow street with a howl of joy and navigated town like a brand new driver.

The effect was short-lived, luckily, and by a few miles out of town, I had already relaxed into the familiar comfort of the truck's cab. Its distinctive smell, born of eleven years of bonding between my body and its seat covers, the smoothness of its steering wheel, polished over countless adventures, its windshield cracks, which sparkled in the sun, and its reliable purr were all the "home" I needed.

Tears of gratitude for this truck I loved so much overflowed from my heart, and I welcomed them. No emotion was absurd; the trail had effectively stripped all social standards of behavior from my psyche.

I didn't feel the need to decide where I was going. The truck seemed to flow south most naturally, and I encouraged it. Sofia and Margaret lived south of Bellingham, and Hobbes was still yurt-sitting in Portland for a few more weeks.

I didn't worry about my financial status, even though the vacuum my bank account had become would have spun me with panic before the trail.

And I was not dismayed when Sofia texted me that I couldn't spend the night in her apartment because she had prior plans, but I was intrigued. I had always spent the night at Sofia's before and after any adventure, and walking the PCT definitively qualified as an adventure. Were the patterns of my old life disintegrating? Had I changed so much that my best friend no longer resonated with whom I had become? Was Life guiding me to stay elsewhere, for a greater purpose of which I was not privy? Or had I simply not yet returned from the adventure?

Speculating seemed pointless, so instead, I took the off-ramp to Margaret's apartment. Before the trail, I wouldn't have appeared at anyone's door unannounced or uninvited; I would have considered it rude.

As I rang the bell, I couldn't help giggling. I loved the image of myself as a roaming feral cat, the kind that brings tall tales from afar in exchange for a shower, a meal, and a level surface to unroll a sleeping bag for the night.

I was still giggling at the thought when Margaret opened the door wide and greeted me with a full-body embrace. She did not seem surprised to see me at all. She even had hot water ready, and offered me my favorite kind of green tea in my favorite tea mug. She also expected I'd be hungry and invited me to rummage in her fridge for anything I might want.

As I sat at her dining table with a plate of tandoori chicken and pasta salad, I noticed the pile of boxes stacked high in the corner of the room. While I was on the trail, Margaret had been an exemplary link with the off-trail world. She had sent me maps, gear, treats and funny love notes I carried in my trail journals. In exchange, I had sent her pieces of bark, feathers, rocks, worn out shoes I didn't have the heart to discard, distressed used maps and five camera memory cards holding thousands of photos. I was shocked at the height of the pile of treasures I had accumulated.

"We carry our fears." LB had said. I must have feared forgetting the trail. After my meal was done, I spread the content of the boxes on Margaret's table, just as I had done with my gear on the lawn at the Kickoff, and only selected those treasures I meant to keep. Most of the bark, feathers and rocks were released back into the wild. I also freed the worn out shoes, but not before hugging and thanking each one. I kept all the memory cards filled with photos and the spare clothes I had shipped home from the Kickoff – including my favorite pair of yoga pants. Except for one small evening in Portland, I had worn the same pair of hiking pants and tank top every day for five and a half months. I was finally ready to give them a rest.

My whole body was ready for a rest. I changed into my yoga pants and sunk into a large pillow on the floor of Margaret's living room with another steaming mug of green tea. I had not yet moved from the pillow when Margaret's husband, Steve, returned from work late that evening.

They shared stories from their lives – working, riding buses, finding time to exercise, caring for aging parents, planting a garden, feeding the cat, dreaming of vacations. My heart grew a little wider with each of their stories and a warm glow of friendship, kinship, a sense of home beyond physical location filled the newly opened space.

I let the flow of the evening conversation carry me like a river. I needed no destination; I understood that I belonged anywhere in the world where someone or something opened my heart. The trail was merely a metaphor for the life path I chose to follow. The "real life" I had dreaded reintegrating was no less magic than the trail. I was just as loved and spoiled in the off-trail world as I was on the trail.

I felt such gratitude at this realization that my eyes watered until big tears rolled down my cheeks. Neither Margaret nor Steve mentioned my tears. They probably assumed I was just tired from my journey. They carried on with the conversation as though nothing unusual was happening. I was also grateful for the space to cry, and I cried about that.

CHAPTER 45

I drove out of Seattle the next morning under a perfectly blue sky, and headed straight towards the white majesty of Mt. Rainer in the distance. The dream-version of the Pacific Northwest was in full effect that day. The hills were lush and green, the air was fresh and clean. Traffic was light and everyone was courteous.

If I belonged anywhere in the world where someone or something opened my heart, why was I driving away from such vibrant beauty? If I stayed in the Pacific Northwest, I could be close to friends and to mountains I loved.

Suddenly, I knew where I was going and why – I was moving to Portland to become a yoga instructor! The thought and the decision were simultaneous, like the realization of an established fact. I could teach yoga to pay off my debts, fall in love with Mt. Hood, find a room to rent and live happily ever after in Portland until the next adventure called. My heart beat faster with excitement. I assumed this meant a green light. As long as I followed my excitement, I knew that the Universe would provide me with exactly what I needed. I didn't have to reintegrate; I could integrate forward into a brand new life, more suited to whom I had become.

Once again my heart overflowed with gratitude and my eyes teared with joy. Within the excitement, I became aware of the tears. I had cried in gratitude when I left Margaret's apartment, when I first caught sight of Mt. Rainier and for every sign I passed that reminded me of the PCT. I sure cried a lot.

Although I didn't mean to reintegrate in the traditional sense, if Portland was to be my new home, a few adaptations would likely be necessary. I would need to shower more often, change clothes occasionally, wash my hands, pee indoors, and curtail this excessive emotional expression of my incessant gratitude while in public.

Luckily, my stay in Portland began with Hobbes, who required none of the common civilities, so I postponed adapting. Good, I didn't feel ready to be civilized yet anyway.

I recognized Hobbes's gait from two blocks away. The familiar confident stride with a slight lateral sway and a playful bounce finish were leading him straight to the street in front of the yurt where we had agreed to meet. We reached the address at the same time. I jumped out of the truck, leaving the door wide open, and ran across the street to jump in his arms.

"You're here!" His whiskers curled.

We walked hand and hand to the yurt talking excitedly about my move to Portland. The yurt was ours for ten more days, he said, which left plenty of time for serendipitous doors to open onto a sunny grass field of yoga teaching and Portland living opportunities.

I dropped my bag at the entrance of the yurt and let myself sink onto the mattress in the center of the room. The sounds of the noon traffic on Hawthorne Boulevard hinted at the fast-pace city life just a few blocks away, but in the yurt, peace and diffused sunlight reigned.

Hobbes lay next to me. Without concerted effort, our bodies found their most natural intertwined position, legs weaved and hands interlaced. We spoke no word. We simply enjoyed the sanctuary of our reunion, the reconnection of our physical forms. Sunlight through the partially translucent yurt illuminated the pink and orange draperies on the walls and ceiling, our very own One Thousand and One Nights palace for ten days.

I meant to kiss Hobbes then, but I was already asleep.

I have very little recollection of the first few days I spent in Portland because I slept through most of them. I knew, as I crossed the Canadian border, that I was tired, but I had underestimated the depth of fatigue my body had accumulated.

The yurt became my personal regeneration chamber. I slept in late every day, gorged on fresh, local, organic produce, napped and only on a few occasions ventured out into the bustle of Hawthorne Boulevard. When I did, I walked to the grocery store and back. I didn't stop in any store, coffee shop or restaurant. On a few occasions, I walked past the homeless hippies I had befriended a month prior, but they didn't recognize me. They asked if I could spare a dollar, and I could. A brief thank you and they had already, again, forgotten me.

Hobbes used my rest time to organize his own thousands of PCT photos and never failed to greet my return to the waking world with the gentlest kind of intimacy.

Without warning, five days had passed, and still I had taken no action towards establishing myself in Portland. I felt I didn't need to. I fully trusted that encounters and events would become manifest when the timing was right, and that the only action required on my part was to stay alert to potential opening doors. I assumed I would recognize an open door by the excitement I felt about the prospect of walking through it.

My heart felt safe, but my mind still wondered. Shouldn't I try a little harder to get a job? Shouldn't I be writing resumes? Or looking for ads in the paper? Or stress about my non-existent yet still dwindling funds? Invariably, my heart's answer was no. I could not make myself worry, not even when I tried as an exercise to see if I could.

I was, however, showing early signs of yurt fever. Until a week prior, I had been walking all day, every day, in pristine wilderness. Now that the collapsed stage of my convalescence had subsided, my body begged me to move. Indoor snuggles and strolls down Hawthorne Boulevard were simply not enough physical activity.

It was perfect! Instead of looking for work the traditional way, I could walk around the neighborhood in search of signs, serendipitous encounters and open doors. I felt such excitement at the prospect that I immediately set out on foot from the yurt in no particular direction.

Despite the lingering physical fatigue, I was still a well-oiled walking machine. In just a few days, I had covered every street in a twenty-block radius from the yurt. I knew all the garden gnomes, friendly cats and artistic stone walls in the neighborhood, and the straightest path to a small street-corner yoga studio with a "7 days for $15"new student deal.

I had practiced yoga on the trail whenever a suitably level meadow invited me to do so but still had lost much of my former yogic abilities. My muscle mass had been eaten for fuel, and my calves and legs were stiffer than steel. If I was to advertise myself as a yoga instructor, the least I could do was reshape myself to bend like one.

To my routine of walks, naps, salads and snuggles, I added a daily yoga class. I was so stiff during the first class that I couldn't even touch my callused toes, but with each session, my body released little bits of its steel scaffolding. I was still far from my Rishikesh abilities by the end of my trial membership, which coincided with the end of our yurt-sitting stint.

Less than twenty-four hours before Hobbes was to fly back east, leaving me yurtless and jobless in Portland, no magic had been performed yet. Like a spectator riveted to the suspense movie of my own life, I couldn't wait to see how the plot line would be resolved.

"I got a job in southern OR, but my roommate is out of town. Can you cat-sit and house-sit 'til he comes back?"

In the early morning of the day when Hobbes was to fly out, Mountain Buddha's text woke me up. I read it and smiled, then rolled over to find Hobbes under the covers and whispered in his ear: "It's taken care of." He smiled knowingly and whispered back "You're a textbook case."

It wasn't a job, but at least my stay was extended. Mountain Buddha lived only a few miles from the yurt, and from his house, I could continue my search for serendipity on foot.

A few hours later, however, as Hobbes and I were sitting in front of our last monstrous tomato basil balsamic vinaigrette salad, the plot thickened.

"Never mind." Mountain Buddha texted me, "Just got hired at local Portland bar. So not heading south. No longer need sitter. Sorry."

I texted back: "Can I have your job down south then?"

It was a silly question. Mountain Buddha was a bar tender; I had no bartending experience. And, besides, I was moving to Portland to become a yoga instructor. I watched myself send the text anyway with curious fascination.

"Maybe. Let me check." My eyes opened wide. That was not the answer I had expected. I showed the text on the screen to Hobbes. He shrugged and shook his head. He didn't know what the Universe was concocting either.

"Okay. You're in. You leave in half an hour. Contact Larkspur. You can follow her down."

Hobbes and I looked at each other intently and silently. The twists in the plot had delighted us, but the storyline was suddenly cutting our time together short, from ten hours to half an hour. Yet, we both knew I couldn't refuse this call. Even though I had no idea what stood behind serendipity door number one, it was the only door I could see open.

"No worries." Larkspur reassured me, "The work doesn't start until tomorrow. As long as you get there before eight am for the beginning of the training, you'll be fine. Your spot will be saved."

I never asked what I was trained or hired for, or how many "spots" there were. I had an intuition that my questions would not be answered until I got there anyway.

Ten days in Portland was the extent of my move there, just a brief passage into the regenerating hatching yurt.

I stood at the door of the yurt one last time in gratitude. I thanked it out loud for the quiet space, the comfortable bed and the opportunity to explore uninhibited heart-centered intimacy. This was just what I had needed. My post-trail peaceful exhaustion had been transmuted into functional vigor, and I was ready to work.

I pointed the truck south and drove through the night, feeling Hobbes's goodbye kiss still on my lips. Although we were physically separated again and had no plan for a next encounter, I felt no loss. Our connection was still constrained by neither time nor distance; it was enriched by the prospect of individual adventures ahead.

By three in the morning, I was still approximately an hour away from my destination. I was to meet a man at a gas station at seven in the morning and follow him to the job site. He insisted that the directions would be too complicated and that our meeting there simplified the process.

All the mystery made me giggle. The Universe was definitely having fun with this one, leading me on a treasure hunt to my next place of employment with still no clue about what I was actually hired to do, where, with whom, or why. I could definitely recognize the stamp of my own creation on this transaction. This was such a better storyline than finding a job in a paper, or even having a yoga studio offer me a teaching position.

I took a random exit off the freeway to catch a few hours of sleep before my first day at work – it could have been strenuous work, after all. A tall grove of willows lined the side of the off-ramp, and the shoulder opened onto a flat dirt lot. I imagined truckers likely used this space as a rest stop on their journey, but that night, it was all mine. I slid the truck under the willow curtain and stealthily crawled into the back of the truck. With my sleeping pad and sleeping bag directly on the bed of the truck and the high canopy shielded by the willow branches, I felt well out of view. I double-checked with my heart before turning my headlamp off and found nothing but safety, joy and trust.

I watched the stars through the back window of the truck until I fell asleep. I loved this unfolding story. I loved being a feral cat sleeping in the back of my truck by the side of a freeway on my way to solve a mystery. Whatever happened the next day, I already knew it wouldn't be any dreaded nine-to-five reintegration. Oh no – an adventure was coming. I could feel it.

CHAPTER 46

"Have you ever seen one of these before?" my new employer asked. His question was directed at a particular plant, a ten-foot tall Blue Dream marijuana plant.

"I have" I said casually.

I had, indeed, seen a marijuana plant before, when I was in my early teens. It was my own.

A friend at school had given me a seed, I think mostly as a ploy to seduce me. He must have been clued in to my predilection to fall for mavericks, and nothing says "unconventional" louder than illegal activities. I had no interest in selling or smoking any of it, but in my curious naivete, placed the seed in water to see if it would grow. It did. When it reached a height of about five inches, I transplanted it behind my mother's ferns in the garden thinking it would blend in and grow unnoticed for a while. I was wrong. I returned from school that day to find my baby plant in a glass on the kitchen table.

"Why did you get my little fern out of the ground?" I asked my mother in a preemptive casual tone.

"How stupid do you think I am?" ended that conversation.

My punishment was to watch it slowly desiccate into a gnarled twig over the course of a few days. Watching it die broke my heart. This was the first and last plant I ever grew and the last marijuana plant I had seen before my first day on the farm in Oregon.

In truth though, I had never seen anything like these plants. These were not just plants; they were voluminous, sticky, fragrant, luxuriant beings with a vigorous energetic presence palpable tens of feet away, a whole small forest of them.

I asked if I could walk through the plants to see the different strands I would be working on in an attempt to conceal my amazement. Larkspur had warned me that the owners weren't pleased with the last minute personnel switch. This was not the kind of place in which to bring a random rooky. I knew I would be under scrutiny until I could make a good impression.

I walked into the heart of the small forest until I was out of sight and let my jaw drop. The energy of the plants enveloped me. The humans weren't the only ones sizing my appropriateness for the task. I felt energetic tendrils palpate my heart with gentle curiosity, then a flash of recognition, and I was held in a motherly, loving green embrace – Mother Nature recognizing its own. Time held its breath for a second as I returned to stillness to meet the plants in that realm as well. I was still aware that the team was waiting for me to start the training, so I closed my eyes and let the sensation absorb throughout my body as an instant imprint of communion. I could have left right then, and the experience of my visit to the farm would have been worthwhile, but I had no other place to be and working on a marijuana farm seemed surreal enough to appeal to me, so I stayed.

As a provider of organic, medical marijuana, the operation was legal, I was told, but still, I was to be discreet. I wasn't the only thru-hiker working there. Thru-hikers are the perfect workforce for a marijuana farm. We are used to long physical days, require nothing but a small patch of level grass, come fully self-sufficient in living gear and skills and have effectively fallen off the world's radar for several months.

Sneaking through Bellingham unnoticed helped in preventing me from having to lie. Only a few friends and my dad asked where I was and what I was doing. Most people assumed I was still on the trail, if they thought about me at all.

"I work on an organic farm in Oregon. It is pear season." was my official answer. I could smugly retreat behind the excuse that both these statements were true, and that I never implied they were related. I laughed with Sofia when she joked about her friend the migrant worker. I was migrant and a worker, even if I didn't match her mental picture of a migrant worker. I also laughed in anticipation at her surprise the next time we would see each other in person and I could reveal what was in fact behind door number one.

I took to the work right away, in part because I had already fallen in love with the plants, but also because I worked outside, in the sun, with a cast of well-traveled eclectic characters. We were not migrant workers; we were swarming locusts. As each plant was trimmed down to buckets of marketable buds under our rapid scissors, the transformation from luxuriant to naked seemed almost instantaneous. When night fell, the buckets were brought in, the music volume cranked, and the scissors continued snipping bud after bud after bud until the harvest for the day was fully groomed into an infinity of small smokeable art pieces.

"She's a good one!" one of the seasoned trimmers said about me to the boss sometime around eleven at night on the first day. After fifteen hours of trimming, on less than three hours of sleep, I showed no sign of fading. Nobody questioned my place on the farm after that first day.

The pay was good, the hours were long – our shortest day was twelve hours, our longest one seventeen. We all understood that when the plants are ready, the window of opportunity for superior quality is only a couple of days, and that the harvest season itself is only a couple of weeks. In two weeks, we, the locusts, had devoured most of the plants at four associated farms.

I giggled my way through the first week. I didn't use the drug myself, so the perk of free marijuana was irrelevant, but the potential for tall tales was irresistible. Just the thought that I had quit a fully-funded PhD in Geophysics to become a locust/migrant-worker on a marijuana farm struck me as hilarious.

I spoke to Hobbes every day after work and shared with him all the delights of my new employment in code that I knew he understood yet that revealed neither incriminating facts nor locations. Speaking in code amused me as well.

Although I loved working at the farm, in the end, the music broke me. I could flow through the long hours, the back-loading repetitive work and the complete surrender of any volition to the directives of the boss. But, after five and a half months of natural silence, the loud gangsta' rap and soulless electronic music overwhelmed my system, even with ear-plugs.

By the second week, I began dreading the evening trimming sessions. I had grown fond of my employers and coworkers and understood that I was a minority in my need for a quiet workspace, so I chose to not complain. I reasoned that I could endure anything for a short period of time and always had the option of retreating into internal stillness.

As the harvest dwindled, fewer workers were needed after dark anyway. I often volunteered to clock out early, allowing others the larger paycheck, and returned to my home-farm, the farm where my tent was set.

The grower at my home-farm was a woman whose code name in my conversations with Hobbes was The Goddess. And she was, to the extent of my imagination, the perfect embodiment of an Earth Goddess. Other growers' plants were beautiful, but none had the vibrancy of the Goddess's.

As often as I could, I left the trimming noise to the boys and relaxed on the Goddess's patio in the evenings. It only took a few conversations for us to recognize we belonged to the same soul tribe.

She lamented the loud soulless music as well, such a harsh environment for plants that had, up to that point, been revered as the sacred beings they are. The Goddess spoke to her plants, and listened to them. The plants let her know what they needed at each stage of their growth. She also protected them from natural and human calamities. She often had to chase thieves off her property with a loaded gun. The dangers and stress inherent in growing marijuana didn't daunt her. She believed that the essence of her true purpose as an incarnated being was to experience life as it unfolds. Growing marijuana was simply the form of the experience. She understood her own timelessness and multidimensionality. She also spoke with angels when she needed guidance, and on many a summer night had recorded extraterrestrial spacecrafts flying over her farm.

The Goddess spoke my language, and I knew that our connection would outlast the end of that year's harvest.

The end of the year's harvest came quickly, and not a moment too soon. By the beginning of the third week, my lower back ached, my throat was coarse and a sharp pain directly below my right shoulder blade sucked all the giggles out of trimming. When Larkspur asked if I could give her a ride to a hot springs resort in exchange for free soaking, I knew the next step in my journey had been revealed.

With a fat envelope full of cash, a triple-bagged load of hash-impregnated laundry and an open invitation for the following year's harvest season, I pointed the truck north and gratefully left the farm.

By the miracle of healing minerals in the hot springs, all aches disappeared from my body within two days of soaking. On the morning of the third day, I became dizzy in the water after a mere ten-minute soak.

"You are done now." the little pool said, "So, go on."

I didn't argue. I hugged Larkspur goodbye and left the resort for some unknown destination.

With $3,000 in cash under my truck's seat, I no longer felt bound by any need to reintegrate. As a feral roaming cat, my only monthly expenses were fuel, food, phone and storage unit. Although my farming income was not sufficient to pay off my credit card debt, I could, if I paid only the minimum fee each month and charged nothing further, stretch my cash over several months. I assumed that soul-fulfilling and bank-account-replenishing activities would appear before the cash completely disappeared. It was an easy leap of faith compared to others I had taken.

I drove the truck to the end of the resort access road, right to the 'T'. I felt no special pull in either direction, so I sat at idle for a few minutes in attentive curiosity to see which way the truck would flow.

Just then, my phone rang. The tone startled me. I didn't think I had reception this far out in the woods. The call was from Marine, a friend from Bellingham who had never called me before. I knew even before I took the call that the ensuing conversation would lead me to my next destination.

"Hey Mel, Yogoman Burning Band is playing at the Frog for Halloween. Do you want to come with me to the show?"

I certainly did, and not just because of the synchronicity of Marine's phone call. Yogoman Burning Band was my favorite band at the time. Unlike the harsh, forceful beats to which I had been subjected at the farm, Yogoman Burning Band's songs were like droplets of concentrated danceable joy.

Before the call was over, I had already pointed the truck north, Bellingham-bound.

CHAPTER 47

10/31/2012 – Bellingham, WA
Excerpt from The Roaming Bobcat's blog
Titled "Flow: an interview with the Bobcat" [edited for length]
We join the Bobcat on this rainy Halloween for a status update and
reality check. A jasmine tea brewing, Railroad Ave. as weird as we had
left it, laptop is plugged in and ready. Let's catch up.

> Good morning Bobcat, it has been a while since you last wrote and
> some of your readers might be wondering about your whereabouts.
> How is your post-PCT reintegration into real life going?

Well, Bobcat, since I am both asking the questions and answering them,
this might be a bit of a redundant interview, but as you know, I am not
reintegrating.

> You mean you are resisting reintegration?

No, I mean I don't believe in "reintegration". Reintegration implies that
the trail was an adventure outside of what you just called "real life" rather
than an integral part of it. I think some people might feel this way because
on the trail a certain flow is established that seems unnatural, almost
magical. This is reflected in the terminology. On the trail, we speak of
Trail Magic when our needs are fulfilled effortlessly, of Trail Angels when
strangers show us kindness and so forth. I believe that the magical quality
of the trail is actually a quality intrinsic to life; it's just that on the trail
people expect it and are therefore more attuned to it. Even pragmatic
hikers who argue vehemently that magic doesn't exist believe in trail magic.
So, rather than "reintegration" to some separate, less magical reality, I am
living my post-trail life as an extension of my trail life.

> Mmh. Interesting. So, what does "living a trail life" actually mean
> in the day to day?

The basic premise is a blind trust that all is well, all is as it should be, I
am always exactly where I am supposed to be, and the Universe is
benevolent and loving in all situations.

> It seems if all is always well and you are always exactly where you
> are supposed to be that you easily could be stuck somewhere.
> Wouldn't you lack motivation to grow and explore if you are always
> content with where you are?

If that were the case, I would not be The Roaming Bobcat, now would I? One aspect of trail life is to follow one's heart. "Heart" is a cat with many names: Universe, Spirit, Inner-voice, Higher Self, Intuition, etc. We actually know what we need, even when we don't know that we know. If it were right for me, I would feel great joy at staying put, but as it is, my own heart, in recent times (everything always changes, including this sentence), has found its greatest joy in random meanderings.

    I see we are going to have one of those "higher" conversations this morning. Would you take it down a notch and give us some examples?

Sure. You want specifics … While I was on the trail, I really longed to be back in Bellingham. I felt it was my home. When I pulled into Bellingham the day after finishing the trail, however, I felt a clear pull to continue south. Many times on the trail I felt that my heart was inadequately small to hold the magnitude of joy I felt. This is how I felt on the drive down to Portland. I was moving to Portland to become a yoga instructor there and felt absolutely sure that it was the right move.

    But that's not what happened, right?

No, as indicated by my presence here, that is not what happened. I had a lovely time in Portland but at no point did I feel a drive or excitement for yoga job searching. I resisted the urge to judge myself for this, even after balancing my checkbook and discovering that my credit card was maxed out. The trail cost me a lot more than I had anticipated.

    This doesn't sound like a "need fulfilled" sort of situation…

Our lower earth-bound-selves are not in a position to judge what needs are fulfilled in most situations. The fact that I have little money is a perfect backdrop to test out the hypothesis that my needs will be fulfilled without any pain on my part if I just believe they will. I am not very receptive to subtleties, so it is easier for me to see the inner-workings of the Universe in contrast to a dire financial situation, if that makes sense.

    So you are planning to continue roaming even though the cash you earned at the farm isn't enough to cover your credit card debt?

Money will come to me whether I roam or not. I think that free-will really only applies to the world of form. I mean, we create our own reality with our conscious and unconscious intents and as a reflection of the energy with which we resonate. Within the physical forms we create, our underlying needs are fulfilled. I will not be financially broke because I do not dwell in "financially broke" energy, so whichever way I choose to go, the Universe matches me. I think that is essentially how manifesting works, but I'm just experimenting, as I said earlier. And it could all fail, and I could go broke, and that's fine. I'll keep on assuming that things will work out until proven otherwise.

So, do you have any intent to work at all? Any wishes for a money making activity?

I am not opposed to working, but I seem to always get my wishes, often with unforeseen twists, so I am trying to neither create nor decide anything. I feel that way the Universe has free reign, unbound by my potentially misguided earthly wishes. I am bypassing the "be careful what you wish for, you might get it" quandary.

And how is that working out for you?

Not so well, actually. It turns out that my brain is a mad wishing machine. I have a hundred dreams a minute. The less I know where I am going and what I am doing, the more I come up with plans to fill the void.

But isn't forcing a void a form of resistance? Shouldn't you accept the fact that you have plans, dreams and wishes?

Maybe. As I said, I'm experimenting. I don't really know how it works. All I know is that I wake up every day with peace and gratitude in my heart. Maybe plans, dreams and wishes are like thoughts; they should be observed but not taken to be absolute truths. Or maybe our conscious dreams are irrelevant, and our unconscious dreams are those being fulfilled. If that is the case, my time is better used looking for signs reflecting my unconscious than in active planning or deciding. Or maybe I'm just completely out of touch with reality. It's all good by me. I'm just learning.

And this perfect life, do you plan on continuing living it solo or are you looking for a life-mate, or do you have someone in heart already? Some of your readers have been wondering and trying to find clues in between the lines.

Ah, yes ... Oh, look at the time! I was supposed to meet Marine thirty minutes ago. Sorry, that's all I have time for. It was nice chatting with you. Love to you. More soon ...

I waited for signs from the Universe for three days after this post on my blog.

I found a theme-appropriate seventies hippy costume in which to exultantly dance the night away at the Yogoman Burning Band show and spent the rest of that night at Marine's apartment. But the next night, I couldn't find any place to sleep. Calls were lost, friends were out of town, or they had company, or prior engagements. I expected some serendipitous phone call or encounter to show me the next step, but none came. After driving around town aimlessly for several hours, I parked in an absent friend's driveway for the night, crawled into the back of the truck and resigned myself to a cold strange night under the neon glow of a sidewalk streetlight. I would have much preferred a willow grove along the freeway.

I woke up the next morning to a bleak November sky from a dream about Logan. The longer I stayed in Bellingham, the more I ran the risk of an encounter with him. He was likely out of town on Halloween or he would have been at the show. Logan loved Yogoman Burning Band as much as I did. I had known this going in, but my intuition had assured me that he would not be there. My intuition wasn't so clear anymore.

I shook the dream off and drove to a coffee shop to warm up. I observed myself hide in a corner and nervously gaze towards the door whenever a new customer entered. Logan likely still drank coffee, and this coffee shop had been one of his favorites. Hiding in a corner felt ridiculous, so I asked for a to-go cup for the rest of my tea and left.

Another day went by and still there was no sign from the Universe, no indication of what my next best step should be. I drove aimlessly around town, avoiding the main arteries in case Logan had returned. He occupied my mind all day. I was aware that I feared my nascent desire to see him more than I feared actually seeing him. As long as I wasn't tested, I could pretend that I could resist him. Doubt was preferable to the potential certitude that I couldn't.

I struggled to keep my mind filled with memories of heart-based companionships and clear any thought of Logan lest I unwittingly manifest an encounter.

Being in Bellingham began to feel oppressive, and if I had known where to go, I would have left.

In the afternoon of my third day in Bellingham, mostly to occupy myself, I visited my storage unit. I was much happier to see my treasures than I had been immediately after the trail. I gathered several thick camping pads, a feather mattress topper that had once graced my marital bed, a down duvet, a soft pillow, a wooden crate with a few books and a small duffel bag of winter clothes. If I was to be a homeless person in the back of the truck, at least I would be a warm homeless person from that point forth.

I drove back to my friend's driveway to find that a neighbor had parked there for the night, so I parked in the street, some distance from the streetlight, and once again crawled into the back. Because sleeping in the street was still awkward to me back then, I didn't dare use my headlamp to read. I lay motionless in my sleeping bag hoping to quickly fall asleep and have that day be over. I was starting to seriously question my claim that I was always exactly where I was meant to be.

A full bladder woke me up at three in the morning. It was drizzling. I rummaged through my duffel bag for a rain coat and climbed out to the quiet street.

That was the turning point. I couldn't find anything giggle-worthy about peeing on the sidewalk in this irritating little rain in a town that clearly no longer welcomed me. I still meant to give the Universe free reign, but in the absence of any sign at all, I decided that it was alright to decide just this one time, and my decision was to leave town at the first light of day.

The sun hadn't even broken the line of the foggy horizon when the last exit for Bellingham disappeared from my rear-view mirror.

A few miles before Seattle, the fog lifted to reveal a heavy sky of rain-pregnant clouds. Only one break in the clouds opened to the blue beyond, to the sun above, and my truck happened to be in perfect alignment with it. As soon as the sun reached my face, any lingering doubts I had about the validity of my place in the Universe instantly dissipated.

I was grateful for the irritating little rain and the sickly glow of the streetlight that had finally shaken me into action. I didn't know where I was going, but the rib-expanding joy and gratitude in my heart had returned, so I trusted that wherever I landed, I would be matched and met with nothing but joy- and gratitude-inducing experiences.

CHAPTER 48

I recognized Sofia's high heel boots' distinctive staccato before I saw her. I reached for my duffle bag in the back of the truck and hurried to meet her with a gleeful bound every couple of steps.

She was a vision, as always. Her long black trench coat cinched at the waist revealed just enough of the playful colors on her dress, and her long hair flowed behind her like a deep brown veil, apparently impervious to wind or rain.

We met half way between the gate to her apartment complex and my truck for a full body embrace. I lifted her off the ground slightly and we both laughed.

"Can I help you carry anything?" She noticed my small duffel bag. "I swear, every time you visit, your bag gets smaller."

"And yet I still have all I need."

"You're correct! You don't need anything because I'll take care of you. How long are you staying?"

"I don't know. Until it's time to go."

She laughed and took my arm under hers as we walked to the gate. "Perfect."

In no time, Sofia had filled the air mattress in her living room, fluffed a couple of pillows, and dressed my new bed with the usual luxuriously soft sheets and warm blankets. She then selected out of her collection a leather jacket to complement my blue jeans and drove us to a small hidden gem of an Ethiopian restaurant in downtown Seattle.

Immersed in the delight of our reunion and the spiced

aroma of beans, meats and vegetables on our shared plate of injera, I couldn't imagine having ever been out of sync with Sofia, however temporarily. Although our lifestyles were diametric opposites, our underlying learning, healing and exploring was identical.

The checkout error on Sofia's expired Nordstrom gift card that allowed her to purchase a classy fabulous coat at the fraction of its cost represented the same magic, the same thought-creation process, as the appearance of a brand new bottle of Gold Bond on the trail when I began chaffing.

The dream she had about a former lover assuring her that he supported any experience she chose to pursue, including that of connecting with other men, strangely mirrored the heart-based connection I had experienced with Hobbes.

Sofia also trusted signs from the Universe, followed her vehicle to surprise destinations, extended her conscious awareness to the city surrounding her effortlessly, and occasionally cried in gratitude when her heart overflowed with love.

I finally understood why she had not cared to hear about the dirty trail, the bears, the hitchhiking, the stars, the perfectly clear natural springs or any trail romance when I visited her in Portland. It wasn't that she had not found my journey remarkable; she simply had remembered what I had temporarily forgotten – that the thru-hiking superhero-cape-wearing Bobcat was merely a role I played, a personality I had chosen to experience for a set span of time, a fun personality very much in line with the highest expression of my true self, but in no way superior to another.

Sofia had little interest in the role or in the stories associated with it. Her own Storyteller was a minimalist. She thrived in bottom lines and lessons learned.

I was aware throughout our meal, and later as we nestled on Sofia's sofa with mugs of herbal tea, of hundreds of stories lurking in the forefront of my mind and on the tip of my tongue, all vying for release. If I let just one flow, I feared the ensuing tidal wave would wash away my audience of one, so I let Sofia lead the conversation. Through careful questioning and tactful containing, she weeded through hundred of lessons of lesser importance to reveal the crown jewel of my PCT experience, that sense of timelessness, stillness, immense joy and ultimate freedom I called Trail High.

"That's your home frequency. How wonderful that you could dwell in it so often!"

"What's 'home frequency'?"

"It's your highest vibrational frequency, what you emit when other clouding energies have been cleared. It's like your personal version of pure love."

She pointed to the book on her coffee table. "I experience it often, but I had no term for it until I read ..."

My eyebrows lifted in surprise "Is that *Frequency* by Penney Peirce?"

This was not my first encounter with *Frequency*.

During the Intensive Sunday School for the Rebellious, Sofia and I came upon *Frequency* in a bookstore in downtown Seattle. Its existence upset me. I then assumed that *I* would write a book about vibrational frequencies. I felt that I was uniquely suited to the task. I was a scientist with an open line of communication with the Unseen and journals filled with lessons on the topic. If the book I assumed I would write already existed, what was I supposed to write?

Sofia laughed at my reaction and called me "silly". She suggested I sit with *Frequency* in a comfortable chair in the bookstore and suspend my preconceptions long enough to see if the book called to me. Maybe I was to write a different kind of book on vibrational frequencies, and this book could serve as one of my sources.

I placed the book on my lap and relaxed my mind to that state of openness in which I received answers from my Higher Self. Was this book for me? I heard no answer. I decided that if I opened the book randomly to a page relevant to my life or journey, I would buy it. I opened it to a page with a graph. The graph looked simplistic and not engaging in any way. I immediately closed the book and replaced it on the shelf.

"This book isn't for me." I told Sofia, "but, maybe you should read it."

"No, I prefer learning these lessons from you, with pinecones in the bay."

She took my arm playfully and we walked out of the store empty-handed and regret-free.

But, the book wasn't done with us yet.

While I was on the trail, it found its way into the hands of Sofia's mother, who read it and loved it. She loved it so much that she bought Sofia her own copy. Sofia assumed that if the book had appeared on her path a second time, she probably should read it. She read it and loved it. So, a year had passed, and it was my turn to consider the book anew.

I lay the book on my lap and once again opened it to a random page. The book opened to the title "How a Relationship Can Oscillate Harmoniously". On the opposite page, a set of sketches illustrated how to shift from a pattern of opposition to one of harmonious flow in a relationship. I read the entire page, and then backtracked to the beginning of the chapter. Where had this book been a year earlier when I was still in the throes of Logan drama? I really could have used that information then.

Out of curiosity, I searched for the graph that had prompted my decision to not purchase it the first time. That graph probably existed in a parallel universe version of the book I then held in my hand, but in my current reality, it was nowhere to be found.

"Sofia, I need to read this!"

She smiled and pointed to the book still in my hands. "I thought so. Keep this one. I know that you won't buy it. I can pick up another copy for myself."

I placed *Frequency* next to my bed in the living room, expecting I'd be eager to read it right away, but for the few days I spent at Sofia's, I was not moved to pick it up again.

I was not moved to do much else either. I slept in late, practiced yoga, prepared dinner for Sofia and walked around town looking for signs of my next best step.

From Sofia's apartment, because of the layout of the freeways in Washington, my choices were really only to continue south or east. I had no desire to roam north into Canada in winter. Although no specific outward sign appeared, after a few days of aimless roaming the sidewalks of the city, I began to sense a physical pull eastward. This also made sense to my cognitive mind, I had already driven south, only to come right back.

The sense of certitude about my next destination increased gradually over the course of a day to full-blown excitement. Yes, east! I could go to Montana and visit Jimmy. I could even drive to Minneapolis, just in time for Darcy's Birthday and for Thanksgiving at LB's.

"Bobcat! How the hell are ya?" Jimmy always began his conversations that way. I had spoken with him a few times from the trail and had officially been upgraded from Hula Girl to Bobcat. I loved the upgrade.

"No way! You're coming to Livingston? I'm in Arizona for a few weeks, but you know the door's open. Haha! Make yourself at home for however long. Tell the ghosts I said hello."

"I'll warn my Mom to make extra." LB laughed.

"One of the rooms just opened in the Arthur house, if you want to rent it and stay for a while. I can't wait to see you!" Darcy added.

So, for the second time in my life story, I left Sofia's apartment in the early morning, with a kiss, a hug and a new inspirational spiritual book, eastward-bound to Minneapolis where a room was waiting for me, with a planned stop of a week at Jimmy's in Livingston. The similarities were peculiar, but I knew that this was a new journey.

As I drove away from Seattle over Snoqualmie Pass, a sentence I once wrote in my journal reverberated in my mind: "All paths flow towards enlightenment, but sometimes loops might be necessary before the journey can continue. These are actually not loops but upward spirals."

CHAPTER 49

I drove through the Palouse of eastern Washington as though for the first time, and because it knew that it was noticed, it exaggerated.

How could I have missed such breathtaking beauty on my prior passage? The freeway meandered through long geometric rows of golden brown crop stems sketched on rolling hills. Old barns in various stages of dilapidation dotted the fields like wooden exclamation marks. The hundred mile postcard was complete with a light dusting of snow on this hill, a low hanging wispy mist on that one, and rainbows – rainbows everywhere.

The further east I drove, the darker the sky became. Montana, big sky country, was capped by an ominous ceiling, but neither the truck nor I worried about it. The massive dark clouds in the distance only accentuated the evening's golden light on the open plains by contrast. I thanked the sky and the plains out loud for their beauty. My heart hummed a perfect home frequency – freedom, joy and preemptive gratitude for the experiences up ahead.

I snuck in Jimmy's house through the garage and landed in a vivid déjà-vu in the silence of the living room.

There were subtle differences. The Christmas tree in the corner was gone, Al-the-alien had moved to the front porch and a different assortment of books were stacked by Jimmy's favorite chair. It didn't matter. I could not shake the feeling that time had collapsed and that I stood at the same threshold, the same gateway to the unknown, as I did two years prior.

Throughout the week, I tried laying in the opposite direction on the sofa and moved my sleeping bag and pillow from the guest bedroom to Jimmy's room. There were no ghostly drums in Jimmy's room, but the creaking and cracking of the house kept me awake just the same. I ate in a different chair and never once sat at the kitchen table where I had written portions of my master's thesis. No physical change made any difference. The déjà-vu was pervasive and persistent.

Because I no longer conceived of enlightenment as a goal or destination, I was not distressed by the apparent backtracking. If I had returned to this place of power, as indicated by the déjà-vu, I was likely ready to climb upward to the next level on my spiritual spiral of growth.

The manual for this transition had appeared just in time.

I read *Frequency* on the same sofa and by the light of the same lamp as I had read *The Power of Now*. I read compulsively, in the bedroom, living room, kitchen and bathroom. I read while shuffling down the corridor like one of the house ghosts and occasionally turned too soon into the wall or a door frame.

The first part of the book detailed the usual stages of the awakening process – from the discovery of a reality beyond the world of forms, through the dramatic and erratic release of emotions, the exploration of dark corners of the psyche, the dissolving of old worldviews, and finally into the joyful silence and stillness of the Now.

I recognized these steps, and understood why the book had not called to me the first time I encountered it. Had I read it earlier, I would have surmised that a seed of self-fulfilling prophecy was planted in my subconscious and always doubted the genuineness of my awakening. Instead, I had found the steps on my own and added flare to the process to make it story-worthy because it suited my current personality.

I had traveled so far, learned so much, flown so freely and felt such joy, and yet, according to Peirce, my awakening had only just begun.

I had found my home frequency. The next step entailed updating all areas of my life to match this frequency. I could work more passionately, love more sincerely, build, grow and flow more organically. I could manifest a harmonious relationship or anything else I desired. I could even, eventually, develop paranormal abilities such as levitation, telekinesis and telepathy.

Peirce offered exercises in each chapter to hone one's energetic skills. Some were designed specifically to practice manifesting a preferred reality, but most were simply tools to deepen awareness through conscious sensitivity. I tried them all.

I carefully read the steps for meditative visualization and the account of the author's personal experience with it. Peirce and a friend had sat face to face, eyes closed to visualize a certain large sum of money. They had imagined the smell, touch and look of this money in the space between them, and held the image vividly in their minds. They then had completely released the idea. A few months later, both had received exactly the sum they had visualized.

I sat on Jimmy's bed in cross-legged lotus position with my eyes closed eager to try this visualization, but could not find anything I wished to manifest. I didn't need a large sum of money; I still had the greater part of $3,000 tucked under my truck's seat. I didn't need a relationship; as a single woman, I was free to roam. I didn't need anything, so I decided to manifest a cookie, just to practice.

In the space before me, I visualized the most perfect chocolate chip cookie, with a moist body and large chunks of tasty dark chocolate morsels. I imagined it so crisply that I became hungry. I immediately ended the exercise, jumped off the bed and walked to the store at the end of the street.

The only chocolate chip cookies the store carried were a packaged generic brand in which I had no interest. I was puzzled rather than disappointed.

I left the store empty-handed, but on the way home, a small side street caught my attention. I had walked to the store dozens of times, but never before had I noticed this side street. My feet turned onto it and straight to a little store where a soft-spoken elderly lady sold therapeutic honey. She gave me a tour of the available flavors and their infused healing agents. I chose a cacao infused honey to stay with the theme of my quest.

Had my visualization experiment failed or succeeded beyond my imaginings? I scooped another nugget out of the jar with my finger and shrugged. Regardless, it was delicious. I'd likely need another jar before I left Livingston.

On another day, I tried deepening my conscious energetic

sensitivity by learning to "feel into" inanimate objects, people or situations. First, because I felt it would be easier than with larger or living entities, I tried feeling into the sofa. Peirce suggested that by merging consciousness with a sofa, you could feel its desires – new foam for its cushions, for example – but either Jimmy's sofa was silent or I could not hear it. I had slightly better luck with the house plant, but only learned that it needed water, which I could have inferred from its pale color. From my truck, I felt deep love and loyal companionship, but this is how I felt about it, so I could have been projecting. Sofia felt wise and witty, Hobbes gentle and complex. These were all energies I could infer from the flow of our daily conversations. I needed to feel into somebody with whom I hadn't spoken in a while, yet whom I knew well enough to gauge the accuracy of my energetic reading.

The image of Logan's piercing green eyes floated up to the forefront of my mind, and a small electric pang sparked in the pit of my stomach. Feeling into Logan was akin to playing with fire, and I knew it, but he was by far the best subject for this experiment. I was safe anyway. The exercise was in my mind. I wouldn't actually be interacting with him.

With rising excitement, I returned to a lotus cross-legged position on Jimmy's bed and followed my breath until my mind was clear. I brought up the image of Logan and left a wide open space around it in which to perceive his energy. I remembered Logan's energy as intense and tumultuous, but in the open space I sensed lightness and a hint of mischievousness. Was I projecting? Was I reading a deeper level of Logan's energy than I had previously perceived? Or had Logan's life changed so drastically while I was on the trail that his energy was transformed?

I shifted my focus to a mental image of us, together but in the present time, and opened a space to perceive the energy of our relationship in its current form.

I was knocked backwards by the force of the incoming energy. It was massive – a multidimensional, multi-incarnations, complex entanglement branded with the stamp of meant-to-be, of victory-against-all-odds, of larger-than-life exceptionality. That energy exploded out of the open mental space and grabbed my heart with both hands. It reverberated throughout my body as loudly as my most attuned home frequency.

Oh sweet addiction! That was the exact moment when I decided to call Logan.

CHAPTER 50

"Melissa Wyld." Logan enunciated his first words to me in six months very carefully, "What is the definition of insanity?"

"Doing the same thing over and over again and expecting different results?" I answered hesitantly.

"Riiiight. So, why are you calling me?"

I had spent the whole day pondering the same question.

The night prior, in a flash of wisdom, I remembered that I had chosen to let the flow of Life guide me. I was not deciding anything. If I couldn't manifest a cookie, I certainly wasn't ready to manifest a healthy relationship. What I could do, however, was withhold preconceptions born of previous experiences with Logan and instead open my heart and mind in the Now to signs leading either away from or towards him, and then act accordingly.

In the morning, before breakfast, I asked a brand new deck of oracle cards what they thought of the situation. The Dragon's Lair was their answer:

Dragon's Lair – Enchanted Map Oracle Cards [edited for length]
"You are about to enter dangerous territory, so tread carefully. Red flags shouldn't be ignored. Don't be seduced into learning a lesson that will only hurt your heart. Your longing has neither substance nor longevity. Choose another path, for your treasures lie elsewhere."

For a first reading, I felt the cards were rather opinionated. The natural flow of Life is gentle and effortless. I believed there was no such thing as dangerous territories, only experiences. The message was unsettling nonetheless, so I turned to my Higher Self, to whom I had not specifically written since the PCT.

11/11/2012
Excerpt from my journal
Dear Love,
If I call, is there any way that Logan and I are not doomed?
The card only indicates a probable future based on your current unconscious beliefs. The card reflects you. You unconsciously believe that you are doomed, but your unconscious is not your Self, not your Soul; it is a representation of acquired patterns. And you are here specifically to dismantle these patterns. The card is not to your liking? Center yourself and do not react to it as you have reacted to bad omens in the past. Thus starts the breaking of patterns that no longer serve you.

My Higher Self was right. As long as I held unconscious beliefs, I would continue to unwittingly create potentially unpleasant realities. I saw that I was teetering on the edge of the abyss of old patterns, and that my mind was enticing me to jump. Before trustworthy signs could appear, I needed to clear these old patterns.

I took my quandary down to the Yellowstone River, right to the apex of a bend in the river where I liked to meditate. I extended both palms upward and closed my eyes. A fine mist engulfed me, a gentle river greeting on my face.

"Good morning, beautiful River. I am here to release patterns that no longer serve me. Please allow me to let them flow away like your water. And in the space that is created, please allow me to see the signs I need to see. Thank you."

I opened my eyes and carefully scanned the river from shore to shore, upstream and downstream. The signs were ambiguous. The stagnant eddy by the shore warned me of unfruitful returns to old places, but the choppy white water in the center reminded me that peril is exhilarating, and that by the essence of my personality I was unlikely to choose safety.

In the early afternoon, I called Sofia. Her perspective had often expanded and clarified my field of vision of a situation and I hoped she'd speak exactly the words I needed to hear.

She listened carefully to my dilemma and to the list of evidence for and against calling Logan I had collected thus far. She confided that she had expected the Logan story thread to continue by the way I still spoke of him. She could also sense the energy of meant-to-be, of victory-against-all-odds about our relationship, though she could have been reading my own energetic interpretation of our relationship. In the end, her advice was the same as it always was – "Follow your heart."

I could follow my heart in most things, but not in matters that concerned Logan. When it came to him, the frantic flapping of the lust butterfly wings created too much disturbance to get a good read on a clear heart.

Or was that yet another hidden belief, another misconception, another dramatic arc in my Logan story?

I had struggled to make decisions in the past, especially decisions that involved taking leaps of faith, but not deciding was just as difficult. The hidden beliefs and acquired patterns that had blindly guided my decision making process up that point could so easily and insidiously pass for common sense. Common sense's opinion was that calling Logan fell under the category of doing the same thing over and over again and expecting different results, the very definition of insanity.

I saw my answer in a flash of understanding. Of course! Common sense assumed a stagnant system with predictable causality, but I was not a stagnant system; I was an evolving being. I was not doing the same thing over and over again; I was using a known benchmark to measure my progress. My approach was in fact very logical and scientific. If indeed I had climbed up a rung on my spiritual spiral of growth, then calling Logan from my new position was a first-time act. Common sense, therefore, did not apply, but curiosity certainly did.

In the early evening, before calling Logan, I carefully reread the chapter on building harmonious relationships in *Frequency*. I cooked a wholesome dinner, danced and sang in the kitchen, drank a full mug of green tea and relaxed on the sofa for a few minutes. Finally, I picked up my phone from the coffee table and mentally checked that my safety belt was properly fastened.

I dialed Logan's number. I still knew it by heart.

With each ringtone, the rollercoaster train clicked a little higher, and my heart beat a little harder. This was a first-time act, but all common sense hidden beliefs throughout my body were waving red flags in a loving yet misguided attempt to protect me from myself.

"Melissa Wyld. What is the definition of insanity?" I had expected he would say something of the sort.

"Doing the same thing over and over again and expecting different results?" Logan lived in a common sense world. I didn't think he'd understand that he had never spoken with this version of me before. It was best I simply follow conversation conventions until I could demonstrate the change.

"Riiiight. So, why are you calling?"

"I just wanted to talk to you. I wanted to hear your voice." At least, this much was true. I had always loved Logan's deep bass voice.

"You are so selfish!" He suddenly sounded furious.

"You barge into my life with no consideration for my preferences. What if I don't want to talk to you? And why do you want to hear my voice now, why not last month, or the one before, or the one before that? Huh? Was it too inconvenient to call me until now? Did you just now get lonely? What the hell, Mel?"

The rollercoaster's first drop felt like free-falling. Logan was furious that I didn't call when I finished the trail, furious for my misspoken words, careless acts, judgmental thoughts, for every time I kicked him to the curb and abandoned him, for every time I returned under the arrogant assumption he would take me back and for every time I callously broke his heart, starting with this phone call and working back to the first time we ever locked eyes. In fact, he would have been much happier had we never met.

I held my breath and the space for him to express himself. I didn't argue. I just listened. I consciously let my heart be wide open with compassion for his hurt rather than defensiveness for his words. Such was the basic building block of a harmonious relationship. Such was the new Melissa.

His anger crescendoed and finally peaked to the concluding sentence: "Damn it, Mel. If you want to be with me, just *be* with me. *Stay* with me."

"I'm here. I hear you." The first drop was over and I had survived it with an intact open heart. For the first time in the history of our relationship, I had stepped out of my own story to really hear Logan's. It didn't matter that his story of "us" was completely different from mine. We each lived the story that we needed to live in order to learn what we needed to learn. The love that filled my heart was in no way diminished by his interpretations.

"Why didn't you call when you finished the trail?" His tone was softer already, so I chanced the truth and hoped it wouldn't anger him again.

"Because you disappeared. I assumed you were done with me."

"I was in rehab. I couldn't take your call. So I set you free. 'Set them free. If they don't come back they were never yours. If they come back, they're yours to keep'. I set you free so you could experience the trail like only a free person can, but I always hoped you'd fly back to me."

Each of his words was a perfectly sized hook into my heart, and I watched myself step down into our common story of longing, passion and dysfunction with cautious curiosity. I watched myself cradle the phone a little closer, lest Logan slipped away in the space between the phone and my ear and I lost him again. Non-attachment was already out the window, but peace and stillness still reign in my heart. I assumed I could still recover.

We spoke for five hours that first night. We shared the stories of our inner and outer journeys over the summer, taking turns describing our adventures and rejoicing with pride in the other's accomplishments. As I suspected, he had been climbing in the Cascades only a few passes away from the PCT while I walked through. He even had given a ride to a couple of my trail family members out of Stevens Pass.

Some parts of our stories were stressful to share and difficult to hear. I hated the length to which he had gone to forget me; he fell silent to the news that I had loved another man, and had sex with yet another.

When the silence ended, he wanted specifics. How soon after our last communication? How many times? In a tent? In a hotel room? Had I liked it? Had they liked it? Did we still speak? How often? I heard his anger rising.

"I don't get it, Mel, you already had a dick to sit on, why on earth did you need to chase another one?"

Of course, I saw the red flags planted on each side of the path that led straight to the entrance of the dragon's lair; I just chose to pretend they were pretty red wild flowers and collected them in a big basket of gratitude.

According to Peirce, any issue that appeared in a relationship field belonged to both parties or it simply would not be – we cannot perceive a vibration that we are not. What an efficient way to bring hidden beliefs to the surface where they can be acknowledged and healed. What a unique opportunity for fast growth.

I had spent a whole summer on the trail purifying my drinking water of contaminants with nothing but love and gratitude. I was certain I could purify our relationship with the same exact ingredients.

11/12/2012 – 3:58 am
Excerpt from my journal
I feel so grateful for Logan. And I feel safe too. Not because he makes me feel safe, but because as long as Logan is in my life, that means we are still vibrating in resonance.
To make the most of this relationship, I must therefore bring my most centered highest home frequency to the field we both create.

I choose to do this by opening completely to him. I will not act from fear in anything. I will have no secret. I will be completely transparent in my life, my schedule and my social interactions. I will provide him with all my passwords. I will also continue to follow my heart and do what is right for me, but without fear of Logan's reactions. If an issue arises, I will know that the issue belongs to both of us. If I clear my side of a common issue with awareness, then Logan either will have to clear his, or find somebody else with whom to tackle it. Either way, if I am clear, I am safe. Either this will be an intense learning process that will in the end split us for good but leave us "better" than we were and more able to attract the relationships we deserve, or, maybe, we actually will rise to the challenge, grow together and have the out-of-this-world-even-better-than-in-my-wildest-dreams relationship we both always suspected we could have. Oh! I feel great, happy, tired, hopeful and grateful.
Thank you!

CHAPTER 51

Logan was dismayed, and I was surprised, when the truck flowed east instead of west out of Livingston. Both on-ramps were available from the main road, and until the truck actually made the turn, I could not have guessed which way it would go.

The truck took the eastward on-ramp with such urgency that my entire body shifted against the driver's door. I braced my knee against the door for stability and held on to the wheel tightly but did not relax the pressure off the gas. By the time we joined the flow of the freeway traffic, we had already reached our usual cruising speed. Apparently, I was not returning to Bellingham right away.

In the miles between Livingston and the town of Wall, just outside Badlands National Park, Logan called five times – an average greater than one call per hundred miles. And what a wonderfully fertile ground for arising issues our relationship was. Issues of jealousy, lack of care, fear of commitment, disrespect, need for space and their associated negative emotions were each in turn ousted from my subconscious so that I might explore and heal them.

The discomfort of the actual conversations had no hold on me. Each time my phone announced a call from Logan, my heart jumped in joyous trepidation. I could clear a mistaken belief in about thirty miles, but one of his "I love you so much, I love you stupid!" could sustain my smile for hundreds of miles.

I had relegated all aspect of navigating the physical reality to my truck, so I was surprised when a large sign announced the exit for the Badlands. How fast had that truck been going anyway?

I stopped by the side of the freeway right before the Badlands entrance and warned Logan that I would be out of cell reception for the rest of the day.

I meant to retrace my steps of two years prior. The Badlands had been the backdrop of my first night alone in the truck in a strange landscape far from home, my first glimpse into the free-roaming lifestyle I had since embraced. I envisioned performing a small ceremony out in the prairie to honor the memory and express my gratitude to the local Grandmothers.

I drove through the empty park in quiet appreciation but was not moved to stop at any of the viewpoints. When I reached the last parking lot, I parked in the space in which I had spent the night and walked to the edge of the prairie.

The landscape was so identical to my memory of it that I almost expected finding my own footsteps in the brown dirt. I stood as still and silent as the sediment spires, waiting for my exploration reflex to propel me forward, but it never did.

"I'm sorry." I finally said out loud to the Badlands. "I feel disrespectful in my sudden lack of enthusiasm about being here. Please be assured that it is by no fault of yours. You're as beautiful as I remember. I just … just thank you."

Without setting a foot further than the paved parking lot, I returned to the truck and crawled into the back. I was asleep before my head reached the sleeping pad.

I slept restlessly. An energetic presence that moved too fluidly to be physical circled the truck. In my dream, a council sitting in a circle discussed my fate, evaluated my safety and speculated about my chances of success. I modified my breathing and shifted my body to wake myself out of the council, but emotional exhaustion sat on my chest like a fat cat, preventing my return to the waking world until the late afternoon.

11/18/2012 (Badlands NP, beautiful evening light!)
Excerpt from my journal
    Dear Love,
What would happen if I approached a relationship with Logan from a fearless open space but he didn't meet me at the same level?
Love and trust begets love and trust. If you fear that Logan is coming into the relationship from a place of fear, if you fear he won't be open enough to receive your openness, then you are not in a place of trust yourself. Only trust begets trust. Fear doesn't beget trust.
Am I putting too much emphasis on the issue clearing process? I mean, am I manifesting a reality where there will be lots of issues for me to explore and mistaken beliefs to dismantle, whereas I could just bypass all this and get to a healthy relationship if I just put my energy on that instead?
As long as you think of a healthy relationship as something to either be earned or waited for, then that is what you will get. As Logan said, if you want to be with him, just be with him.
Well, sometimes I really do, and other times I worry that I am making my life harder and more complicated than it needs to be by being with him.
Yes, and he is a very clear mirror for you in that. Sometimes he's all in; sometimes he wants someone else. You cannot do anything to change the situation. You cannot make him do something or force happiness by your actions. You must live in the state in which you want to live and believe in miracles. And they do happen.

A few days before Thanksgiving – and Darcy's birthday – I parked the truck in its former location in the driveway of the Arthur house. The house still creaked and smelled of old, experienced wood, but the energy that permeated it was much different than when I called it home.

Both of the post-doc ladies had returned to their respective countries. Darcy had moved to the large bedroom on the third floor. A quiet new geology post-doc researcher had recently moved in the corner room, and Darcy's brother and his contagious booming laugh occupied my former bedroom. Studiousness and worldliness had been replaced with glee and shenanigans – once again, perfectly matching my needs for an environment.

I slept in the room that could be mine if I decided to stay and was woken up on my first full day in Minneapolis by a combination of the sun on my face through the large window and the sound of laughter in the kitchen downstairs.

I smiled with my eyes still closed, but my moment of bliss was quickly overshadowed by an inopportune thought: "If I return to Bellingham to live with Logan, how often would I wake to sunshine and laughter?"

I preferred not to answer. It was irrelevant anyway. I would flow where I was meant to flow and experience what I was meant to experience. In the meantime, the delicious smell floating up the stairs informed me that my next best step was to get to the kitchen and join the rowdy crowd before all the pancakes were gone.

I was greeted with cheers, hugs and a warm plate of cakes and authentic Vermont maple syrup. Life was so glorious in that instant, that I gave Darcy a check for the rest of the month. I knew there would be repercussions, but their time had not yet come. Friends, laughter, sunshine and warm cakes occupied my Now.

From the outside, my life in Minneapolis seemed even simpler than it had been two years prior. I had no thesis to write, not deadlines and no plan. I took long walks by the Mississippi, occasionally drank vodka in polka bars with LB, and walked Darcy to school for the pleasure to do so.

My internal world, however, was once again on a fast upgrade track. Logan and I spoke every day, several times a day, and I never hung up empty handed. In the fertile space of our relationship field, issues bloomed to the surface like an invasive species. Although I welcomed each one with gratitude for the opportunity for growth it offered, the upkeep of the field was draining, and I often crawled in bed in the early evenings feeling more exhausted than I was after hiking forty miles in the Cascades.

11/25/2012
Excerpt from my journal [edited for length]
Titled: Thinking out loud
 Why Logan? Why not anyone besides Logan?
Because I have found my highest joy in epic adventures. I want to associate myself with someone who has a "larger than life"-ness about them, and so far, Logan is the only person I have met that feels "large" enough to hold my dreams.
If that's the case, why the hesitation? I should return to him. All experiences are valid and beneficial in the grand scheme of things. Aren't they?
I don't live in the grand scheme though; I live in the experiential realm. What if the energetic environment living with Logan becomes so toxic that it lowers my frequency to such an extent that I can't even stay centered anymore?
That could happen, yes. But I refuse to approach this relationship with fear in my heart. If I stay open, he will mirror me.
So, do I expect him to change?
I guess I do, but not in the sense of "change for me". If I respond differently to the same triggers, if I change, the relationship field will change automatically. The environment will be completely different than what we have known, so necessarily Logan will be different as well. Those parts of him that resonate with a higher vibration relationship will naturally be brought out.
So, what do I expect from this?
I think if I go in with any expectation at all, I'm setting myself up for disappointment. Of course, I hope for a healthy relationship, but I will take what comes. That's all I can do: take care of myself, be centered, learn and grow.

So, am I set to return?
Yes, I am. I feel the greatest love through him. I want to pursue this.

I sat back and stared at the words I had just written.

Now, hold on a minute! That looked like a decision. I still had an entire corridor of potential open doors at my disposal, and there had been no sign that returning to Logan was the best next step. For over a month, I had purposely not decided anything to give the Universe free reign with the creation process. Clearly, one of the other doors would call to me – *any* of the other doors besides the path back to Logan's Dragon Lair. I could go to Rishikesh and be an assistant for Tribe yoga. I could write a book. I could become a barista in Montana and climb ice all winter or stay in the fun Arthur house for a season. I could go to Death Valley or chase the sun across the deserts of Utah, Arizona and New Mexico. I could live in my truck full time and meander from town to town until I found one to call home. I could move to a new place and enjoy a completely blank slate on which to create whom I was going to be next. I could fall in love again … Couldn't I?

Intimidated by the insinuations in my own writing, I closed my journal and placed it in my duffel bag. I was done writing about Logan, I hoped for a while.

Maybe I had been so cooped up in my over-analytical brain that I had lost all sense of perspective. I remembered times on the trail when my eyes could see in all directions unhindered and longed for the scope of perspective available in wild places. I had no mountain to climb in flat Minneapolis, but I had the Mississippi. There was wisdom in all rivers, and I already had a history with this one. I had learned trust and faith along its shores, and it had let me live. I knew it could be trusted.

I climbed down the stairs to the path I had once followed on my one-day fast. The river had then been frozen, but in late November, it was still flowing – at least, if I fell in this time, I wouldn't risk my life. I followed the shore to the small beach where I had found a feather, but without the snow to embellish its banks, the river and beach seemed dirty and brown. No feather stood out against the murky background. I climbed back up to the paved road and walked along the row of religious buildings. The particular concrete square in the sidewalk where I was struck with the revelation of my mandatory PCT walk looked exactly as I remembered. I stood within its boundaries, closed my eyes and opened my heart to receive guidance but was only struck by the gratitude of adventures past.

I understood. Although the geography was the same, this Mississippi was a different river than the one along which I walked before the Vision Fast because I was a different person, with a different task. To celebrate the shift, I crossed the river on one of the bridges to the opposite bank. I had no history with the eastern bank, no energetic leaks into past memories to distract me from my current search for guiding signs.

I paid no heed to the noon-traffic congesting the road next to the walking path and asked out loud, "Please, can you send me a sign to help me see what my next best step from here is?" I then remembered a few miserable days spent in search of invisible signs in Bellingham and added, "Oh, and please make it obvious, you know I don't get subtleties."

No sooner had I spoken the words that the ring of my phone startled me. I held the phone at arm's length as though God himself was calling. Wherever He was calling from, I didn't recognize the area code.

"Hi. This is the Longmont Humane Society. We have your cat, Smaug, here with us."

My cat! – As in, my ex-cat who had run away from Jack's house two years prior, my ex-cat whom I had not seen in four years by then.

I stopped walking and looked at the phone again, this time expecting some indication that this was a joke.

"I'm ... sorry, can you repeat that?"

She did. Same sentence, same cat.

"Okay then. Huh ... Well. I'm in Minneapolis right now, but I'll come down and get him. I guess it'll take me about two days to get to Colorado, so Friday?"

"Friday is great. We'll see you then."

CHAPTER 52

The journalists were likely still able to see me from the front door of the Humane Society, so I carried the handsome black and white cat who no longer answered to the name "Smaug" back to my truck as nonchalantly as I could. He didn't move, but he was a large cat, and I struggled to fit the cat carrier onto the passenger seat. I walked around the truck casually, sat behind the wheel, checked my surroundings once more, looked over at the cat and cried.

There had been two journalists waiting for the woman who loved her long-lost cat so much that she had driven two days to pick him up. The Humane Society wished to use the story to incite more pet owners to place a chip in their beloved animals. We had been photographed, interviewed and congratulated. All fees had been waived.

I loved Smaug very much when he lived with Jack and me. He was just a feral kitten I had found on a hiking trail and brought home, but in the ways he approached the world, he was one of my greatest teachers. He was fearless and fierce, independent and self-sufficient. He disappeared often on adventures on his own, sometimes for days, weeks or months. I was not surprised when he ran away from Jack's comfortable home.

But the cat that had treated me like a sibling, attacking my legs in the morning and falling asleep on my chest in the evening, was long gone. The full-grown fella in the Humane Society's cage recognized me as little as I recognized him. We both played along for the camera, but once in the truck, we dropped the masks. His gaze towards me was completely vacant. Why would he care? He had just traded a cage for another. What did I gain? I had a cat. I had spoken with Jack. His rental agreement had a firm no-pet clause. So the responsibility was mine. I couldn't see living in my truck with a responsibility. Having a cat meant needing a home, which meant paying rent, which meant getting a job. My destiny was as black and white as the markings on his fur. My roaming days were over.

I allowed myself a few minutes to grieve the loss of the gypsy life I had barely tasted. The cat seemed undisturbed by my weeps. After a few spells of tears, my heart returned to its home frequency. I was always exactly where I needed to be, so I could trust that whatever happened was for my Greatest Good, including this cat in my life. One dream was gone, but I could create a new one, maybe even a better one.

I wiped my eyes and, with a wave of the hand, cleared the last wisps of the vanishing dream of a roaming life. The new dream included a home-base and a cat, local roaming with the benefit of a community and indoor plumbing – suddenly, that last part really appealed to me. The new dream involved Logan. I could see it clearly. I was going to Bellingham. That was the next best step, and I had needed the cat to appear to eliminate all other options.

Right on cue my phone rang.

"What's wrong? I just sensed you were sad." Logan said.

This was not the first time that he called to comfort me out of the blue accurately. I told him about the cat and the loss of freedom it represented. He interpreted my distress as fear of commitment, but I had already explored that particular issue in our common field, so I ignored his comment.

"Would you take a woman and a cat?"

"The door's wide open. You're both welcome."

It was already too late in the day to start driving towards Bellingham. I called my friend Ben in Denver and appeared within a half-hour at his front door with a cat-carrier filled with mewing discontent. If I had any illusion about the feasibility of roaming with the cat in my truck, I was cured of it. Within a mile of the Humane Society, I recalled Jack's horror story about moving to Colorado with Smaug – something about nearing his wits' ends and needing to stop at a random veterinarian's office for some feline sedation.

Having accomplished his task in making me decide to move back to Bellingham to be with Logan, the cat then decided to stay in Denver. He carefully avoided having any sign of affection towards me, going as far as deflecting the straight path to a food bowl around the sofa where I sat. Ben, on the other hand, he covered in purrs and head rubs, all the while looking at me, pointedly. He knew what he was doing, and so did I, so I respected it. Only once my bag was already in the truck, and he was certain I wouldn't take him away in my awful moving machine, did he come by for a quick rub on my leg with a purr.

"Thank you, cat." My love for him was intact, I discovered, now that he was no longer my responsibility. "It was nice to see you again. I hope you have a good life here."

Less than a week later, he was gone from Ben's. That cat sure had a lot of roaming in him.

I drove north back to Livingston and spent one night at Jimmy's. He was off on a flight to Florida, but we overlapped by half an hour – the most we had ever seen each other – and I once again had the haunted epiphany-house to myself.

For once, I was able to sleep there, a deep sleep filled with vivid dreams. The last one lingered as I woke up on the day when I was to drive back to Bellingham to take my rightful place in Logan's arms.

12/04/2012
Excerpt from my journal
Dream: Dead and Six Feet Deep.
I was going somewhere important. I was a reporter on a mission to interview a great wise man who lived in a remote alpine area. To get there, I had to jump from roof to roof to get across a city's skyscrapers, then cross a precarious suspended bridge into a jungle, where I had to bushwhack until I reached the top of the tree line, where I had to rock climb, then ice climb, to reach the wise man. I was very much looking forward to the adventurous journey, but I was still only on the roof of skyscrapers when the dream started. Before I went on, I realized that I was dreaming. I

thought, "Oh, since this is a dream. I can do whatever I want. I have full control. Mmmh. I've never jumped off a skyscraper before." I ran to the edge and leapt. This was a full sensory dream. I could feel the rush of falling, the wind, the sounds, the fear, the exhilaration. The ground was coming up fast. I thought, "I'll probably wake up soon now. I think that's what's supposed to happen in falling dreams." WHAAACK! I hit the ground full force, breaking every bone in my body. In fact, I hit the ground so hard that I became embedded in it, about six feet deep. I was dead. Dirt flowed in from the side of the hole my body had created to cover me. "Huh. That's interesting. I'm broken, dead and buried. Well, I guess I got to experience that" I thought. I blinked and was instantly returned to the roof of the skyscraper. I grabbed my pen and pad of paper and continued on my journey. I woke up feeling as though somebody had taken a bat to my ribs. It still hurts now.

CHAPTER 53

Considering that it rained non-stop for twenty-two days, and that during that time Logan and I were both unemployed in a four-hundred-square-foot studio, the fact that we even lasted twenty-two days qualifies as a miracle.

Living with Logan was at first greater than I could have imagined. We slipped into our roles effortlessly and played house so well that we even fooled ourselves about our chances of longevity. He made space for me as a token of welcome. I moved some furniture in to confirm my intent to stay. We cooked meals together, watched movies, made love and spent our evenings on our respective computers looking for job openings.

Outwardly, we fit the mold of our shared idea of a "normal couple". I aspired to a life much larger than normal, but I also expected surprises from the Universe. What if I accidentally found happiness in being a settled loving housewife? I had met more than one adventurer to whom it had happened. Besides, I consoled myself, I wouldn't be a full-time housewife; I would teach yoga and make a difference in the world that way. Maybe freedom wasn't my quest, nor adventure my path. That was just a line I wrote in another lifetime. If I wanted to pull my own weight in our relationship, it was time I reintegrate.

I visited every yoga studio in town. Unlike my quest for serendipity in Portland, I was very active in this search process. I pestered yoga studio owners with my resume and multiple follow-up calls, created a website, designed future classes, created yoga music playlists and sketched potential logos for my eventual own yoga studio. The market was oversaturated though, and on the few occasions when I was offered a sub position, the class was canceled for reasons unrelated to me.

According to the new worldview I had been taught on the benches of the Intensive Sunday School for the Rebellious (the name of which I always enjoy spelling out fully) and which I had embraced on the trail, this swimming-up-stream feeling in my job search was a clear indication that I was not flowing in an optimal direction for maximum growth and joy. But this was the real world, the world of grown-ups. I had my fun believing in magic and flowing aimlessly; it was time to buckle down and make it happen for myself.

Eventually, my dedication paid off. I was offered a few classes in a studio. All I needed was to get my own yoga teaching insurance and sign a six month rental contract with the studio. Luckily, this offer was extended on day twenty of my return to Bellingham, two days before Christmas. I set both the studio and insurance contracts aside until after the holidays. They are probably still sitting in a box labeled "Melissa's treasures" somewhere in my storage unit.

12/25/2012
Excerpt from my journal
I have not written in a while. Today is Christmas day and I have the flu. Logan is napping with his head on my leg; I think more out of boredom than tiredness. The weather is dismal and depressing and has been since I got here. Of course, this is a judgment call on my part based on my current mind-set.

I have failed to remain centered. I did at first, but the more centered I was, the more triggered Logan got, and eventually we tumbled down the old hill together. I could process hidden beliefs revealed in the mirror of constant criticism, false accusations and unfounded suspicions for only so long. The first time I lost myself, I was saved by a trip down to Sofia's. She reminded me that my intent when I came here was complete openness with no preconception or judgment or expectation. Take was IS and love it. I came back ready for a lifetime with the man I love, no matter what. Within a few days, the drama had returned, but I wasn't even his trigger this time. His wallet was stolen, a drugged-up man attacked him while he was filing the report about the stolen wallet with a police officer, then a man we didn't know threaten to key his truck in the grocery store parking lot for no reason I could see, and another man was rude to him in the store, again, for no obvious reason. Although that seems like an incredible set of bad-luck events in one person's day, it actually makes sense to me, considering the level of anger lurking in Logan at all times. The fact that he even functions as cordially as he does is a testimony to the strength of control he has. But the energy of anger is still there and by the law of resonance he attracts any anger-trigger anywhere within a mile radius. He lost control then, but because I've mostly cleared my own anger issues, I didn't react to him. It took him two days and one night to break me down. I might have lasted longer if I had been physically healthy, but with my immune system down with the flu, I just didn't have the strength. Though, I suppose strength is necessary only for resistance. Maybe that is where I went wrong. Any resistance is an indication of my ego being triggered. Just as I thought I was centered and peaceful ("Holier than thou" as Logan calls it), I was actually sucked into the drama game anyway, and I didn't realize it until right now, writing this.

It only took a small crack in my defense system for the whole game-plan of non-response to triggers to disintegrate – a small comment from Logan about a photo of one of my beautiful girlfriends.

"Wow, look at her. Why can't I be with a girl like that, a fresh young one instead of you?"

I felt the contraction in my heart. Yet another issue I'd have to explore. I probably had hidden beliefs that I was old and ugly. My immediate task, however, was to not respond.

I shook my head dismissively, but I knew that he would gauge my deflated stance and realize he had gotten through.

From that point forth, the onslaught was incessant. I could see the attacks as the pain that it was. I could reason that it had nothing to do with me – I had only aged by one year since the day when he had left a poem on my mirror about the most beautiful of them all. I could see the sabotage for self-preservation. I could even visualize the love behind it all. But I could not process my own feelings fast enough to clear our common energetic field, though I tried.

With my energy completely drained in a futile attempt to keep the tide of issues at bay, I fell ill. That is exactly what Logan's pain-body had hoped for. Any fight we had ever had was revived and new ones, real or invented, were thrown in as sacrificial fuel. I was incapacitated. My throat closed up to such tightness that I could barely swallow, my body ached and my temples pounded any attempt at handling the situation rationally into oblivion. On Christmas eve, the pain-body snarled at me when I asked for tea and left for the bar taking my key.

There was a girl at the bar. A young, beautiful girl, the pain-body told me repeatedly – the kind of girl he'd dream to be with – at two in the morning, through a Nyquil-medicated brain. I sat up to leave calmly, but the pain-body became agitated and punched a wall, so I lay back down to keep myself safe.

Morning came at last. I got up and got dressed, unsure of what my next best step should be, and decided to drive down to Boulevard Park to find solace and counsel by the bay.

"Can I have my key back?" I was already by the door.

"No. If I give you your key back, you'll wait for me to be out of the house, take your stuff and leave me again."

"That'll be perfect. You'll then have room to have a fresh young one move in as you wished."

"I never said that…"

I crossed the space between us without a step and came to

my senses one hand pushing him back on the desk chair and the other suspended in the air along the axes of a bent elbow perfectly poised to break his nose in one blow. I saw the destructive rage in my own eyes reflected in the surprise in his and stumbled back in shock.

Without another word, still carried by the strength of my emotions, I turned around and fled without the key. The swirl of emotions coursed through my body and gradually dissipated while the truck carried me to the bay. As we crested the hill before the final descent to Boulevard Park, my eyes caught a patch of blue sky, the first break in the clouds since my return to Bellingham.

"Arizona."

A one-word thought floated through my mind. There was a rainbow on the horizon. That word with that rainbow combined rang of reclaimed freedom.

I parked by the bay and walked to the water's edge.

"Yes. Arizona."

There was also a rainbow on the other side of the bay.

Ah, but I still loved Logan so much. Was it too soon to give up? I had come back to be open. If I closed my heart as soon as times were rough, then I had not broken any pattern.

I wished I could talk to Sofia, but it was Christmas day and I knew that she was with her family. Sofia never answered phone calls when visiting family. I dialed her number anyway, maybe this time she'd answer.

"I had a feeling I needed to take your call. Are you okay?"

I related the details of circumstances quickly because we both understood they were irrelevant. Only the feelings triggered and hidden beliefs exposed mattered.

"I don't know, Sofia. What if I just stay and work through all the triggers? There must be a place beyond them where all is cleared and Logan and I can live happily ever after."

"Melissa," she said gently, "you have jumped off the building, you have crashed, you are dead and buried six feet deep. It is done. Let it go."

She patiently waited until all the tears I could cry in one

sitting were exhausted and repeated it, "Let it go."

"I'm going to Arizona." I sniffled and wiped my nose on my soaked sleeve, "And there's a rainbow over the bay."

I drove back to Logan's with the peace of known departures in my heart, but the man I found was not the one I had just left. The spell was broken, the pain-body had left, and my love sat in his place, utterly sorry for what had been said.

"Please don't leave. I know what happened, and I can't promise you that it won't happen again, but please don't leave."

Arizona could wait. If there was an ounce of a chance this actually could work, maybe I wasn't six feet deep yet.

"You know what – I always leave, and you always ask me to stay, and when you do, I never stay. This was about breaking patterns. So, okay, I'm going to stay, but you're on probation with zero leeway from that point forth."

We kissed a strange kiss, forceful rather than passionate, with a dash of desperation.

Probation lasted less than three hours, at which point even Logan saw how hopeless our situation had become.

"I think you should go, Mel, before one of us gets hurt."

From his desk chair, he extended his hand to bring me closer. I sat on his lap with my entire torso cradled in his strong arms. For a full minute we looked at each other's faces solemnly and silently. Finally, we both stood up. I turned to the closet to start packing, and he simply walked out the door.

I gathered the belongings I could carry in one truck-full and left, never to return. What I couldn't carry, I simply donated to the lost cause of fairy-tale romances that can never cross over into experiential reality, yet are the most potent gift anyone on a path of self-discovery can ever receive from their Higher Selves.

Part 7

REINTEGRATION

It's not denial; I'm just selective about the reality I accept.

- Calvin -
(Bill Watterson's *Calvin and Hobbes*)

CHAPTER 54

01/07/2013
Facebook status update:
FYI: the first Joshua tree one encounters when driving south on I-15
is located exactly 1,258 miles from Bellingham. Now you know.

I drove through rain, snow and sleet for two days before I found the sun. The truck understood that we were not stopping for any inclement weather. I barely slept and fasted for most of those two days to reduce the need for stops. Finally, somewhere in southern Utah, I saw it – a glow on the horizon, a straight line in the clouds as though sketched with a ruler to demarcate the boundary between the life in the rain I had just left and the one in the sun calling me forward.

I was on phone with LB when I first saw the glow in the distance.

"LB! This is it. I see the sun. Hold on … I'm almost there. Five more miles … two more miles. I'm in it! I'm in the sun! Oh, my God! It's so bright and I don't even know where my sunglasses are. Wooohooooohooo!"

I howled and laughed, and LB celebrated with me. I had

just won the jackpot of life. I was unstoppable, immortal and magical. I didn't need a rainbow to know there was a pot of gold waiting for me wherever I was heading.

In fact, I didn't know where I was heading. I was going to Arizona. If Arizona didn't suit me, I'd continue to New Mexico or return to Nevada, maybe even explore California. It didn't matter.

Since I had found the sun, I wasn't in such a hurry to get anywhere. I left the freeway for a smaller road down red canyons bathed in the sunset's orange light – the first sunset I had seen in over a month.

As I neared the end of the canyon road, the landscape opened to a flat wide area covered in surreal lights. There is only one place in the world so flat and bright and strange at night, and that is Las Vegas.

I'm not a gambler, but my heart was glowing at such high vibrancy that I almost expected winning some monetary jackpot to finance my move. The money I had earned at the farm had served me well, but with rent in Minneapolis and Bellingham and travels in between my once fat envelope was looking meager. I calculated that I had just enough left to travel to Flagstaff and survive for a week or so once there. Then? Then I would see. Maybe my stop in Las Vegas was a well-orchestrated plot from the Universe. If it wasn't, that is where the truck was decidedly headed anyway.

I left all the details of my arrival into the city to chance. I looked for neither directions to the Strip nor a hotel. The truck flowed into town with a left turn here and a right turn there, and soon we landed in the parking lot of a perfect little hotel on an uncharacteristically quiet street within a few blocks of the Strip's main attractions.

I dropped my bags in the room and set off on foot. I allotted myself a twenty dollar budget. I bought a burrito, gambled two dollars, lost two dollars, and realized I didn't enjoy gambling after all. Instead, I found a dessert shop with a chocolate fountain in which to invest my allotment. A few minutes later, a lemon honey crepe drenched in chocolate was catapulting me into a giggly state of bliss. The leftover change I distributed a few dollars at a time among the donation jars and open guitar cases of street musicians.

Las Vegas was exactly what I needed, the antidote to the Bellingham episode. Musicians sang songs in praise of my smile and beauty, men opened doors and offered me drinks, and women complimented me on my earrings – the same dangling blue earrings I had worn on the PCT.

Maybe musicians honored all donations with compliments, and maybe the pervasive appreciation was alcohol induced, and maybe I stood out primarily because of my hiking boots and hiking pants with zippers at the knees in a town where everyone dresses to the nines. It didn't matter. I felt noticed, bright and beautiful.

On my way back to the hotel, around eleven at night, I met a man who was walking in the same direction – in hindsight, he might have been following me, but in the state of bliss in which I walked, I would have never assumed any ill intention from anyone.

We began talking, at first about my blue earrings, then about our lives. He had escaped a dreadful existence in Detroit in a daring move to follow his best friend to Las Vegas. Nobody else in his world back home had moved such a distance. Nobody else in his world understood what could possess him to want to live in the Sin City. He liked it, for the most part, but feared he might not find a suitable love partner in a town reputed for its liberal promiscuity. I understood him well. Many of my friends were also baffled by my lifestyle choices, and living out of my truck, for a while anyway, would not be very conducive to attracting a long-term relationship.

By the time we reached my hotel, we were both so

engrossed in our conversation that we were unwilling to say goodnight.

"C'mon!" He took my hand and turned me around, back towards the Strip. "I'll show you the backside of Las Vegas." He worked at one of the Casinos and had the keys to most back doors.

Through back alleys, closed off corridors, kitchens and managing offices, my sudden guide introduced me to Las Vegas's non-glittery underbelly.

"This is my friend, Melissa." He told the cooks, dish washers and janitors we met. No one questioned the duration of our friendship; we walked in close proximity and laughed at each other's jokes as though we had done so for years.

When we finally returned to my hotel, around one in the morning, he leaned forward to hug me. I anticipated that the moment when he'd ask for my phone number was next and noted my own anticipatory resistance. But when he retrieved a phone from his jacket's pocket, I couldn't find a logical reason to deny this lovely man's wish to stay in contact. I gave him my number.

I had barely closed my eyes off to sleep when he called the first time.

"Melissa, I must see you again. When will you be back in Vegas?"

"I don't know. On my way to Death Valley sometime, probably, maybe." The evening was over. Las Vegas was over for me.

"This doesn't happen. Strangers don't meet randomly in the street and have the kind of chemistry we have. Strangers don't bare their souls to each other the way we just did. You were meant to come here. You were meant to meet me. Surely, you must see this."

"I'm sorry. I can see this is unusual for you, but I have this kind of chemistry and soul-baring conversations with strangers quite often. I was meant to meet you, yes, and then I was meant to go on. I'm grateful for the wonderful evening, thank you, but this is it."

Like a guitar suddenly out of tune, my new friend's song turned desperate and scratchy. I politely hung up, but he called back again and again. He became angry that I was leaving him. This was fate, he said. We were meant to be, he insisted. I hadn't even given "us" a fair shot.

His words resonated in my head with a different voice. There was another man I had left with a broken heart, repeatedly. In this reenactment of potent parts of my Logan story, I saw my own guilt, and I saw that it was misplaced. I was neither too flirty nor too friendly. I had led no one on. I was not too promiscuous. I was not abandoning anyone from fear of commitment. I was simply a free-spirited woman not interested in dimming her own light to accommodate other people's insecurities or needs.

A wave of anger towards Logan rose up from the pit of my stomach, that nest-locus of deceptive lust butterflies, and I was grateful for it. At last, I could be openly, unabashedly angry. I cursed Logan to Hell, and it felt wonderful. I indulged in "how dared you" sentences, in full awareness that nothing was actually done to me. I knew that eventually I would look at all the points of indignation one by one and find that the issues were mine as well, and that Logan had merely helped bringing them to the light. At which point, my heart would hold nothing but unconditional love for him – which required neither physical proximity nor verbal or written contact for the rest of this lifetime.

But, for the time being, I was to honor the anger, the frustration and the indignation. I was to show Melissa that she was my priority, and that I would never again put her in harm's way, not in the name of passion, not even in the name of enlightenment. My inner knight in shining armor's sword was unsheathed and ready to trim any weight-inducing drama in my life – starting with the incessant calls from this man I had just met.

"Look, there is no 'us'. We are severely ill-matched." I told him, "Don't settle for the first shiny person you meet. There's somebody out there that'll match you, and I'm not her."

"How? How are we ill-matched?"

"Would you hike three-thousand miles?"

"Maybe. I don't know. I've never tried."

This was ridiculous. He had never even hiked a mile; he had told me so himself.

I glared at the phone from the length of my arm and fumed through the constriction of frustration in my throat. This was exactly the kind of nonsensical argument that no longer served me, and all I had to do was not partake.

"No, you wouldn't. Please stop calling me. Goodbye."

I hung up, turned my phone off and checked the locks on the door. It took a few minutes for my breath to dissipate the adrenaline out of my system. Seriously, what a strange story – it sounded like one of mine alright. I shook my head and suddenly laughed at my own creation. The laughter dissipated the frustration instantly, leaving it its wake nothing but gratitude for the expedient and necessary lessons of the night. With the shift in my energy, I knew I was safe from any unwelcomed visit to my hotel room.

"Thank you stranger." I said out loud.

"Thank you for seeing me, for showing me my own bright light, for unlocking trapped anger. But, most of all, thank you for ushering in the new era with a bang."

CHAPTER 55

Just in case Flagstaff was to become my new home, I wanted to imbue my entrance into the city with extra meaningfulness. I took the first exit into town, pulled over by the side of the off-ramp and retrieved my iPod from underneath the pile of maps and snacks on the passenger seat. I needed a special song – something classy, flowy yet grandiose, with a dash of finality. Strauss's Blue Danube was the obvious choice. Of all the songs on my iPod, I felt it alone afforded enough space to adequately hold the memory of a potential homecoming.

There were no false notes in my waltz into town. The sidewalks were luminous from the ice and snow, the air was clean, crisp and cold, and the sky was impossibly blue. Peace permeated the tranquil downtown.

The truck led the way through town as though it had always lived there and finally parked in front of a coffee shop. I looked up to the sign – Macy's European Coffeehouse – and laughed.

I knew of Macy's from a poster in Jimmy's kitchen in Livingston. I had studied the sketch of a woman in a coffee cup as an art piece but never linked it in my mind to an actual physical location in the world, and here, I was parked in front of it. What an amazing coincidence this would have been, if I believed in coincidences.

Macy's barista welcomed me as an old friend and brewed one of the best cups of Genmaicha green tea I have ever had. Every man who walked into the coffee shop was ruggedly handsome; every woman was outdoorsy and friendly. I sipped my tea quietly and allowed Flagstaff to seep in and soak my experiential field.

As the closing hour grew nearer, I began to ponder where I might spend the night. Sleeping in the truck was not a comfortable option in the woods of Flagstaff because the temperature was still below zero at night. I didn't worry; I assumed a solution would appear. When I felt it was time to leave, I thanked again the barista and returned to the freeway.

The truck most naturally glided down the edge of the Colorado plateau, away from the pastel palette of Flagstaff towards the desert and Sedona, where the temperature was still in the tolerable teens.

Sedona – what a sight! I had no idea. I had heard the name but had never seen a photo or read a line about it. Suddenly, after miles of expected brown and beige desert, a wall of deep dark blood-red rocks appeared right ahead. My jaw dropped as my eyebrows rose. "Holy …" I swore out loud. The truck caught the next exit to a trailhead parking lot and stopped at the foot of a massive monolith.

"Bell Rock", the sign said. I turned off the engine and stared upward in disbelief. Was I dreaming? Such beauty was impossible.

I left the truck in a trance and followed my feet down the trail, pulled intractably forward by the red intensity of Bell Rock. When I reached its base, a juniper called me to the side, and I knew that the proper and right thing to do was to sit in its shade. I buried both my hands in the soft red dirt – a ritual whispered in my mind by the juniper or possibly Bell Rock itself – and cried tears of gratitude.

An hour passed like a minute. My hands remained in the dirt. Shadows lengthened, and each layer of rock in turn reached its most surreal shade of saturation. A muted version of the scene was reflected along the black body of my truck. We looked at each other in full agreement; Sedona was home for the night.

We drove through West Sedona in the dark. Very few stores were opened. I asked a lady at the grocery store for a recommendation on where to camp. She sketched a simple map of town and up to Oak Creek Canyon. Although the road up Oak Creek Canyon was dark, narrow and enclosed in trees, I could feel the beauty I could not see surrounding me.

I had packed the truck in haste when I left Bellingham, and although I had all the elements to create a comfortable mobile bedroom, none of them were in place yet. I set up a tent by the creek and hoped that exhaustion overruled the cold in the canyon.

The cold didn't wake me, the buzzing did.

It must have been no later than four in the morning. The forest was still dark, peaceful and quiet. My body, however, was buzzing as though I were lying on an electric table. A steady hum filled my ears and forehead. A pang of fear sparked in my belly. I saw it and breathed through it until I had regained composure. I then extended my hand outside my sleeping bag and through the door of the tent to bury it in the dirt, as I had done under Bell Rock. It made no difference. The buzzing was in me, not in the canyon.

I moved my hand to my carotid artery to check my heart rate. In my younger years, I had battled bouts of thyroid hyperactivity. I knew the symptoms well. But this was a different kind of buzzing, and my heart was only fast from the spike of fear, from which it had already recovered.

I returned my hand to the sleeping bag to keep it warm. It couldn't have been vibrations from the creek. I had slept on the shores of much larger rivers without buzzing. I had drunk nothing but green tea and had eaten a wholesome vegetarian dinner. I had no electronic device near me and there was neither nearby human habitation nor traffic on the road. I was puzzled, but my heart assured me that I was in no danger.

I lay still with the buzzing sensation and explored it one body part at a time. It was consistent throughout, from my feet to my fingertips, and really only uncomfortable in my head, because I didn't trust it. Little by little, I relaxed in the sensation and eventually fell back asleep.

The buzzing was still present but barely perceptible when I woke up in the morning light. I asked the camp host if he knew of this buzzing or what might have caused it.

He shrugged and looked away.

"Never heard of it".

I didn't believe him.

"Are there any good hikes around here" I asked him, in part to change the subject. He seemed grateful that I did.

One of the best hikes in Sedona was just up the canyon. I rolled the tent and packed some granola in a Ziploc bag to eat as I hiked and drove up the canyon in search of the trailhead. I never found the trailhead. Instead, I drove right back to Flagstaff.

Flagstaff? I had not yet looked at the map and believed that I had been driving away from Flagstaff since I left Macy's. What was going on? Had the red rocks anything to do with this? Was my reality so precarious that mere contact with a massive monolith could send me into alternate states of perception?

Well, why not? I once read that the human brain was most plastic during major life changes. This allowed new neural pathways to be created quickly and was the reason humans were amongst the most adaptable of all creatures – although still second to bobcats. Some people could learn languages at an accelerated rate in this state. I, apparently, could quantum-leap or curve the space-time continuum. This didn't bother me. Inexplicable circumstances were nothing more than serendipitous magic, of the same kind I had experienced on the trail. In this case, I assumed that if I had returned to Flagstaff, I was probably meant to be there.

And I was – I met Mikhael that day.

My request for a couch on *Couchsurfer.com* had caught her eye. She didn't have a couch or room to offer because she had recently lost her partner and needed her grieving space, but she could meet me for lunch and welcome me to town. It was perfect – I had placed a couch request for the sole purpose of meeting locals anyway. I had always intended to sleep in the truck.

Mikhael and I met at noon at an Indian Restaurant. She was as intense as the red rocks of Sedona. We sat facing each other, skipped any form of chit-chat and dove headlong into the exploration of my buzzing from a spiritual perspective. I knew I had found a soul-sister within five minutes of meeting her.

"There's strong energy in those red rocks. That's what you felt. Depending on sensitivity, it can be enticing, addicting or flat out overwhelming."

Mikhael had lived in Sedona for several years. She knew well of the buzzing I described. She had experienced it herself.

"Sedona's a place of healing. You go in, heal, and get out. For most people the energy there's too intense to make it a permanent home."

Luckily, the antidote was right up the canyon. Flagstaff was the antithesis of Sedona, the yin to calm the yang. If I chose to live in Sedona, Mikhael recommended that I periodically reconnect with Flagstaff in order to keep myself balanced.

I was grateful for the mind-bending beauty of Sedona so close but had no intention of moving there. I envisioned myself living in peaceful Flagstaff. I could teach yoga, work at a local gear shop, climb in the summer, ski in the winter, and eventually meet a ruggedly handsome local over a perfect cup of Genmaicha.

When the Indian restaurant closed, Mikhael and I moved our conversation to Macy's. She never made it to work that afternoon. When Macy's closed in the late evening, I followed her home where we continued exploring our past dark relationships, transformative experiences and subsequent epiphanies.

Mikhael was a sharp mirror for me, one unlike I had ever met. Whereas Sofia and I had navigated our storylines by gently holding each other's hands as we leaned our heads behind the curtain, Mikhael's questions encouraged me to rip the curtain off the rod and scrutinize the raw emotions behind it. This was a Sedona kind of healing – intense, efficient and unavoidable.

I woke up late the next morning and found Mikhael sitting in the sun in the living room. The empty cup of coffee on the table suggested she had been awake for a while.

"I've been thinking …" She leaned forward to place a deck of tarot cards on the coffee table. There were several other decks already there.

"Why don't you move in my spare bedroom until you can get yourself situated here with a job and a place of your own? You don't need to pay anything. I've checked with my heart, and it feels right to offer."

I sat down in the sun on the carpet, thrilled and speechless. Did the generosity of strangers know no bound?

"What about your grieving space?"

"We'll keep it open. If I feel I need space, I'll let you know."

I noted my own hesitation under the excitement, and so did Mikhael. But I had no reason to refuse; this offer was a gift beyond even my expectations of magic at every corner.

"Let's ask the cards." I ran back to the spare bedroom to get my own deck of oracle cards.

Mikhael and I carefully lay three spreads on the coffee table, one for her, one for me, and one for us, asking for guidance in this situation. The cards were explicit – "no" for me, with a warning about closing options, "no" for her, with a reminder about the need for solitude, and "no" for us, with a "trust the process".

We were both disappointed with the results and spent the rest of the morning discussing light-hearted ways we might ignore the cards. Cards merely reflect our own internal energies, after all. Couldn't we just acknowledge the warnings and craft a communal space in which both our needs were accommodated? In the end, our commitment to our growths superseded any loophole we devised, and we decided to trust the process.

I left Mikhael with a promise to visit often and drove away with a hint of sadness under curious excitement about those options I was to keep open.

Of its own accord, the truck flowed back down the edge of the Colorado plateau to the desert below where the temperatures were warmer, and I let it because I had no opinion about our destination.

The truck followed a dirt road to a clearing with a view over the low brush desert, miles from either Flagstaff or Sedona. This was a perfect remote and quiet home for the night. I emptied the content of the truck in the clearing and leisurely repacked each item to craft a comfortable living space.

On one side, I placed a stack of sleeping pads, my warm sleeping bag and a soft pillow. This was the bedroom side. On the other half, I used a plastic bin filled with climbing equipment as a nightstand and secured the food and camping stove box between the duffel bag and a small suitcase of clothes. On the back seat of the cab, I created shelves with wooden crates secured by seatbelts to hold my books, maps, lion, tigers, dragon and art supplies. Only the hula hoop slept outside.

I had just crawled onto my sleeping bag to test the comfort and ergonomics of my new living space when a coyote entered the clearing. It walked along the truck, less than ten feet away, with its nose to the ground. I silently leaned over the edge of the tailgate to make eye contact and greet it, but it never looked up. I was no more incongruous to that coyote than the shrubs, cacti or rocks in its territory. Its complete lack of interest brought a wave of gratitude to my heart. I could not have imagined a more welcoming omen. I had found a place in the world where I simply and naturally belonged.

CHAPTER 56

I never returned to live in Flagstaff. I visited occasionally but always flowed back down the hill, drawn by Sedona.

I sold $3,000 of some investments I had carefully saved in case I break a leg on one of my daring leaps of faith and suddenly had enough money to survive for months. I trusted that my heart would let me know when it was time to rejoin civilization and the working world. I trusted that this call would come before I ran out of money. But, until such time, I joyously disappeared into the desert.

My roaming territory extended westward from Sedona, beyond Dry Creek Road, and covered the open plain between the red rocks at the edge of the Colorado Plateau and the Verde River. I had hundreds of miles of dirt roads at my disposal, endless hiking trails, lizards, cacti, silence and sunshine.

I woke up every morning to the first rays of sun shining through the intricate crystalline structure of the frozen condensation on the truck's windows. The transition from my warm cocoon to the chill desert air was the only hardship I faced all day, and it was well worth it.

I stretched in the morning light, honoring the red rocks in the distance, and inhaled the whole universe into a tight ball of love I could fit into my heart.

"Good morning, beautiful world!" Sometimes I yelled it,

sometimes I whispered it, and sometimes I silently bowed. I felt my greeting was returned. I always felt welcome.

"Good morning, my love!" I also greeted the truck with love and gratitude every morning. It was the companion of all my adventures. It kept me safe, mobile and free. It was my home and sometimes, when I was willing to disturb the peace and silence of the desert, it was my dance partner.

With both doors wide open, the music from the truck's stereo was amplified in the vastness of the desert. And I danced around it with complete abandon, followed in my frenzy by puffs of red dirt to mark the contact points between my soaring feet and the earth.

Out in the desert, all discipline was abolished. My only responsibility each day was to follow my heart with exact precision and no argument. I danced and hula hooped for hours, read books, napped in the middle of the day, practiced yoga on flat red rocks, hiked every trail on my corner of the map, or just sat in awed contemplation at the beauty of the land. Once a week or so, I drove up to Mikhael's for a bit of social contact. Each shared meal, conversation, shower and fresh load of laundry was imbued with the preciousness of rare events.

Time dissolved into a collection of unique and exquisite moments with neither chronologic nor hierarchical order. But this was no numb blissful state. A full range of feelings – from the painful oppression remnant of past heartbreaks to the gleeful exuberance of my free-range inner-child – ran through my body like wind over the chaparral. I cried or laughed without specific reasons. The desert accepted me with no judgment. It reflected back to me my own core equanimity and patiently reminded me to just be. It guided by example in the settled stillness and openness of its land and the composure of even its smallest inhabitants. Why would I fuss if that tiny cactus at the entrance of my mobile bedroom could be covered in frost in the morning and gloriously bathed in sun a few hours later?

Impermanence was the only constant.

My world shifted slowly but inexorably. The morning frozen condensation grew sparser, the noon sun hotter. Jeep tours increased in my territory and other campers appeared along previously deserted roads. Civilized life was coming to meet me out in the desert, and I began to feel a pull to rejoin it.

Without any conscious decision to do so, I drove to town more often and for longer stretches of time. I stopped using my camping stove and instead visited the market daily to fill my food box with fresh vegetables and home-baked deserts. I traded my morning ritual of drinking green tea on the tailgate of the truck for the exploration of little coffee shops.

Java Love Café quickly became one of my favorites. It was the quintessential Sedona watering hole, frequented at any time of the day by an assortment of purple-wearing angel-channellers, dreadlocked travelers, Native American elders and far-west tour guides in cowboy attire. It also had several tall tables and matching chairs near the front door, perfect for people-watching and feet-dangling.

Whereas Rishikesh had worn the robe of spiritual Mecca modestly, Sedona flashed its psychics, tarot readers, reiki healers, shamans and aura photographers like shiny lures to the tourists. Yet, in spite of the blatant commercialism, every shopkeeper, palm reader or psychic healer with whom I spoke radiated genuineness.

They came from all over the world to be in Sedona, drawn by intuition or by mystical forces beyond their reckoning. They came for healing, then fell in love with the land and stayed. Yes, the land was beautiful, they all agreed, but the sense of uplifting power they felt in the red rocks, and especially near the vortexes, was the true draw.

"What are vortexes?" I asked each one, but no answer was the same, and I was left with only a compilation of vague impressions.

In a small bookstore at the edge of town, right next to Dry Creek Road, I found the perfect manual to fuel, rather than assuage my curiosity: "Scientific Vortex Information" by Pete A. Sanders Jr.

According to Sanders, the vortexes of Sedona were the source of the area's palpable power. Some vortexes were male, outward, or yang, most conducive to feelings of oneness and expansion, and others were female, inward, or yin, perfect locations for introspection. Only a few vortexes had both qualities. These were best used for gaining balance. There was no measurable change in the electromagnetic field because the energetic distortions happened in a dimensional reality outside of our field of sensuous perception and beyond the scope of our existing instruments of measurement. Empirical evidence, however, was abundant. Thousands of people reported feeling a sense of peace, swirling energy, elation, goose-bumps, spine-tingling, déjà-vu, or sudden epiphanies in the field of vortexes. There were documented cases of miraculous recoveries from addictions, illnesses or injuries that could not be otherwise explained.

I read the whole book in one sitting and blinked in fascination when I finally looked back to the desert.

Was the buzzing I felt on my first night vortex-induced? Would I be able to perceive these higher dimensional energetic disturbances? Could I raise my vibrational frequency simply by standing in one of these power centers?

In the abundant vacant space the desert had opened in my mind, scientific curiosity was suddenly wide awake.

The next morning, I began collecting data. For my first experiment, I returned to Bell Rock, recognized as one of the most powerful male vortexes, and again buried my hands in the soft dirt. I made a mental note of the level of buzzing in my body, and then walked away one hundred feet at a time, each time checking the level of buzzing with both hands in the dirt. I could not detect any significant change.

I drove back to the open plain, miles from any towering red rock and sat on the dirt I called home. I definitely felt more peaceful out in the open, but I still could detect a slight buzzing, which could have been residual.

In the course of the next few days, I braved busses of tourists, souvenir vendors and fee-based parking lots to visit every vortex on the sanctified tourist map of Sedona.

Most male vortexes were located atop towering red rocks, most female vortexes deep in cool canyons. Of course, I felt a difference in the quality of my energy – I felt more powerful atop a red hill and more introspective by a green bubbling brook. But how much of these effects could be attributed to higher dimensional energetic distortions when the terrain was so obviously different?

The only consistency across the greater Sedona area was my level of buzzing: anywhere within the red sandstone, regardless of the distance from a known vortex or the type of vortex, I buzzed. Anywhere in the open plain or above the red sandstone – such as at the top of Bear Mountain, composed of quartz-rich and iron oxide-poor Coconino Sandstone – I didn't. The buzzing increased and decreased gradually as I changed environment.

My Higher Self had once written that everything was energy. The oscillation of quantum particles in and out of our reality, in accordance with our level of awareness, determined our vibrational frequency. During the Yoga Teacher Training, I had learned to observe and sublimate this energy, Prana, or Life Force.

If my vibrational frequency could be modified with applied breathing techniques and mindful meditation, surely it could be affected by a vortex. Where were the quantum particles going when they oscillated out of "reality" anyway? Could they simply be oscillating between perceptible and imperceptible dimensions? And if Sedona was located in a field of higher energy in an imperceptible dimension, could my quantum particles reach an excited state as they periodically entered it? Is that why I was buzzing?

I felt the experiential data gathering phase of my investigation was over. It was time to raid the Sedona library's Quantum Physics section for answers.

With a pile of books on the tailgate of the truck, including several by Michio Kaku, I let my body lounge in the sun of the desert while my mind surfed the wave function – which is not a wave at all but a mathematical quantification of probability describing the state of a system. I followed the wave to the beach of wave-particle duality, where I stopped to pet Schrödinger's cat, and finally swung away on one of the strings of the string theory, only to land back in multidimensionality.

When I closed the last book of the pile, I felt none the wiser. I understood the concepts – albeit sometimes with much mental gymnastics – but still, I was missing a link, a map or a broader view of how it all fit together.

My cognitive mind was utterly confused, but my unconscious mind had absorbed the nectar of the concepts and already drawn its own conclusions. It patiently waited for me to tuck myself out of the way to express itself.

The desert must have known that I needed help. That evening's sunset surpassed all I had yet seen in Arizona. The wide canvas of the sky usually painted with smooth color gradations was filled with hundreds of tiny puffs of clouds gathered in long rows. As the sun descended behind each layer, the sky exploded with silver linings and crepuscular rays.

I dropped all mental explorations – I had no choice. I

leaned back against my food box and allowed the experience of that sunset to permeate every particle in my being, in this and any other dimension. When the spectacle finally subsided, I retrieved my journal and pencil.

01/23/2013
Excerpt from my journal
    $E=MC^2$. What if C is Consciousness, instead of Celerity. The energy in the Universe is in square relationship to the level of consciousness. If the consciousness (awareness) of an entity with a form (mass) increases by 1, the creative potential, which is reflected in the overall vibrational frequency (energy) of said entity, increases 10-fold. Reality is vibrations. All pasts, futures and alternate presents exist. The material reality that gets collapsed is that which resonates with the current vibration of the observer.

    "What?"
    I read again what I had just written, carefully and mindfully. What did this have to do with buzzing and vortexes? I read it a third time and started to catch a glimpse of a fragment of understanding.
    $E=MC^2$, my favorite equation of all time, was the key to creation. If the buzzing was an indication of increased vibrational frequency of my internal energy, then, if I understood correctly, being in Sedona increased my potential for creating physical reality by a factor of ten.

CHAPTER 57

In the early morning chill of the open desert plain, I woke up to the sound of the sky breathing. The sound was soft and indistinct at first, and I believed it part of my dream, but as my consciousness emerged gradually into the waking world, the forceful exhalation increased and sharpened.

A dragon was flying overhead. It was true – incredibly, the energy of one of my fantasy realities had densified to a full sensory physical experience.

I got dressed quickly and opened the back of the truck to see the creature. How disappointing – It was only a green and yellow hot air balloon floating against the backdrop of majestic red rocks bathed in the sunrise glow.

My eyes followed the balloon's progress for a moment, but I was much more fascinated by my own disappointment. I really believed in magic. I really believed that I could create my own physical reality with applied consciousness.

But was I wrong in that assumption? I crawled back to my sleeping bag and cocooned myself with my thoughts. Could I create a dragon? Could I believe that I could create a dragon enough to create a dragon? Was Einstein implying anything about dragons when he penned his famous formula?

The breathing overhead became increasing louder, but I barely noticed. I was completely absorbed in my analytic musings, until one breath was so close and so loud, that I jumped up and out of my sleeping bag.

With hundreds of square miles of available flat land, that hot air balloon was landing on my truck.

At the last minute, it exhaled a few more puffs, and gracefully glided to the ground less than twenty feet away from my bedroom.

"Did you order a balloon for breakfast?" One of the men in the basket playfully yelled. While the basket-full of tourists laughed, two men jumped to the ground to secure the balloon.

"Do you ... need any help?" It seemed like an odd question, but I had no prior experience with balloons landing on me and was unsure of what to say.

"Sure. We'd love some help."

With a few instructions and much mimicking I learned to

gently bring the envelope down, fold it, roll it and load it onto the support vehicle when it found us. I welcomed the delighted group of tourists to my desert and photographed each family and couple in front of the basket while the men secured the load to the trailer. When I felt that my help was no longer needed, I walked home, twenty feet away.

The tourists were already loaded in a van and the balloon trailer truck had driven away, when one of the men approached my truck with a glass of champagne, a piece of cake covered in strawberries and sweet cream and a business card.

"We really could use a female crew member on our team, and you seem like a natural. If you have free mornings, here's the boss's name and number. I already told him about you, so I hope you'll call."

01/24/2013
Text to Sofia
A hot air balloon just landed on me in the middle of the desert and offered me a job. They also had breakfast for me, champagne, cake, strawberry and cream. It's not even 9 am yet!
Text from Sofia
Your stories are getting ridiculous ☺.

Not only was the story ridiculous, it was delicious. The Storyteller was so excited about sharing this one with the world that I could not even contain it long enough to finish my cake, strawberries and cream. I poured the rest of the champagne in the dirt and, within a few minutes, the truck was packed and bouncing down the dirt road to town in the cloud of dust left behind the tourist van.

The library was not open yet, so I drove up 89A towards Java Love Café. But I never made it to the café.

While I was waiting at a stop light, a mere two blocks away from Java Love, a pink jeep turned right in front of me from a side street. The pink jeeps of the Pink Jeep Tours Company were ubiquitous by this time of the year. I had seen them, eaten their dirt, passed them and maybe even occasionally cursed them, but I had not yet looked at them as I did that morning through my brand new "I could get a job, and it could be a fun one" goggles.

People were getting paid to drive off-road to breathtaking locations throughout the Sedona backcountry and share with tourists from all over the world their love of the desert southwest, its geologic wonders and mysterious vortexes.

When my light turned green, I followed the jeep.

This particular jeep drove straight to the Pink Jeep maintenance and repair shop.

"Hi. Good morning. Could you tell me how one goes about driving one of these for a living?" I pointed at the jeep.

The mechanic's gaze swept from my dusty boots to my dusty hiking pants to my disheveled hair under a dusty hat. He looked amused.

"You've just missed the hiring season for Sedona, but we're still hiring for Grand Canyon. You should hurry though; I think the application process closes today."

He gave me the name of the hiring manager and directions to the main office and wished me good luck.

The Pink Jeep Tours' main office's large glass entrance doors opened automatically past a couple of thigh-high pink cement balls on the side of the door. I stepped my dusty boots in the clean and spacious reception hall. Across a curved granite counter, a professionally-dressed receptionist was talking with a man in a Pink Jeep cap and a Pink Jeep buttoned shirt. They both turned and smiled as I entered. I had not expected such a corporate look from a company whose main business was to drive in the desert dirt. But this was my reality, and I would not have created it any less paradoxical.

"Good morning. I just followed a jeep to your repair shop, and the man there suggested I come here to fill out an application."

While the receptionist searched her files for an application, I turned to the man in the Pink Jeep outfit.

"Are you one of the guides?"

"I am – best guide in the company for ten years running. My name is Mike."

The receptionist laughed.

I read once that, within fifteen minutes of a meeting between two strangers, each party would manage to insert into the conversation those parts of their life story they found the most interesting. It never failed.

Within fifteen minutes, I had learned that Mike had claimed the title of best guide for ten years running within a month of his initial employment, seven years prior, that he loved Sedona, his job and his geo-cashing adventures. And, above all, he loved his wife, the fabulous Julie, whom I would undoubtedly love, if I were to meet her.

In the same span of time, Mike, and the receptionist by extension, had learned that I was living in my truck in the desert and loving it, that I had walked from Mexico to Canada the previous summer, and that a hot air balloon had just landed on me and offered me a job, but that I could see myself happier at the wheel of a jeep than suspended under a hot air balloon.

In the same span of time, the receptionist had quietly decided that I was just the kind of energy the company needed and had asked the hiring manager to come to the reception to meet me. Within five minutes of meeting her, I had mentally resigned from my potential position as a hot air balloon flight attendant. I already knew that the jeep-driving job was mine.

I didn't return to the desert right away that day. My timeless idle days in the desert sun had finally birthed a financially advantageous adventure. With the prospect of work on the horizon, I no longer needed to safeguard my budget. I made reservations to fly back to Seattle at the end of the next week and booked a moving truck to relocate my stored treasures to Arizona.

The time for action had come. In the span of a couple of days, I drove to Mikhael's for a shower and a load of laundry, convinced the Pink Jeep Grand Canyon branch manager that I was an ideal candidate for the final late-February in-person interview and drove to Grand Canyon to explore my new territory.

The Pink Jeep Tours office in Tusayan, just a few miles south of Grand Canyon was almost deserted when I walked in. Tourist season had obviously not yet started. The only tour that day was a Sedona-Grand Canyon tour led by none else but Pink Jeep's best guide running for ten years, Mike.

"That's great! You'll be part of the family." Mike said when I told him I was one of the candidates scheduled for the final interview. "I'm sure you'll get hired. In fact, why don't I take you on a private guided tour and show you my favorite spots?"

Mike's excitement about the canyon was contagious, even if some of the tales he told seemed too tall to be true. A good guide, I understood, is primarily a good storyteller, and Mike was exceptional at it. We dropped below the southern rim for a short hike, where Mike pointed out some petroglyphs in the rocks above. Hundreds of thousands of visitors each year walked this trail looking down into the canyon, but how many ever looked up? I couldn't wait to surprise my guests with such insider information.

By the end of the tour, we had laughed so hard that we had already transitioned from colleagues to friends. The next best step was to meet the fabulous Julie of whom he spoke so fondly. The timing was perfect. Mike invited me for dinner and offered that I stay in their spare bedroom the night before my flight to Seattle. He could drive me to the shuttle in the morning, and my beloved truck could safely stay in their driveway until I recovered the treasures.

Julie was, indeed, fabulous. Her energy was immense, crystalline and invigorating like the ring of a gong. She was a closet medium – a skilled psychic able to communicate with the dead, angels and spirits, but not yet willing to share her gift with the world. Yet another instant soul-sister!

Mike and Julie's world was as magical as mine. They did not earn money; they manifested it by following their hearts and placing intents to the Universe. They did not encounter problems, only opportunities to learn and grow. Mike and Julie were soulmates on a common journey of exploration, and despite my love for unbridled solo freedom, I was envious of and inspired by their relationship.

I explored this new longing on the flight to Seattle. Was I even ready for a relationship? Did I have any lingering Logan energy clinging to me? The position at Grand Canyon offered medical, dental and housing benefits. Trading my free-range lifestyle for a roof and a schedule – and a paycheck – was likely to be a sufficient shock to my system. Maybe I was wise to not even think about a relationship, lest I manifest one with applied consciousness.

The stealth recovery of my treasures was a complete success. I neither dreaded nor hoped seeing Logan, and because I fed the thought of him no energy, I knew I didn't risk creating an encounter. Bellingham's sky was as grey and oppressing as I had left it. Mt. Baker was hidden in the clouds. Construction obstructed much of the view of Bellingham Bay from Boulevard Park. I left without even a glance in the rear-view mirror.

I drove the moving van through rain, fog and snow for two and a half days. I missed my truck, but the moving van kept me safe, going as far as getting a flat tire to ensure I spent the night in a hotel in southern Idaho instead of driving on as I had planned. I would have driven into a massive snow storm had I not stopped then.

I crossed the southern Utah line delimiting the cold and snow to the north and the sunshine awaiting me to the south with the same exuberance as the first time. The glow of my home frequency was fully activated. Joy and gratitude overflowed to tears; I was coming home to Arizona.

With the treasures safely tucked in a storage unit in Flagstaff, I hitchhiked back to my love in Mike and Julie's driveway. Mike had left a note and a key for me, but with all the gratitude in my heart for these wonderful, generous, Trail Angels, I still meant to spend my remaining days of unbridled freedom out in the desert, where I belonged.

I disappeared for five days into the backcountry, and likely would not have come out for another day – just in time for my in-person interview at Grand Canyon – if the truck had not insisted that I do.

CHAPTER 58

"Hi Love, why is your 'check engine' light on?"

I dragged a finger across the red dirt on the instrument panel to uncover the warning light. In eleven years of shared adventures, not once had the truck worried me with a mechanical problem.

I placed both hands on the steering wheel and opened my mind to feel into the truck's energy, but all I could detect was a subtle wave of mischievousness. I had never really mastered feeling into objects – or into anything else for that matter – and didn't want to worsen a bad condition with a false interpretation of the truck's energy, even though I felt relatively confident that nothing was wrong with it. I trusted that the truck would not activate its warning light idly, so getting it checked instantly became my priority.

The first mechanic I called had a full schedule for weeks, but lo and behold, somebody had just cancelled their appointment for nine that morning. It was about eight, so I just had enough time to drive out of the desert.

And as creative awareness would have it, the mechanic's shop was directly across the street from my favorite Sedona coffee shop. I dropped the truck off at nine am and walked across the street to Java Love Café.

Peace permeated the café when I first entered it. The few patrons dispersed in the room were engrossed in their respective laptops and books, and the welcoming soft music filled the resulting silence.

I sat at the only tall table available to dangle my feet while having breakfast – hot Sensha green tea and a decadent Java Love Bar.

I had just bitten into the suffocating squishy sweetness of the Love Bar, when an elderly gentleman approached the man at the table directly behind mine. A sudden conversation erupted mid-concept, and I could only assume that their debate was an ongoing one.

The older gentleman was still convinced that he was an alien from another planet in a human body; the younger one argued, as he had before, that there was no evidence for the hybridization of human DNA and that his interlocutor was in fact, still, a primate, from earth. The older gentleman had a new argument: he had clear memories of his home planet; the younger one dismissively invoked spiritual delusion.

I suspended biting further into the Love Bar to direct my attention to their surreal conversation. The alien made sense; Sedona was filled with spiritual eccentrics from other planets, dimensions or realities. But who was this incongruous science man so confident in his dismissal?

I stretched my back to the right, then to the left, and finally weaved a stealth twist of my spine to get a glimpse of him. In an instant, I noted the shoulder-length dark hair, curly underneath, graying and distressed on top, the bumper sticker on the back of the laptop that read "unSpirituality.com", the strong working hands, the square jaw and the reading glasses, above which dark eyes under heavy eyelids were fixed on mine.

I turned back quickly to my own table with a pounding heart. His eyes had the intensity of inevitability, but I wasn't interested. No, I wasn't. I wasn't interested in anything romantic or complicated or time-consuming or that required me to alter my free-spirited life in any way. Besides, I was moving to Grand Canyon in just a few weeks. My only interest here was mere curiosity about unSpirituality.com.

I typed the address in my phone's internet and read the headlines on the site: Christopher Loren, a one man army against spirituality was about to publish a book dismantling the religious and spiritual conspiracy to free the human primate from centuries of oppressive delusion.

My heart had just relaxed back to its preferred single reality when the elderly alien finally left. Without mindful volition, my body turned back to face the unspiritual man.

"So, do you make a living out of arguing with people about their spirituality?" I smiled in mock defiance.

"No, I just challenge assumptions. Would you like to discuss it?" He smiled back and pointed a hand to the chair across the table from him. I watched my body change chair and barely had time to snatch my tea and Love Bar.

"So, how can you be certain that this man is not an alien?"

I could stretch my imagination to believe anything.

"Show me evidence. I can claim that I'm a member of the Orion council just the same. I can create any subjective landscape I choose in my mind, but that doesn't make it reality. There is, however, ample evidence for the theory of evolution. The greatest minds in science, from evolutionary biology, DNA schools of research, brain science, all support the theory."

"Who's arguing against evolution?" Because I was raised in a science-minded secular home, evolution had never been in question for me, not even in light of my spiritual awakening.

"Spiritualists are! They suffer from cognitive dissonance. Once you have created an identity for yourself as a 'spiritual being having a human experience' then simply being human isn't enough. You must instead get on a 'path', follow guidance from 'God' or your 'Higher Self', which always lives in an invisible realm that is always so much better than the natural world. The 'lowly physical self' is devalued in favor of a grandiose mental construct. Who wants to bother with real life when you can imagine yourself an eternal multidimensional being with infinite creative power?"

My jaw opened to answer, but then closed again. Wait a minute – *I* was one of those eternal infinite multidimensional beings guided on a path by the Invisible. And I was not willing to be anything less.

"What if 'real life' *is* a personal creation? What if each person's physical reality is the result of applied consciousness? If that man believes he's an alien, then that's the experiential reality he creates for himself. If I believe I'm an energetic being, then I am. Consciousness wanting to experience itself could create any physical reality simply by applying itself, including the physical reality where one is the pinnacle of evolution. $E=MC^2$! Straight from one of the greatest minds in science."

I knew that this was not what $E=MC^2$ traditionally meant, but the formula was fresh on my mind and I felt I needed scientific backing.

Chris leaned back on his chair and carefully placed his glasses on the table. He crossed his arms, pensive for a moment, and then slowly looked straight up at me under his eyelids with the same intensity as when I first spied on him. He smiled and nodded, though I couldn't determine whether in agreement or mere appreciation of my retort.

"I actually don't know what E=MC² means, precisely. For over thirty years of my life, I was shielded from science. I walked many paths of spirituality, from the most orthodox religion to the most occult branch of metaphysics, looking for enlightenment. Then, two years ago, I discovered the scientific method and the concept of evolution. I discovered that, as humans, we were grown through five billion years of natural selection. Now, *that* is more impressive to me than any spiritual story I was ever fed. Evolution makes sense. I was finally awakened to my true self as a human primate."

I extended my hand to shake his.

"Hi. My name is Melissa; I'm your opposite. I have been a scientist for over thirty years. Two years ago, I awoke to the awareness of my true self as an infinite multidimensional energetic entity, manifested at the grossest level as a human body for the purpose of experiencing Life. It's nice to meet you. If you want, I can explain E=MC²."

We debated all day – a battle of wits and big words. By noon, we had covered religious delusion and oppression, the fundamental laws of physics, energy, mass, celerity, consciousness, advantages and flaws of the scientific method, Jesus – whom Chris called the Jewish Zombie – alien life, the subjective mind, and what actually constitutes physical reality.

"You can't argue that this table is right here between us." He leaned forward and placed both palms down in the center of our shared table. "You can claim it's a unicorn, but if ten people approach it, the consensus will be that it *is* a table. And … and also, would you have lunch with me? I know a great

Indian buffet."

"I would love to have lunch with you. I love Indian food. And using consensus to determine reality is too unreliable. What we perceive depends on our state of mind. Ten people subjected to the same mind alteration could very well agree that this table is a unicorn, or a grizzly bear swimming across a river and about to be hit by a boat."

He did not question my reference, and I, surprising, did not offer that I had kayaked four hundred miles in the Yukon and experienced full sensory hallucinations.

In fact, we had both violated the fifteen-minute rule.

We stepped out of the café side by side, as comfortable as an established couple, and yet I still knew nothing of this man except for his unabashed invalidation of core spiritual concepts I had just discovered and embraced.

He courteously opened the passenger door of a dirty old rusted GMC truck and invited me in. The truck bed was filled with rolls of black poly tubing of exactly the same weight and diameter as those Darcy and I had once used to create hula hoops.

"Are you a hula-hoop maker? I thought you were a writer."

"I am a writer, but I also own an irrigation company. I maintain and install irrigation systems. I build water features and sometimes take on stone projects, like patios, stairs, and garden ponds, whatever comes my way."

I was disappointed. I would have enjoyed creating a paradoxical reality in which I met an unspiritual professional hula-hoop maker, but irrigation did make more sense in the common reality.

Once we were both fully enveloped in the exotic aroma of the Indian buffet, Chris steered the conversation back to the science of reality.

"There are limits to the natural world. Laws of physics can't be violated. Any story of supposed performed miracle, levitation or resurrection is always second hand. People talk about it, but have you seen it? I once asked a guru who claimed he could heal by touch to plant a knife through my hand and heal it. He wouldn't do it – said I didn't have the right 'mindset' for it. Maybe I can believe that at the quantum level reality is made of waves that become matter when there is an observer. I just don't think that's how it works at the level of solid, physical matter. Reality is reality, with or without an observer."

Chris's worldview felt like cobwebs – sticky, inconvenient, non-magical cobwebs. I believed in miracles, levitation, resurrection and healing by touch. I believed anything was possible. I noted the constriction in my heart and handed the dilemma over to my brain. It would know how to silence this born-again scientific man.

"Actually, quantum physics doesn't claim that reality is made of waves. The wave function is a mathematical expression that describes the state of a system of particles. At the quantum level, all configurations of reality exist. The wave function predicts the probability that a particular configuration will exist if measured. But the very act of observing or measuring the system reduces the set of probabilities to just the one observed. As long as Schrödinger's cat's still in the box, he's got an equal chance of being dead or alive. If we open the box and look inside, we collapse the probability to either a 100% live cat or a 100% dead cat. That's the simplest representation of the Copenhagen interpretation of the wave function collapse."

I could easily sound smart and knowledgeable on the topic; I had recently spent a few days surfing the wave function on the tailgate of my truck. I casually continued eating throughout my discourse to conceal the fact that I barely understood the concepts myself. When I finally looked up, I found Chris staring at me, his face as flushed as the tandoori.

"*That* is the sexiest thing any woman has ever said to me."

I laughed much louder than the remark warranted. I felt a little flush myself.

"Anyway ... I believe any reality can be created by conscious application of awareness, but the source of creation is our Higher Self, not the ego part of ourselves. And ... and would you like to go for a hike with me this afternoon?"

"I don't hike, but yes, I'll go for a hike with you. Let's all go – you, me and your invisible Higher Self!"

We selected a short hike, mere minutes from Chris's house, but spent most of the afternoon sitting on rocks debating physical reality.

"Show me evidence. Be the president of the United States tomorrow by four pm, and I'll believe you can manifest reality."

"It won't work because I don't believe I could and don't need to be the president. If I had the belief and a need, then yes, I could be the president of the United States tomorrow by four pm."

"That's the problem with the spiritual story. It's a treadmill. It creates guilt. If you don't manifest your preferred reality, you must not believe enough. The spiritual ego constantly needs to be stroked so that spiritual fantasies can be attained, but they never are. Meanwhile, the mind is so engrossed in divine narcissism that the precious 'here and now' is completely missed."

"So, are you saying that manifestation isn't possible?"

"We are primates – highly evolved creatures with body wisdom beyond our reckoning. Why create a spiritual story for our natural abilities? If I decide to buy a blue VW van, suddenly I'll notice all the blue VW vans in town. I can create a spiritual story that says, 'God is sending me signs.' There are hundreds of other cars on the road I'm not noticing. No invisible being came down to put VW vans in town. I just notice them because I'm attuned to them. It's called patternicity. We recognize patterns. That's how our ancestors survived in the wild – leaf moves equals predator in bushes. Now we live in cities, but we still have this deep-seated knowledge of natural patterns, like wind, rain, prey, predators, subtle body language ..."

Sticky, inconvenient cobwebs! The wind *had* been stopped for me. Signs had been sent. Magic had graced every step of my journey, from the Gold Bond on the trail to hot air balloons with job offers to sudden mechanical warning lights precisely crafted to facilitate this very meeting. Was meeting Chris part of the magic, part of the path? Why? Why would my Higher Self arrange for the magic to be dismantled?

"I don't like what you're saying."

Chris's face softened with a smile and he extended his hand to take mine.

"I know." He said gently. "I went through denial too, at first. Spirituality is really just an expression of the reclaimed shamed imagination. Imagination is part of a child's natural development. If the parents squash the child's creations with discipline, shaming, punishing, invalidating, then the lessons from the fantasies aren't assimilated and we develop an obsession with the Unseen. As adults, when our spirituality is challenged, it feels like the original shaming of our childhood and so we fight for our right to create."

I didn't take his hand. Images were flashing in my subjective creative mind – ghosts in the house, discipline in the house, "She has too much imagination." the child psychologist had said, playing in the woods with imaginary friends that did not come home, speaking to God in my head, in secret. Oh no! I was a textbook case.

As we drove back into town, I felt obligated to ask Chris if he wanted to have dinner with me. I longed to return to my solitary magical den and let the desert smooth my frazzled mind, but I also felt compelled to continue our debate until all cobwebs were dismantled and cleared. Chris must have felt my ambivalence.

"No, I think I'll go home now. Thank you though."

No sooner had he declined my invitation that a text from Mike and Julie appeared on my phone.

"Come on over, Kiddo. Julie just made a huge dinner. You can shower before your interview tomorrow and sleep in a real bed."

At least, even if magic was only the result of my shamed imagination, I still had friends in the physical world to help me sustain the illusion.

Chris dropped me off at the mechanic's right at closing time. As I had suspected, there was nothing wrong with my love, just a small hiccup in its catalytic converter sensor, a common occupational hazard of desert dirt dwellers.

CHAPTER 59

"I intend that $100 finds their way into our home today, if it is in line with the Highest Good. I trust and remain open to receive from both expected and unexpected sources. With trust and gratitude ~ Love, Julie."

I looked up from the small note Julie had just retrieved from the kitchen drawer dedicated for checkbooks, notebooks and notes to the Universe.

"Show her, Mike."

With a grin from ear to ear, Mike reached two fingers in his Pink Jeep guide shirt and flicked out a small wad of cash, his guide's tips for the day.

"Exactly $100." Julie said smugly, "For aesthetics' sake I would have preferred one crisp $100 bill, but we're always open to receive, in whatever form it comes."

There was magic in Mike and Julie's home. There was magic in the delicate balance of flavors in Julie's vegetarian tacos, magic in the small attentive gestures of two people in love for several decades, and magic in the sincere and unguarded generosity they had showered upon me from our first meeting. But still, the light of their bright hearts could not dissolve all the cobwebs.

If the best guide for ten years, running trips to the most popular destinations on the map, with that genuine grin, sharp wit and magnetic charisma brought home $100 in tips, could we really call it magic? Or did Julie, through some innate primate body wisdom, absorb the ebb and flow pattern of customer tips based on the weather, time of year and Mike's mood that morning and unconsciously infer how much he was likely to bring home?

I lay in bed for hours that night, tossing and turning. Whichever way I faced, the awful possibility that the past two years of my life had been fueled by delusion stared me in the face. I frantically searched through my memories for just one example of a miracle that could not be explained by natural intuition, coincidence or hard work. With each memory, my heart sunk further.

"Relax, my love," I heard in my head, "All is well. Your meeting with Chris is only designed to expose those areas within you that still doubt the process, so that you may enlighten the shadows and fly ever freer."

"Blah blah blah." I whispered back to the voice with rolled eyes. It always said what I wanted to hear, like a good imaginary friend locked up since childhood would.

Sometime shortly before dawn, I realized that Chris was right; I needed evidence. I would not despair until I had fully tested competing hypotheses using sound scientific methods. If I could manifest a sum of money so large that it could not be attributed to natural causes, then I would know that I was indeed an infinitely creative energetic being whose needs were covered. If I could not, then I would be wise to seriously reconsider finishing that PhD.

$6,000 in a month – It was enough to completely pay off my credit card, it was more than I had in savings and investments, and there was no way I could earn that much as a guide in training. I relaxed into the comfort of knowing that, one way or the other, my doubts would be cleared and fell asleep for the remaining thirty minutes before I had to get up and drive to Grand Canyon for my interview.

02/05/2013
In my little notebook
Dear Love, Dear Universe.
I intend for $30,000 to appear in my bank account within a few months. When the full sum appears, I will donate it anonymously and entirely to the Make-a-Wish Foundation so that a child or several might experience magic in turn.
Thank you, with all my love and gratitude.
~ Melissa

Three other women and one man sat in the lavish lobby of the Canyon Plaza Resort waiting to be ushered into the interview room. According to Mike, over a hundred candidates would pass through these doors in one week, but only ten of us would have the privilege of driving pink jeeps along the rim of one of the seven natural wonders of the world.

The numbers did not intimidate me. Either through the sentience of my Higher Self or the innate wisdom stored in my DNA, I already knew that I was to be one of the lucky ten. This interview was only a formality, but of the outcome of my existential investigation depended the rest of my life, so while others tapped nervous fingers on armrests, I concentrated on my intent.

During the drive to Grand Canyon, I had imagined a few non-magical ways that $6,000 could come to me, so I gradually increased the sum until the number was too large for my imagination. $30,000 was the final sum. I, however, did not need that sum except to validate my faith, which should not have needed to be validated if it were truly faith. An intent born of doubt I knew would not work. If I were to give the money away to charity, however, I could spark my intent with the joy and excitement of giving. I didn't need this money, but the Grant-a-Wish Foundation always did.

I closed my eyes and recalled the steps for meditative visualization I had read in *Frequency*. I let my mind quiet and my heart return to stillness by visualizing my home out in the desert plain, and then focused my mind on the intent. There would be no cash, so I visualized the numbers on my bank statement online. Income: $30,000. My mind navigated to the Make-a-Wish foundation website and clicked on the donate button. I traveled to that emotional moment in space and time and let the energy be as real as I could create it. Incredulous awe, inhibited excitement, tears of gratitude, faith restored – I embraced the feelings, letting my mind climb to a crescendo of joy, holding on, holding on, then finally letting it all go, with trust and gratitude that it was already granted.

I slowly reopened my eye and had a slight jolt of surprise. I had strayed so far that I had forgotten all about the Canyon Plaza and the interview. Several of my potential co-workers were staring at me curiously. Who smiles in beatitude before an interview?

"Melissa?"

I was saved from explanations by my future manager. He led the way to a curtained room where I sat, beaming, across a panel of interviewers. My heart still radiated so much magnificent peace, joy and gratitude from the visualization exercise that I could have sat there quietly and still been offered the position. I left Tusayan certain to return in a few weeks as a Pink Jeep Tours guide.

CHAPTER 60

Despite the trust and preemptive gratitude applied to my intent, I feared facing my doubts alone in the desert, so instead of driving back to Sedona, I retreated to Mikhael's haven of grounded spirituality for a few days.

We dispelled the energy of doubt and confusion in the smoke of wild harvested sage fanned with owl feathers for added wisdom. While the sage cleared my energy, Mikhael read what lay behind it.

"The lesson here", she said, "isn't about uncovering whether Chris's philosophy is right or wrong, but exploring your resistance to it."

I knew that she was correct, but after a good night sleep and several walks through the woods of Flagstaff, Chris's philosophy faded behind the scent of pines and under the crunching of needles. Exploring resistance felt like work, and I preferred to just play. I did not expect to see him again anyway, and figured that, if I did, I would simply greet him and not engage in any philosophical debate.

So I was surprised when my truck parked next to his, right in front of Java Love Café, within a few minutes of my return to Sedona.

Although the café was crowded, Chris sat at the same table as when I first met him, brow intensely furled just a few inches from his computer screen. He continued typing furiously for a few minutes, oblivious to my presence. When he finally looked up, in search of the next sentence, his eyes met mine and his face instantly flushed.

"Hey, you blushed without quantum physics this time."

His head rolled back in laughter. He stood to welcome me with a hug and invited me to join his table. I purposely sat in a different chair, as a reminder to myself to not fall into the trap of a debate.

"You really threw me for a loop with your unspiritual ideas. I think I've recovered now, but I was frazzled and lost for a few days."

"Yes, I understand. Truth is more important to me than comfort, but sometimes I still miss the blind bliss of spirituality. It's not lost though. It lives in my subjective imagination and I can visit at will. Here, hold on, let me get into 'Stillness', you know, that place where it feels like 'God' is hugging you."

Chris closed his eyes and took a deep inhale. On the exhale, his face changed. Peace suddenly smoothed the lines on his brow and a soft glow illuminated his skin from within. His features were the same, but a new, irresistibly attractive magical being now sat in his chair. A sharp pull tugged at my heart.

"Anyway, I can get there whenever I want, and sometimes I do, just for the heck of it." The magical being had left as suddenly as it had appeared, and I was left staring at casual unspiritual Chris. I stared so quietly and intently that Chris blushed again.

"Say ... I need to return to editing my book now. But ... hum ...Would you have dinner with me tonight? I'll cook fish. You'll like it."

My mind said "No, no, no!", but my heart said "Hey, maybe that magical being lives with him. Let's go see!"

"I'd love to have dinner with you, and I love fish. Does five pm work? I need time to drive back to the desert before it gets too dark after dinner."

The truck seemed pleased with itself when I returned.

"I'm not interested. I just like fish." I told it.

Even in the soft glow of candlelight, Chris did not appear as attractive as his spiritual alter-ego, but I kept searching his face for even a glimpse of it across the dinner table. He let me stare.

"Are you handsome?" I finally asked.

He laughed and blushed again. "That's an odd question. I don't know. When I was younger and a rock star I was told that I was handsome often, but I always attributed it to the draw of the music. So, really, I don't know."

"You were a rock star?"

One innocuous little question and the rest of the evening disappeared into a storytelling blur. We traveled through the mental, emotional and physical abuse of his childhood, the Christian born-again awakening that ended his rocketing career as a teenaged guitar sensation on the Hollywood rock scene, his missions in Haiti and the fervor with which he lead his own televangelist show. I held my breath when he escaped on foot from a religious cult, worried when he descended into the depth of the metaphysical dark arts, and marveled when he rapidly rose through the ranks of Scientology. I was envious when, at his spiritual peak, he could shoot energy out of his fingertips, and proud when he donated his truck and all his possessions to charity, surrendering all volition and care-taking to the Universe. I walked down the streets of Los Angeles with him, in my mind, as he met his inner child and childhood dog in the flesh, and then entered a tiny chapel to attend his own funeral.

There he was, inconspicuous on the back pew of this tiny chapel, his childhood dog by his feet, his inner child pressed against him for safety. The procession of mourners was barely illuminated by the hazy southern California sun streaming through dark indigo stained glass. I waited for Chris to stand up and approach his own casket, but suddenly he was quiet.

"Then what happened? What happened after you attended your own funeral?"

"That's it. The magic left, so I came home. I think I was tired of spiritual toiling anyway. The constant upkeep of faith and trust was such hard work. Sure, all my needs were covered, but I never knew how until the last minute. Always living on the edge was exhausting. Now I have a business, and I don't have to journey through non-physical realms to clear shadows, negative thoughts or doubts in order to 'manifest' my next paycheck. I work for it. It's easier that way."

I sat in silence for a few minutes, feeling jet-lagged from my journey through Chris's life, while he cleared our empty plates off the table. I was still in a trance when he returned from the kitchen with a large piece of carrot cake to share.

"I made an intent to manifest $30,000 to see if I could. But it's not for me. It'll all go to charity."

I shared with Chris the details of my experiment and the thought process that had led me to it. This was not about proving him wrong, but about testing my own beliefs.

"Ah, yes!" He smiled and nodded. "I used to visualize swirling violet flames whenever I wanted to manifest money. That was a good spiritual story. Well, it sounds like you have applied the scientific method honestly. I look forward to hearing the results of your experiment. You know I'm always looking for evidence."

By then it was well past midnight, but I felt fully awake and agitated from the intensity of his life-story and the post-carrot cake sugar rush.

"Shall I play some music to relax us both?" I assumed Chris meant slipping a CD into the player for ambience, but he uncovered a guitar from behind the bed and settled into a chair with a pick in his mouth.

"Never let them play the guitar for you on a first date," my friend Margaret scolded me the next day, "or you'll fall in love with them in spite of yourself."

Chris closed his eyes as he drew the guitar against his chest, but I kept mine wide open. Nobody had ever played the guitar for me before, and I meant to honor his gift with undivided attention. In my vulnerable post-story state, it only took a few notes for the music to capture my heart. My breath quieted and deepened, matching the undulations of the melody, and still I kept both eyes riveted on Chris.

Across from me, in the blue chair, one hand held the music in place while the other caressed it. The stroking grew faster and louder, matching the beat of my heart. Beyond the wounds in our stories and the doubts in our minds, the room vibrated with a new frequency, a transparent, transgressing, transcendental frequency. Unguarded and exposed, Chris's face swayed behind dark hair, back to stillness within motion, that place where we all dwell in moments of true love. There was the magical being my heart had sought. My fingers began to tingle. My stomach was queasy. I was paralyzed, held captive in a space-time singularity so vast that it was vulnerable, so graceful that it was overwhelming. I shuddered and fell. Inevitability had found me after all.

This was not my first time falling in love, but it was my first time doing so in full and complete awareness of the process as it happened.

A few more strokes straight to my heart and, at last, Chris leaned back into the blue chair, releasing me back to myself. We were silent, locked immobile through unwavering eyes. Chris spoke first.

"Are you okay? I felt your energy shift."

I became aware that my hands were shaking.

"Yes, I'm fine. It's just late and I'm tired. I should go now. Thank you for the delicious dinner."

It was too late to flee back to the desert, so I crawled into my sleeping bag in the back of the truck parked in Chris's driveway and zipped it shut all the way. I wondered if he would come get me during the night. I wondered if I would welcome him. I fell asleep confused and frazzled, but slept the rest of the night undisturbed.

CHAPTER 61

In the early morning light, still buried deep in my bag, I devised a plan of escape. I had two dangerously idle weeks on my hands until the start of the guides' training. If I stayed in Sedona, I was sure to forfeit freedom and peace of mind. My truck would continually find Chris and I would lose myself, as I had the night before.

I needed a short but intense adventure, maybe even slightly life-threatening, to remember whom I meant to play in the world and recalibrate my energy to that frequency.

There were no alpine mountains to climb and I had already hiked to the depth of Grand Canyon and back. I scanned through my mental files of adventures for a few minutes, searching for an activity I had not yet tried and landed on canyoneering. The excitement in my heart was all the sign I needed. I signed up for a three-day "Art of Canyoneering" class in southern Utah right from my phone inside my sleeping bag and left Sedona within the hour.

Rolling in the red Utah dirt, sleeping in the back of the truck in random parking lots and dangling on ropes over narrow abysses was just the cure for cobwebs and romances. By the end of the first canyoneering class, I once again occupied my body, my place on earth, fully and exactly. Melissa the Roaming Bobcat, Melissa the Explorer was back in sharp focus.

"I have enjoyed our philosophical debates and delicious dinner, thank you, but I'm not interested in anything further."

I told Chris. "I need somebody epic, somebody who shines in the wild, thrives in hardships, and defies the laws of physics, especially gravity, because he believes he can."

Sitting in my truck in front of the canyoneering school, waiting for the doors to open for the second class in the series – Canyoneering level II – my life path was evident and obviously incompatible with falling in love with a sedentary unspiritual man.

"Fine then. Go find your fantasy lover. Goodbye." Chris's tone was calm, but he hung up abruptly.

I held the phone to my ear for a few minutes after he hung up and observed my heart sinking into sadness. Had I made a mistake? Was I resisting a relationship out of fear or was sadness a natural side-effect of any separation of energies, without greater meaning, simply the experience of a feeling like countless others?

I opened the gear bin in the back of the truck and gathered my harness, helmet and climbing rack. The familiar metallic jingle of carabiners rang like a wake-up bell. Oh, right! Here was whom I played in the world. Any potential partner of mine would need his own climbing rack. He'd have to be untethered, fearless and larger than life.

Chris was afraid of heights. He would neither climb nor rappel with me. He was afraid of bears. He would never hike thousands of miles or sleep under the stars for months at a time with me. Chris was a non-hiking unspiritual man. I had a choice in this. I could create a partner that matched me simply by keeping my awareness on the possibility.

But the truck – oh, that truck! – drove straight back to Chris's driveway the moment I returned to town, only fifteen hours before the start of the Pink Jeep Tours guides' training.

I stepped in the entrance of his room without knocking, leaving footprints of red Utah dirt on the entryway carpet and through the kitchen.

Without a word, Chris left the editing of his book midsentence and met me at the door. We faced each other, smiling at the joke being played on us.

"The Universe is a sick puppy." Chris laughed and shook his head in disbelief. "Are you staying?"

"Sure. Will you cook fish?"

"Of course. Do you need a shower?"

"Probably, yes." We both laughed. Chris took my hand and led me into the room, past his desk and to the shower. He handed me a clean towel and sat back at his desk to continue editing his book.

This room, this shower, this man and his book – it should have felt all wrong, but instead it felt strangely familiar, as though I had already lived it or was always meant to. Later that evening, we kissed and held each other. There was no awkwardness. I ran my hand along his jaw and let my fingers tangle his hair.

"This – us – it feels karmic." Chris said. I could feel his hand on my back but was mostly held by his eyes.

"I agree, which means it's probably going to be one wild ride. It might not be too late, you know. I can still go find my fantasy lover."

It was too late, and I knew it, but I let Chris ponder the option for a few minutes anyway.

ॐ · ॐ

Karmic, *adj.* An intense kind of relationship to which we agree at the Soul level, designed to rattle us, crack us and open us so that more light might get in. Karmic connections are always wild rides, and the fastest way through is surrender.

ॐ · ॐ

With a pensive moan, Chris pulled my body closer to his until I lay in his arms the way the guitar had on our first fish. I could feel his heart beat like an earthy drum against mine and

345

waited for his response. Finally, he leaned back to look into my eyes.

"Okay. Let's do it. I'm in."

"Okay. I'm in too. I'm not sure we have a choice anyway."

We agreed to an experimental long distance relationship. Chris would drive north to Grand Canyon and I would drive south to Sedona on alternate weekends.

This arrangement lasted less than a week.

My highly creative mind concocted a hundred reasons why this dream guiding position was suddenly unsuitable. There were schedules, rules, forms, required reading lists, mandatory meetings and group jeep rides – I called these "corporate subjugation". Trainees were housed for free in individual rooms in one of the fanciest hotel at Grand Canyon; I drove to the woods and slept in my truck most nights. I convinced myself that I simply did not resonate with Grand Canyon. The light in the canyon was always flat, not vibrant like on Mt. Baker. The geology was interesting, but so repetitive. I preferred the variety of structures in Death Valley. And, no offense to the Canyon, but I just did not find it as beautiful as Sedona.

Under the eyes of my two flabbergasted managers, I turned in my first and last time-card in full understanding and agreement that I was forfeiting any chance of working for Pink Jeep Tours again.

The truck flew back south, and my heart swelled to its full size home frequency. Although quitting made no financial sense – I had used the last of my sold investments to retrieve the treasures – being in Sedona felt right, bright and expansive, and therefore I knew that all my needs would be covered. I didn't need to know how. I figured, if all else failed, I could still call the hot air balloon company.

Without a worry in mind, I sang at the top of my lungs

songs of joy non-stop from Tusayan to Sedona, while the truck purred high RPM harmonics.

CHAPTER 62

"You're coming back? Perfect! I just started building a flagstone patio and I need help. Do you want a job?"

Less than two hours after quitting my job at Grand Canyon, I was developing strong arm muscles and a dark Sedona tan shoveling gravel under the watchful eye of red towering rocks. There were no forms, no clean lunch rooms and no meetings – just a handful of power-tools, a whole stack of two-hundred pound flagstone slabs, Chris and me. It was perfect indeed.

That first night back in Sedona was cold – it even snowed a little – so I stayed at Chris's. The next night was cold as well, and the next one not much warmer, as was the following one. Eventually the nights warmed up, but we began work so early in the morning that it was more convenient for me to stay at Chris's.

My possessions surreptitiously migrated from the truck to his room, one item at a time, until I had my own side of the closet, my own desk and my own bookshelf.

Suddenly, I had an address, a partner and a job – the full reintegration package.

03/14/2013
Email from my Dad
"Congratulation on your new position, that of woman in love. 'Guide at Grand Canyon' was already a romantic proposition, but now you're swimming in pure romance. I bet you love it! And Chris too. The man has found both a companion and a physical laborer. How much does he pay you? Ha!

I think that your unconventionality has reached a level well beyond the usual meaning of the word. In these times of global crisis, while millions of unemployed people in all countries are desperately trying to survive, you, my daughter, get a hot air balloon to land on you with a dream job (and breakfast) and then leave another dream job to mix cement with a man you just met ...
I must ask, what is wrong with this picture?"

Chris and I loved each other, of that there was no doubt, but swimming in pure romance we were not. In fact, if we had loved each other any less, Chris would have fired me from the patio project or I would have driven back to the desert within a week – both of which were possibilities we kept within reach, just in case.

Not only were we challenged by diametrically opposed philosophical views and incompatible lifestyles, but our main commonalities were fierceness of independence, passion in debates and a need for space so vast that it should have been mutually exclusive – I had only just gotten out of the desert, and Chris had been purposely single for nine years before I appeared at his doorstep.

And yet, as romantic partners, we flowed with surprising harmony. We both believed in respecting the planet, in the value of work well done and projects completed on time, in honoring our intuition, learning from our mistakes, looking inward for answers, keeping open lines of communication, and treating each other kindly, patiently and respectfully. We believed in unguarded love and in the creation of dedicated romantic moments each day, several times a day.

We agreed to sleep in separate beds in the same room to maintain a semblance of personal space, but at first light we crawled in each other's beds. We showered, worked shopped and cooked together. We danced in the kitchen, ate by candlelight and made love every day. For the first three months, Chris and I walked through the world as one loving and undividable unit – one endlessly debating undividable unit.

Spiritually, we both believed in a non-dual, unified source of consciousness, but whereas Chris's concept of reality was defined by sensuous perceptions and scientific measurements, I considered these limiting factors in our perception of reality. In Chris's worldview, the body was the source of consciousness; in mine, the body was the result, or grossest layer of manifestation, a mere tip of the iceberg of the true, complete self. Consciousness, in my view, was pervasive and unlimited.

We held fast to opposite sides of the debate fence on any philosophical topic that appeared in our relationship field. The human brain created God, or the human brain perceived God. Science could prove facts, or science was evolving and not to be taken as dogma. Magic was an imaginative interpretation of natural phenomena, or magic highlighted the existence of unseen realms beyond the natural. Some things were certain, and the truth needed to be shared; Nothing was certain, and yes, still, each person's truth should be shared, but not imposed at the exclusion of all else. Atrocities were committed in the name of religion, and spiritualists were too self-absorbed to be bothered with helping others; only by raising the overall vibration could the world become a better place, and my own growth was the only aspect about which I had control.

Well, wasn't that convenient? Would I tell *that* to the starving child or the raped young woman?

Although Chris and I strived to remain level headed, sometimes we failed to keep our debates at a simmer. We both growled in frustration and stormed out in wild flurries of unpleasanteries. I was fired and rehired regularly. But always we returned with apologies and love.

349

When we returned, before we could again hold and kiss each other, we each took turns in the blue chair.

The blue chair in which Chris had so eloquently played the guitar on the day when he first captured my heart became our relationship's talking stick. Whoever sat in the blue chair had the privilege of being heard. Whoever sat on the bed or on the floor listened with an open heart, and for even a brief moment stepped in the other's shoes for a change of perspective.

This worked well for us. No conflict could withstand the volition of two people committed to clearing their relationship field of anything but pure love and I believed that, over time, all our differences could be resolved, set aside or accommodated.

But while Chris could step in my shoes and back to his own unscathed, the process rattled me every time. Embracing a magical worldview was simply an exercise in applied imagination for Chris. He never lost sight of his newfound truth. My reality, on the other hand, was so plastic that each time I stepped in Chris's primate shoes, a little bit of fairy dust fell off my wings, until, one day, I realized I could no longer fly.

"What's wrong, hon'?"

I had not meant to wake Chris up. I had meant to dissipate the oppression on my chest with deep breaths before the alarm set off. Unfortunately, a rogue tear had rolled along my cheek, past my ear and onto Chris's shoulder, where my head rested.

"You took the magic away!" The words burst forth before I could inspect them.

"Oh, c'm here …" Chris rolled over, cradled me in his arms and rocked me gently. My tears turned to sobs.

"I never meant to write a book to hurt anyone and you least of all. I've been where you are. I know the feeling of complete trust in something greater, else, out there. I've lived in complete surrender to some Greater Power that protects, inspires, guides, and loves unconditionally. But, hon', I'm only saying that *you* are the source of all that magic – authentic magic, without the story, without the bullshit."

I could not hear him.

If Chris was right, if joyous applied consciousness was not the source of creation, if I had placed my trust and faith in delusions, then my life as I lived it was not sustainable. Eventually, I'd run out of money and have to rejoin the Old World, the nine-to-five, the grind, the need for discipline in order to survive, with no greater purpose whatsoever. The mere thought sent shivers of horror along my spine and blocked my throat.

"What if Chris is right?" I had asked Ana.

"He's not, love. Even Chris doesn't believe Chris's message. Look how antagonistic he is about it. He's just arguing with himself. Chris is hurt, so he's angry. Truth doesn't come from anger; it comes from Love."

"Of course Chris is right." Hobbes had answered, "All truths are valid, all worldviews are important. The Universe doesn't discriminate."

"Yeah but, how do I know what's true for *me*?"

"You do what you always do: Follow your joy. Whatever makes you happy is what's true for you."

"But what if I'm actually fleeing from reality and calling it 'roaming' because I'm spiritually delusional?"

To aggravate matters, "fleeing" seemed to be the consensus about my lifestyle amongst friends who had known me as a successful scientist, before the roaming.

03/24/2013
Email from Jack, in answer to my sharing that I had begun to feel restless again.
　"I'm going to make an observation. Do with it whatever you wish…seems to me it is time for you to sit and figure things out in terms of what you want to do and who you want to be. Dancing around from place to place is an intoxicating placebo, but it's not life. I'm certainly not saying one must embrace the 9-5 grind, but it looks like you are fleeing the decision making process. I do hope you figure it out."

　I didn't want to believe that my life was just an intoxicating placebo built on spiritual delusions. Jack couldn't be right. Chris couldn't be right.

CHAPTER 63

　On the morning of April 5th, 2013, I drove out of Chris's driveway bound for the desert. I meant to regroup there, I didn't know for how long. I wanted to sit on the tailgate of my truck and gaze over the dusty vastness or reds and browns, visit my former bedroom and its ornamental cacti, and see if I could find Magical Melissa again, somewhere out there.

　Chris understood. He said that he also needed the space. His book was finally published and our relationship was distracting him from the all-important initial marketing. He insisted that the time apart would do us both a lot of good. His goodbye kiss told another tale, but I left anyway.

　Instead of turning left on Dry Creek Rd, however, the truck continued for half a block to the parking lot of that little bookstore in which I had found the scientific manual on vortexes. How curious! I had not planned on stopping there, but since my quest was to retrieve lost magic, I knew to embrace seemingly random events with an open mind. There must have been a book I needed to take with me to the desert.

My feet walked me straight to a shelf in the back corner of the store where my eyes and hand fell on *The Little Prince* by Saint-Exupéry. How odd! I had expected to be led to a new book. I knew *The Little Prince* very well. As a kid I had loved it so much that I had memorized entire chapters to ensure they would always be available to me, lest I find myself stranded somewhere, someday, without a paper copy.

I remembered my Prince. If I were ever lost in a desert and a small caped boy with golden hair greeted me, I would draw for him a sheep. I would believe that he came from a small planet with only four volcanoes and one rose. And if the world of grown-ups dismissed the tale of our encounter as pure fantasy, the result of mind alteration brought on by dehydration and starvation, I would simply smile, and I would write the tale to safeguard it, impervious to skeptical criticism.

I never made it to the desert.

"You're back already?"

I walked through Chris's room with the determination and fervor of higher callings, straight to my desk in our shared corner office. I dropped my keys on the corner of the table and opened my laptop.

"I'm writing a book. It's called 'Crazy Free.'"

"Nice!" Chris smiled and turned back to *UnSpirituality*, a mere five feet away from the start of my spiritual tale, as though he always knew this day would come.

I plunged back down the Rabbit Hole and met again the Grandmothers. I traced my steps back from Mark's office to Minneapolis. I heard again the ghostly drums and felt the icy fingers of death around my immersed body in the Mississippi River. Each moment, each frame, each scene of my journey flashed in my mind's eye. I could barely keep up. My keyboard and three typing fingers – total, not on each hand – heated up from the strain. I forgot to eat, drink or sleep and might have perished had Chris not kept a regular supply of protein-enhanced green smoothies on the corner of my desk.

I typed so intensely and incessantly that by the time I arrived back in Bellingham after the Vision Fast, Chris moved my desk to the living room so that he could sleep. His own writing process had been similar, with words gushing out at all time of day or night for almost three months straight. I assumed that writing *Crazy Free* would take longer because I also had to sieve through voluminous notebooks of conversations with God and my Higher Self.

Not until I had quit the PhD twice again and held my ticket for India firmly on paper did I begin to notice the discrepancies in my story.

That file that was lost when I was writing my thesis, which I was promised would be saved (p.78) had never rematerialized. The written intent to never see Logan again (p. 90), which was to be the only requirement to set myself free, had been worthless. I had returned not once, not twice, but thrice since that intent. I had even moved in. Oh, right, but I didn't have the words to understand the concepts at play in our pandimensional relationship. Well, wasn't that convenient?

Some of the conversations even failed the test of logic. Hadn't my Higher Self written that the sum of all energies was the Soul (p.74) and that the amount of energy that constitutes Life was finite (p.105)? If the Soul was energy, and the amount of energy was finite, wouldn't the Soul be finite? How could the Soul be bounded but infinite (p.102)? Again, maybe I did not have the capacity to understand these esoteric concepts. Maybe something was lost in translation as I wrote the conversations. I did remember that, in those early days, I sometimes struggled to know who wrote what – me, God, my Higher Self, or a split personality version of myself that enjoyed playing the part of an omniscient being.

My story, however, was as accurate as I remembered it. I

was there. I really had felt my own infinity in Death Valley and witnessed wind miracles. I had written records in my journals of these events.

03/28/2011
Excerpt from my journal – The part before the excerpt on page 43.
I sat on one of the goblins' head and attempted to meditate, more to absorb the place than anything else. I saw all the details in the rocks, the different colors and cuts and shapes, the tall ones, the phallic ones, the precarious ones. Then I noticed that the Goblin on which I was sitting was actually not all that stable either. With each gust of wind, I could feel it wobble under me, tremble, shake, and then rest again. The wind was blowing intermittently. I concentrated on just being, and suddenly began to cry – big tears! The wind increased. I said "please take my pain away. I give it to you." And the wind became even stronger. Straight in my face, as though it was trying to dry my tears. I stopped crying and thanked the wind. I then climbed down from the goblin's head, but then started crying again. I guess I wasn't done being sad. I found a small cave and sat in it to cry a while longer. I also laughed at myself for crying so senselessly.

What did I mean by "I climbed down from the goblin's head" and "I found a small cave"? I had no recollection of climbing down and into a small cave. I remembered clearly sitting on that goblin's head and watching the wind match the volume of my tears. That was the miracle.

I turned to the next miracle. Even with a faulty memory, I knew where to find that piece of triangular glass with a heart in the center that God had given to me in Death Valley right before the fast.

The very next day, I drove up to my storage unit in Flagstaff and recovered a box labeled "recent treasures". Between the feathers and pieces of bark I had collected on the PCT and the prayer beads and sacred incense I had acquired in India, a simple white envelope held my precious divine gift.

Unfortunately, I could not see its heart.

I actually knew the heart was gone before I drove to Flagstaff. I had noted its disappearance months earlier. The white envelope had lived in the back pocket of the truck's driver seat since I had found the piece of glass. When I first noticed its disappearance, I casually dismissed it to the account of my farsightedness and the low light. I also reasoned that with the truck's vibrations, over time, the rubbing of the paper against the glass could have muted it. I had just hoped that enough of it was left to ease my growing concerns about the veracity of my story.

"I can't see the heart anymore." My own heart weighed a ton as I walked back into our room with droopy arms straight to Chris's.

"It doesn't matter, hon'. It's your story. You craft it however you want."

I would have likely found solace in these words, had they been spoken by anyone but Mr. UnSpirituality. Instead, I heard: "You can imagine whatever you want." and became increasingly dismayed.

I even stopped writing for a while. What was the point?

So Chris did exactly what a fantasy lover of mine would do – he packed the truck.

"Let's go to Death Valley. The valley can't be erased. Your canyon with the flowers will still be there. You'll see your Sacred Mountain again and you'll find what you're looking for. Besides, I've never been and it's about time you and I go on an adventure together."

Less than six hours later, I sat on the flat red sandstone slab that had been my bed for four days and contemplated the canyon. Every rock and every plant was exactly how I remembered. The lizards and flies still lived there. The Sacred Mountain, the black basalt, the hill where I spent my last night, the flowers to which I had recited my memorized speech — the stage was still there, but the play was over. The Grandmothers had moved on.

Was I disappointed? I checked the feeling in my heart and found no disappointment. Maybe I had known all along that the magic was in me. Maybe the desert had only provided me with a loving holding space while I traveled through my own imaginings or through parallel realms.

Everything was possible, and my story was still neither confirmed nor invalidated.

CHAPTER 64

Regardless, Death Valley, land of my conception as both a primate descendant and potential spiritual being, still held the magic of wild places. And since this was Chris's first visit, I made a plan to introduce him to my favorites of the valley's features.

For our first stop, we walked across the Badwater salt flats, past the end of the tourist path and onto the immense, blindingly white salt honeycomb. I felt the rising heat swirl upward and around our interlaced hands. I smelled the ancient salt so deeply that I tasted it on my tongue. I closed my eyes to get lost in the silence of its vastness.

"Is that it? There's more to the valley than this, right? I think I'll go back, but you take your time. I'll just go read in the truck until you're ready."

Maybe mind-bogglingly beautiful flat vastness wasn't everyone's cup of tea, I consoled myself. If Badwater was too featureless, I still had grandeur up my sleeves.

I bypassed all the little canyons and secret hikes I knew on the way and drove us straight towards the Mesquite Flat sand dunes — my dunes. By then the sun was already high in the sky, and the tapering snake of asphalt seemed to slow dance through the desiccated land to the beat of its own heat shimmers – Dry rock plains, bushes of grass bleached by the sun, black basalt outcrops, dry lake beds and finally the dunes.

As soon as we reached the sea of warm sand, frozen in sensual perfection by the geologic timeline of its creation, I kicked my shoes off and gave them to a Creosote bush for safe keeping.

Oh, the ecstasy of sand between the toes, likely the closest intimate communion possible between the earth and our physical human bodies! My old friend the wind swirled soft sand around us, filling our eyes and ears, and I returned its greeting by laughing and dancing in the swirl.

Chris kept his shoes on, in case there were bugs in the sand, but I didn't notice right away. When I cleared the first wave of sand out of my eyes and looked up at him, I stopped laughing and dancing mid-step – He looked miserable.

"It's alright." I told him. "We don't have to go far into the sea of sand. We can stay right here at the first dune, if you want."

I checked under a tall Mesquite bush for bugs, lizards and snakes and extended my hand to invite Chris to join me in the shade. He sat down cautiously.

"Mel, I don't like it here. I wasn't sure how to tell you. I love you and I want to share your important place with you, but it's just too barren, hot and uncomfortable for me here."

Suddenly, he spoke very fast, as though the levees of politeness had given way under the weight of scary truths.

"I don't like driving aimlessly on bumpy dirt roads or sleeping on an uncomfortable skinny pad when I have a soft bed at home. I don't like the way you drive for miles with your fuel light on because you have an 'intuition' that there will be a gas station ahead, and I don't share your excitement about the prospect of hitchhiking into town if we run out of gas to make an adventure of it. Don't get me wrong, I love traveling, and I love the desert. I just don't like traveling the way you do, and I much prefer the Sedona desert. Can't we just go home?"

We were both silent for a moment as I pondered his last word. Home — Was Sedona home? In Sedona, the buzzing had accumulated during the months since I moved in with Chris into an omnipresent distraction. It sapped my energy, it messed with my system. I suspected, but could not prove, that it was the cause of the inexplicable bouts of rashes, bladder infections, fevers and dizziness that had plagued me. I suddenly realized how vibrantly healthy I felt in Death Valley and remembered it as my natural state.

I also felt trapped in Sedona. I had grown to resent the big red walls I had once found so beautiful for obscuring my view to the open plains.

"You know, Chris, Sedona is beautiful, but it's not home for me. Those red rocks are too just confining."

"I love the confining red rocks. It's like being in a mother womb — warm and protected."

"A mother's womb? Ugh! What a nightmare. No wonder I feel trapped. I've left that place a long time ago. Freedom to roam! Freedom from the mother's womb!"

We laughed in spite of the knots in our throats and moisture in our eyes.

"We are *so* ill-matched. And I love you." Chris said.

"Yes we are. We are *ridiculously* ill-matched. And I love you too."

"Well then, now that that's settled. Let's go home."

I wasn't thrilled to reintegrate Sedona, but Chris was so grateful to be home that I found joy in our return in spite of myself. We settled back into our routine and turned the discovery — or confirmation — of our immense incompatibility into a joke to amuse our friends.

We both avoided the blue chair and the scary truths. Chris buried himself in the marketing of his book; I surfed the internet in secret, looking for images of Mt. Baker, snow-capped mountains and green lush forests. I stopped hiking; I didn't want to be in the red rocks anymore. I stopped debating; we had already covered all topics related to our differences. The seed that was planted in Death Valley, however, slowly germinated over the course of a few weeks until we could no longer ignore it.

"Let's ask the oracle cards about what we should do about our relationship."

The idea, of course, was mine, but we were in such a state of confusion about what to do, that even Chris, Mr. UnSpirituality, pulled up a chair to receive the guidance of the cards. I hoped for one of those cards that advocated patience, or finding silver linings, or even healing wounds.

We each pulled a card.

Chris's card, the Dry Desert card, portrayed a woman who looked like me walking alone away from the viewer across a set of sand dunes very similar in hue, color and patterns to the Mesquite Flat Sand Dunes. The message was so clear that we felt no need to read the card's accompanying words.

I pulled the Sad Embrace card, on which a woman dressed in blue was holding onto her knees, head bowed, and crying.

Sad Embrace – Enchanted Map Oracle Cards [edited for length]
"You may be entering into a period where loss is a theme.
Relationships based on faulty foundations are meant to end at this time.
Disappointment is a form of perception. If a sense of loss arises, along
with sadness and grief, express these emotions. Tears are like healing rain
that can restore life to a parched inner landscape. Growth is always
assured. Whatever the loss is, let it go, and experience your feelings so that
you may soon see the beauty that lies ahead."

"Never mind the cards." Chris quickly shuffled our death omens back into the pack and guided me around the table closer to him. "We get to choose if we want to be together or not. If we both want it, then we can have it. Let's see a couple's counselor. I'm sure we could do it on our own, but with professional help, we might be able to expedite the process … In the meantime, let's take a quick shower and go out for sushi and forget about all this. What do you say?"

I said nothing until we were in the shower.

"So, you don't think that we're doomed? You don't think that all the signs indicate that it might be time for me to pack up the truck and resume roaming?"

"Not yet."

Under the warm water of our shared shower, Chris kissed me until I believed it.

CHAPTER 65

Long after I had left Sedona, Robert shared with Chris that, in over thirty years as a psychotherapist, we were one of the most intriguing cases of couple therapy he had encountered.

I believe that Robert was part magician – with the power to speak to each person in exactly the language of his or her own unique, individual heart.

But that first day, I was nervous. The last time I had seen a psychotherapist, he had suggested I take the red pill that precipitated my fall down the Rabbit Hole.

I sat in the mostly silent waiting room and tapped my fingers on the sofa's cushion to an internal songless beat. I had walked to Robert's office faster than I intended and had fifteen minutes to wait for Chris's first individual session to end and mine to begin.

Muffled voices dribbled under the door. Only a few words were clear, all in Chris's voice.

"But she …", "she …"

I surmised I was "she" and tormented myself with imagined descriptions of how grandiosely delusional and restlessly ungrounded I was. I searched the wicker coffee table by the waiting sofa for a distraction.

My eyes fell on a copy of *National Geographic*.

"EXPLORE" – the word filled most of the front cover, right below "why we" and slightly above a bright flash of light at the edge of the blue earth. I quickly turned the pages to find the article on why we explore. I found it next to the grainy photo of a man trudging through a swampy jungle – the kind of adventure I'd love.

Excerpt from National Geographic – January 2013
Article titled: "Restless Genes"

"If an urge to explore rises in us innately, perhaps its foundation lies within our genome. In fact there is a mutation that pops up frequently in such discussions: a variant of a gene called DRD4, which helps control dopamine, a chemical brain messenger important in learning and reward. Researchers have repeatedly tied the variant, known as DRD4-7R and carried by roughly 20 percent of all humans, to curiosity and restlessness. Dozens of human studies have found that 7R makes people more likely to take risks; explore new places, ideas, foods, relationships, drugs, or sexual opportunities; and generally embrace movement, change, and adventure."

I had just learned about the 7R variant of DRD4, when Chris appeared in Robert's office doorway.

I jumped up from the sofa, magazine in hand.

"Look! There is scientific evidence – I *have* to roam and explore alternate realities. It's in my DNA! It's called 7R!"

I held the magazine up, pointing to the photo of the man in the jungle, but Chris only glanced at it before turning back to Robert. I sensed that I might have just confirmed a point discussed under the door.

Robert simply smiled. He invited me in the room and offered me a choice of chair. I chose the big leather chair next to the door and by the box of tissues. Robert sat in a white rocking chair by the window.

"Hello." He rested a small notebook and pen on his lap, and smiled calmly.

I returned his greeting, and expectantly waited for a prompting question, but he remained silent.

He could have asked about 7R. I was disappointed that he didn't. I wondered why I was disappointed and realized I was fiercely attached to my self-identity as "the Explorer". My attachment likely fueled part of Chris's and my discord. Nice! I had just dismantled my own disappointment, exposed an unhealthy attachment and claimed and cleared part of my side of the dysfunction. But my, was I analytical! How long had Robert been sitting patiently watching me? I hadn't even noticed that I was twirling my keys between my fingers. Their metallic clinging was the only sound in the room.

"Be here, my love!" I heard in my head, "Breathe ... Relax... Chill."

With a long inhale, I swept the room with my eyes, from the long leather sofa to my right, across the bookshelf that held several books I also owned, to the soft light shining through white blinds and back to Robert. On the exhale, I landed in my chair. Robert was still silent, so I draped my arms on the armrests and accepted that we might just be silent for a while.

My relationship with this silence traveled slowly through awkward, then peculiar and past the giggles before finally landing in stillness. I understood that I held the talking stick.

"Where did Chris choose to sit?"

Robert pointed to the far end of the long leather sofa.

"I see that he gave you a copy of *UnSpirituality.*"

"Yes, he did."

"But the books on your shelf tell me that you might believe in magic, as I do?"

The lines at the corner of Robert' eyes smiled slightly deeper as he scanned the bookshelf.

"Yes, I believe in Soul, or Spirit, or the innermost voice of our psyche. It is all one and the same, really."

"I'm writing a book about an epic spiritual journey." I caught the catchy subtitle for my book in the corner of my consciousness and mentally noted it for later consideration.

"It's a story of exploration – exploration of geographic locations, world perceptions, concepts of self and personal limits and edges."

Thus began the conversation. I briefly recounted for Robert the journey that had led me to Chris's unsettling unspiritual arms. He wrote a few notes at key moments, which I correlated to the most animated parts of my story.

Robert believed that all answers, guidance and help resided in our deep inner psyches, stored in our physical bodies as feelings waiting to be heard. His approach therefore, was simply to hold the space for feelings to express themselves and facilitate communication between our conscious mind and the deep wisdom stored in our bodies.

"Chris must have liked your methods; healing by tapping into the innate body's wisdom reinforces what he preaches."

I noted the irritation in my voice on the word "preaches" and I knew that Robert would have noticed as well, so I addressed it.

"I love Chris, but ..."

"No 'but'." Robert interrupted. "You love Chris. That is an undiluted fact. If you want to add information besides that fact, you can do so without minimizing it. "I love Chris, and, also ...""

"I love Chris, and, also ..." and, also, I was suddenly

crying.

"Follow the tears down to their source. See if you can find the lake at the end of the tears. See what it has to say."

05/16/2013
Excerpt from my journal
Titled: 1st session

    I cried in Robert's office today. He led me to follow the tears to the lake, to the source. I found the source in my heart. I sat next to the lake and allowed it to speak to me. It gave me the image of a blue glowing orb in a rusted cage that once was golden. The blue orb was not distressed, however, it just was, and it was fine. I told Robert that the blue orb is my joy, that feeling of freedom I experienced on the PCT and in the Sedona backcountry. The cage is not Chris. The cage is fear. It is not malicious. The door is open but the orb can't get out or it will get ripped by the metal bits protruding at the door. It would be okay though, if it tried to go. It would only hurt temporarily. How did the orb get in the cage? It went in out of curiosity, and inadvertently got stuck. Sure, it can grow and glow past the cage, but not much. It needs fresh air and open space to survive. The blue orb would eventually fade if it stayed in the cage. And, it is MY responsibility to ensure the orb gets plenty of fresh air and open space.

"What is the fear? What is the cage?" Robert asked.

"I fear the possibility that Chris might be right, that my spiritual journey was nothing but an inner-hoax orchestrated by my overactive imagination, that my free-spirited lifestyle is built on delusions."

Two and a half years after separating from my physical body during that January phone conversation with Logan, I knew that I had reintegrated and that I was whole again. I no longer conceived of myself in dualistic terms, with a Higher Self (which I had also called God, the Universe, Love, etc.) and a lower self (my personality, the role I played, Melissa, the Bobcat, etc.).

But had I reintegrated up or down? Was the source of creation a unified field of consciousness common to all things in our awareness and beyond or the result of chemical reactions in our neural synapses applied to natural pattern recognition? Was the world of physical form that I could perceive with my five senses the result of concentrated energy ($E=MC^2$) in a timeless realm or the self-evident material result of billions of years of evolution? Was I an eternal multidimensional being or a simple earthling destined to return to dust beyond my inevitable death? And, most importantly, was I writing a memoir or a fictional tall tale?

"Does it matter?" Robert's gentle tone hinted that he didn't think so.

My mind stopped abruptly like a startled wild animal. Before I began writing *Crazy Free*, Chris's worldview had felt threatening – deadly even – to my lifestyle. I believed that the magic was gone. Writing, however, was an act of magic. These words that flowed out of my fingers and onto the keyboard were merely passing through me; they were not created by my intellect. I was sure of it.

Did it matter? I scanned my body for any stored reaction to Robert's question, but my usual centers of opinions remained uncharacteristically quiet.

"I don't know."

"Did you have fun?"

"Oh my God, *yes*, I had the best time *ever*!"

Images of my journey flashed before my eyes, and my hands joined in the storytelling.

"I've been epic, fearless, up and down. I've lived so much larger than I would have thought myself capable. I've learned so much. And I loved – Man, did I love! I loved like crazy, and sometimes I really was crazy. I think I secretly loved being crazy – Okay, maybe not so secretly. It's like this adventure wanted to be had and it picked little old me to have it and to write about it. I feel so grateful and so spoiled for it."

I stopped for a breath. I could feel the blue orb glow past the cage, bending the golden rusted bars under its joyful pressure. It was only a matter of time before they burst.

I relaxed in the leather chair and settled in the sudden peace of certitude, of decisions made, of quandaries solved.

"I'm going to write my story, Robert, even if no one else reads it or believes a word of it, because some day, when I'm grey and old, I'll want to snuggle down in a rocking chair with a mug of green tea by a fire and read again about the adventures of Melissa and the legend of the Bobcat. And when I'm done with that book, I'll read the next book about adventures that haven't even happened yet, but which I bet will be just as fun, crazy and wonderful."

Robert smiled and nodded. "I look forward to reading your book. You do have a vivid imagination, and that is an essential trait for a writer."

EPILOGUE

On the morning of June 12th, 2013, Chris and I walked hand in hand to my beloved truck in his driveway for the last time. We had made love and cried in each other's arms that morning, but we had not driven to Java Love Café for our usual breakfast. Those days were already gone, absorbed in the continuum of my personal story.

Chris understood I had to go. In fact, he supported it.

"A moving ship is easier to steer than a parked one. There are so many opportunities for exploration for you out there. You would get stale if you stayed here. I love you. Go!"

As a parting gift, he built a set of elaborate shelves for the back of my truck, snugly fitted to a firm mattress under a two-inch memory foam topper – by far the best sleeping surface I have experienced. Some shelves held my camping gear, others my books, journals and stuffed friends. A sliding board allowed me to convert quickly from driving mode to sleeping mode. Chris had built me a home after all.

I was driving north in search of mountains and pine forests, such was the extent of my plan. I wasn't looking to settle elsewhere and I had no intention to stop anywhere for an extended period of time. My only professional aspirations were to roam and write.

I would write *Crazy Free* on the road, in libraries and on friends' couches, a different place for each section. I didn't know how I was going to finance this mad plan of mine but had an intuition that I didn't need to know. Work would appear where I landed, in sufficient amount to allow me to thrive and roam on.

If you are holding *Crazy Free* in your hand right now, in my linear future, then, – wow! – I actually made it.

A FINAL NOTE
FROM THE INSATIABLE STORYTELLER

The day before my departure from Sedona, Chris and I attended to a bit of business that involved the sale of his irrigation company, the IRS and complications that have long since been resolved.

The accountant's verdict was that the easiest way to solve Chris's problem was to transfer $30,000 to my bank account temporarily. The amount had not been previously discussed. The accountant probably assumed that Chris and I were in a committed relationship of sufficient depth to warrant this level of trust. Most people would have; we did not have the energy of a couple about to separate.

During the drive back to the house – my last ride in Chris's old truck – a funny thought floated through my mind.

"You know, if I stayed here, $30,000 would appear in my bank account, exactly as I intended to manifest when I first met you."

Chris pointedly blinked twice in mock surprise and laughed.

"You Silly Fish! You are not staying, so we are not transferring $30,000 to your bank account, so you didn't manifest anything, except a lovely story in your brilliantly creative imagination. And, if my theoretical $30,000 somehow ended up in your bank account, you would most certainly *not* give it all to charity!"

I laughed too, and took Chris's hand in mine to kiss it.

That is all we said about it.

The warm desert air tickled the hair on my arm outside the passenger window as my hand sliced through it in undulating motions, and I thought no further of the $30,000.

ACKNOWLEDGMENTS

I am grateful to *Crazy Free* for pulling me forward to create it,
for giving me a purpose, a rudder by which to navigate an
infinity of delicious life options and for the challenges and joy
through which I have continued to learn, heal and grow.

I am grateful for all the incredibly generous souls who have
stepped forward when I needed help and who have become
part of our communal creative process. I could not have
dreamt a better cast of allies to bring *Crazy Free* to life.

I am grateful to all my Trail Angels in over dozens of towns
for supporting my dream and roaming ways.
Thank you for the conversations, the showers, the meals.
Thank you for the office space, the quiet corner table, the level
driveway, the key under the mat, the open garage door.
Thank you for your support, patience and love.

"I have often felt that my greatest superpower is in
the quality of the people I call friends."

♥

REFERENCES

Baron-Reid, C. (2011). *The Enchanted Map Oracle Cards* . Hay House; Tcr Crds/P edition.

Loren, C. (2013). *unSpirituality: Permission to be human*. CreateSpace Independent Publishing Platform; First Edition.

Peirce, P. (2009). *Frequency: The Power of Personal Vibration*. Atria Books/Beyond Words.

Tolle, E. (2004). *The Power of Now: A Guide to Spiritual Enlightenment*. Namaste Publishing.

Selected influential favorites...

Bodanis, D. (2001). $E=MC^2$: *A Biography of the World's Most Famous Equation*. Berkley Publishing Group.

Cox, B. and Forshaw, J. (2011). *The Quantum Universe*. Da Capo Press.

Emoto, M. (2011). *The Miracle of Water*. Atria Books.

Feynman, R. P. (1977). *The Feynman Lectures on Physics, Vol. 1: mainly Mechanics, Radiation, and heat*. Addison Wesley.

Kaku, M. (2006). *Parallel Worlds: A Journey Through Creation, Higher Dimensions, and the Future of the Cosmos*. Anchor.

Swami Satchidananda (2012). *The Yoga Sutras of Patanjali*. Integral Yoga Publications.

Made in the USA
San Bernardino, CA
10 June 2015